"Grounded in evidence yet deeply accessible, this research-rich guide empowers neurodivergent learners to understand how they learn and advocate for what they need to thrive. Clear, affirming, and practical, it is essential reading for students entering college and the educators and families who support them."

Lauren Hough Williams, *Executive Director, NYU Steinhardt's PINE (Program for Inclusion and Neurodiversity Education)*

"This book feels like a warm hug from a supportive friend during the most stressful hours of college madness."

Jasmine Mueller, *Student, University of Lausanne*

"*The Complete College Skills Guide for Neurodivergent Students* is a wealth of information for students and for those who support them. The guide is clear and helpful and reinforces a holistic approach to learning and success, including the importance of sleep, fun, and belonging."

Cristine Donovan, *Racker*

"Ardon has combined decades of teaching neurodivergent students effective learning strategies with a broad knowledge of the research to produce an extraordinary book that helps ND students navigate the college environment and advocate for themselves. It's a must read for all ND students."

Dr. Saundra McGuire, *internationally recognized learning specialist*

I0805838

The Complete College Skills Guide for Neurodivergent Students

Discover why effective learning depends just as much on being physically, mentally, and emotionally prepared as it does on study strategies, and learn how to harness that knowledge for academic success in college and beyond. *The Complete College Skills Guide for Neurodivergent Students* goes beyond generic study tips to reveal the neuroscience behind how we learn, empowering you to understand why certain strategies work so you can adapt them to your unique brain and lifestyle.

Through evidence-based insights on everything from sleep and nutrition to motivation and metacognition, you'll learn to design flexible study systems that actually stick. Written in a direct, no-nonsense conversational style, this book features real student experiences, expert-reviewed content, and practical "In Brief" summaries that get straight to the point. Rather than prescribing rigid techniques, you'll explore the science behind your need to take breaks, sleep, move, and much more, giving you the freedom to create personalized approaches that evolve with your needs.

Perfect for neurodivergent college students and lifelong learners who benefit from knowing the "why" behind learning strategies, and for educators, professionals, and parents working with neurodivergent college students who seek evidence-based approaches to academic support.

Florencia Ardon has taught study skills courses and provided academic advice to undergraduate students at Cornell University for over a decade. She founded and leads Neurodiversity @ Cornell and advocates for neurodiversity celebration and inclusion. For her efforts, she was recognized as a Stephen H. Weiss Provost's Teaching Fellow, which recognizes sustained excellence in undergraduate teaching and mentoring.

Also Available from Routledge Eye on Education

www.routledge.com/k-12

Successfully Launching into Young Adulthood with ADHD: Firsthand Guidance for Parents and Educators Supporting Children with Neurodevelopmental Differences
Chris A. Zeigler Dendy and Ruth Hughes

Autism, Identity and Me: A Practical Workbook to Empower Autistic Children and Young People Aged 10+
Rebecca Duffus and Lyric Rivera

Autism, Identity and Me: A Professional and Parent Guide to Support a Positive Understanding of Autistic Identity
Rebecca Duffus and Lyric Rivera

The Complete College Skills Guide for Neurodivergent Students

Understanding the Science of Learning for Academic Success

Florencia Ardon

Routledge
Taylor & Francis Group
NEW YORK AND LONDON

Designed cover image: Linda Joleigh Johnson

First published 2027
by Routledge
605 Third Avenue, New York, NY 10158

and by Routledge
4 Park Square, Milton Park, Abingdon, Oxon, OX14 4RN

Routledge is an imprint of the Taylor & Francis Group, an informa business

ISBN: 978-1-041-26423-1 (hbk)
ISBN: 978-1-041-26421-7 (pbk)
ISBN: 978-1-003-75024-6 (ebk)

DOI: 10.4324/9781003750246

Typeset in Optima
by SPi Technologies India Pvt Ltd (Straive)

For Didier and Marisol, who daily teach me how to be a better person

Contents

About the Author

Florencia Ardon is an educator passionate about supporting students' learning through evidence-based teaching. Her personal and professional paths have given her intimate knowledge about the challenges faced by a variety of student populations including international, graduate, and neurodivergent students.

Originally from Mexico, she pursued her MS and PhD in Germany after working for a genetic improvement company. After returning to Mexico, she continued working in life sciences research, first as a postdoctoral fellow at the National Autonomous University of Mexico and then as a tenured professor at the Autonomous University of Baja California.

In 2010, she and her family moved to Ithaca, New York, where she continued working as a researcher at Cornell University for a few years, until changing career paths to teach and to provide academic advising to Cornell undergraduates. Her scientific training shapes her approach to teaching, advocacy work and daily life.

As a neurodivergent educator whose family is also neurodivergent, and through her conversations and collaboration with multiple neurodivergent and disabled students and peers, she has gained a deep understanding of the needs of neurodivergent people in higher education. That understanding, and her interest in evidence-based teaching and learning, are the backbone of this textbook.

Preface

It all started with *saving trees*.

When I started teaching my summer study skills course over a decade ago, we didn't use online learning management systems. I would give printed handouts to students, with my explanations about current evidence for the topics we were discussing.

My students pushed back against the printed handouts, as they felt they were contributing to cutting down trees and the subsequent environmental problems. However, I felt that printed materials were important for learning, so I decided to create a little handbook with all the handouts. And it worked, my students didn't complain anymore.

A couple of years later, I wrote a more formal handbook, then added more recent research findings, and kept improving it, updating the information as needed. Students found my handbook useful; I remember one of them telling me he had given it to his dad, thinking it would be helpful for him.

A few years went by, with me improving the handbook each year. Some of my colleagues asked me for copies to use in their own teaching or learning. (By the way, I should add that it is truly valuable for you as a student or a colleague to offer words of encouragement to your instructors or peers. Your words may be the validation they need to strive for more).

A couple of years ago, I thought it was time to write an actual textbook instead of a handbook, with the most current research, good visuals, and engaging prose. The table of contents was ready; I had written some on all the chapters it would contain, but there was always something more urgent coming up, demanding my attention.

The textbook project had to be pushed off but was never out of sight or out of mind. It would be a way for my students to have the material accessible anytime, presented in a cohesive way. And it gave me the opportunity to offer my teachings to a really wide audience.

So there I was, in the middle of slowly writing my textbook, without a clear idea of how to publish it, when I was told that Dr. Saundra McGuire was coming to campus. Dr. McGuire wrote *"Teach Yourself How to Learn,"* which is one of the textbooks for my class. I was fortunate to have her give a talk to my students. My students were fascinated by her presentation and very thankful for her words, as I was.

Talking with Dr. McGuire about my course, I mentioned that I was working on a textbook, and she encouraged me to reach out to Routledge. She introduced me to her editor, who introduced me to another editor whose focus was closer to my project's idea. My editor was very friendly and encouraging, and since I had been working on the textbook already, I was able to immediately send her a sample chapter and a description of the textbook, along with its table of contents.

By the time I signed the contract with Routledge, I had a bit over four months to write the textbook. That was very ambitious, as several of my colleagues warned me. I thought it was doable since it was based on my curriculum; I was familiar with the material and knew what I wanted to convey. Additionally, since new research findings are continuously being published, more time would create the risk of getting into a never-ending cycle of having to update the information with every passing month.

But, in true ADHD fashion, I added complexity to the project because shiny ideas tempt me. My general idea was to create an evidence-based textbook that included the most current scientific data, was easy to read, and would help students feel empowered and eager to improve their learning strategies. And I wanted to involve students and neurodivergent people in the process.

One of my shiny ideas didn't come to fruition. I wished to have a neurodivergent student draw doodles to make the textbook more fun. However, the contract set a maximum of 20 illustrations, which meant that doodles throughout the textbook were simply impossible to have.

Some shiny ideas did become a reality: I was able to conduct a survey of my former students regarding their study habits to obtain data and quotes for the book. You can read about their experiences throughout the book. I was also able to send chapters to subject matter experts to make sure I was not misinterpreting research findings or missing crucial information. Finally, I sent the manuscript to test readers to ensure the accessibility and friendliness of my writing.

Two incredible artists improved the visual quality of the book. The illustrations in the book were created by Julia Felice, who is a professional scientific data designer and is passionate about supporting students. Julia helped me translate my ideas into reader-friendly, clear visual information. She constantly amazes me, and I'm honored to be her friend.

Linda Johnson, a former student of mine, who intends to become a scientific illustrator, agreed to create the cover. This project required her to explore new techniques and technology, and she invested a great amount of thought, time, and expertise into crafting a cover illustration that represents this textbook's vision. I'm thankful for her talent and support.

The contributions of multiple people enriched this textbook. At the same time, the collaboration with all of them implied more time, effort, and planning than what I envisioned at the beginning. It was all very much worth it; I would not have been satisfied with the textbook otherwise.

Throughout the writing of this textbook, I've been trying to follow my own advice, going to sleep at a reasonable time the majority of the days, limiting the time spent looking for a particular piece of information or improving the way I wrote a given sentence, recognizing when I'm going into rabbit holes and forcing myself to get out, spending time with my family and friends, and so much more. It has been a true challenge at points and has made me empathize with my students and with future readers even more.

This textbook is by no means perfect. A perfect one would never be published, if you consider *perfect* having the most current data and flawless phrasing, or containing all the information available on all topics, or even all my own thoughts and advice on each topic. The short period of time between signing the contract and the submission deadline kept in check my perfectionistic tendencies and prevented me from procrastinating. I did take breaks, which supported my well-being and helped some ideas become more tangible and expressible. My thoughts are normally extremely abstract, and breaks allowed my brain to "massage" my ideas and turn them into words and phrases that make sense to others and to myself.

My wish is that you'll find some of the ideas applicable to your studies and life, and that you will keep refining your learning strategies. And, as I mentioned earlier, new evidence comes out virtually every day; hopefully, reading this book will lead you to keep up to date with research and information on a few of the topics I discuss in the textbook.

Writing this textbook was possible thanks to my children, Didier and Marisol, first of all. Witnessing their developmental journey, as humans and scholars, has been key in my understanding of learning, well-being and love. I deeply admire and love them, and I'm grateful to have their wholehearted support in all of my efforts, including test-reading the manuscript.

My supervisor at Cornell, Amy Godert, has been instrumental in my professional development. She's a true leader, empowering me while simultaneously guiding me to ensure my vision can become a reality.

Michael "Mike" Chen is one of my main role models; his caring and stress-free teaching style is cherished by the lucky students who attend his course or workshops.

Melanie Fraser and Cate Thomson are dear friends who offer me caring advice, support and collaboration. Their belief in me when I doubt myself, and their enthusiastic championing of my projects, make the impossible

possible. The contributions of countless colleagues, students and friends across Cornell and beyond have improved the work of Neurodiversity @ Cornell and have ensured that a myriad of programs and ideas become a reality.

Without Dr. Saundra McGuire, this textbook would not be in your hands. I am deeply grateful for her friendly and wise advice, as well as her willingness to connect me with editors at Routledge. Dr. McGuire also gifted me her time and expertise, carefully reviewing Chapter 4 and offering valuable recommendations.

I'm thankful to the students that answered the survey and to all who have taken my courses, been my long-term advisees, or met occasionally with me. They have trusted me to hear their experiences and support them. They have made me a better instructor, advisor, and person.

People who I admire and consider subject matter experts offered thoughtful and useful feedback on the textbook chapters. I'm deeply grateful to Antonia Pellegrini, Clara Matton, Julie Edwards, Michael John Carley, Wendy Strobel-Gower, Beth Parrott, and Rachel Gunderson for their invaluable recommendations and ideas.

The feedback from test readers significantly increased the readability of this textbook, and their ideas enriched it. Sarah Bonawitz and Jasmine Mueller, in particular, helped me see other perspectives and notice topics I was inadvertently omitting. I'm deeply grateful to you both.

Lastly, I am thankful to you for reading this book. I hope it helps you throughout your learning journey.

Introduction

The content of this book arose from the curricula of my courses, which have evolved based on students' reflections, discussions in class, and conversations with countless students, both those enrolled in my courses and others whom I have advised. One of my goals was to focus on what science is telling us about how our brain works, which can help students understand their own learning process and take full advantage of their strengths. The other goal was to demystify the college experience and encourage all college students to embrace this adventure, taking advantage of all the resources, programs, and knowledge available to them, while supporting their well-being and maintaining a balance between their academic and personal life.

Before addressing the different areas that influence your capacity to learn, I offer next a brief overview of the history of higher education and how that relates to "knowing how to study in college."

Learning in Higher Education

Considering how long humans have been around, higher education is very new. The first bona fide university is believed to have been Plato's Academy in Greece, which operated between the years of 387 to 86 BC. Except for two women, all the students in the academy were male members of the Greek upper class. Although there were no fees or explicit access limitations, it is believed that only wealthy men had the luxury of spending their time learning (Haake, 2020).

It is important to consider that knowledge is constantly added to the curricula, and increasingly more populations have gained access to higher education. An example of knowledge being added to the curricula in college, which in time "trickled down" to high school, is that Harvard University was established in 1636, before calculus was invented. The consensus is that both Leibniz and Newton invented calculus in the period between 1673 and 1676 (Sastry, 2006). Calculus was first taught at Harvard

DOI: 10.4324/9781003750246-1

around 1720, 80 years after Harvard was founded. Teaching advanced placement (AP) Calculus in high school started in 1955; in the 1980s, only around 30,000 US highschoolers took calculus each year. The number increased to ~800,000 in 2023. Access to high school calculus is still limited, curricula vary widely, and its efficiency in preparing students for college math is controversial (Burdman et al., 2024). While some STEM-focused institutions such as the Massachusetts Institute of Technology (MIT) and the College of Engineering at Cornell require applicants to take calculus in high school, Harvard and the University of Chicago—to name but two renowned institutions—do not require calculus to apply.

I found another historical gem while doing research for this book, specifically about the stress continuum (discussed in Chapter 2, the stress continuum is a visual representation of the difference between good stress, which motivates people to act, and toxic stress, which decreases well-being and productivity). The stress continuum curve is based on a study by Yerkes and Dodson, published in 1908. David Diamond (2005) created the graph commonly used for the stress continuum, explaining that Yerkes and Dodson didn't report statistical analysis, because "statistics had not yet been conceived." This is not completely accurate. Statistical analysis did exist; Carl F. Gauss, for example, who created the bell curve, died in 1855 (Kronzon, 2011). While there were early attempts by several universities to teach statistics in the US (Fitzpatrick, 1955), Zieffler et al. (2018) states that statistics education in colleges became more common only after the Second World War, and in 1954, it was first recommended to be taught in high schools.

As you see, the material learned in college in the past is objectively less than what you are expected to learn now. In Plato's Academy, students learned philosophy, the basis of scientific research, politics, ethics, and a few other subjects (Haake, 2017). Harvard's initial three-year bachelor of arts degree, where the instruction was in Latin, focused on what a gentleman should know about: philosophy, classical languages and literature, rhetoric, and a bit of history, astronomy, and botany.

Comparing what people currently learn in college to more recent years, you can consider that, for example, in 1970, people could only learn what was already proven or discovered by that year. I went to college in the early '90s; there have been a myriad of scientific discoveries since then, which are now part of the curricula. This is noticeable in high school too: my children learned in regular biology some concepts I learned in AP biology in 1989-1990; they also study some techniques that did not exist when I graduated from high school (e.g., CRISPR DNA editing, Jinek et al., 2012).

The purpose of college has been changing too. As mentioned earlier, Plato's Academy was mostly attended by well-to-do Greek men with enough time at their disposition. The inaugural graduating class at Harvard, the first university in the US, took place in 1642 and consisted of nine White men. The goal of their education was to acquire the knowledge that was considered socially necessary for a gentleman. There were no practical considerations, and the curricula was fixed—adding new knowledge was not deemed necessary (Geiger, 2014).

Cornell University, the younger of the Ivy League universities, was established in 1865 with a very different goal, as described by Ezra Cornell: "I would found an institution where any person can find instruction in any study." By any study, he meant

> an institution which shall combine practical with liberal education, which shall fit the youth of our country for the professions, the farms, the mines, the manufactories, for the investigations of science, and for mastering all the practical questions of life....
>
> (Ezra Cornell's address at the opening of the University, October 7, 1868)

Since then, many college majors across the US have focused mostly on the knowledge needed for the workforce.

Finally, people attending college are more diverse than ever. The US college population has evolved from ten White male students starting college at Harvard in 1638 (Geiger, 2014), to 15.4 million students enrolled in 2021. Of these, 58% identified as female and 42% as male, 50.6% as White, 21.4% as Hispanic, 12.3% million as Black, 7.1% as Asian, 4.3% as Multiracial, 0.59% as American Indian/Alaska Native, and 0.26% as Pacific Islander (National Center for Education Statistics, 2023).

The academic background of current students is incredibly varied; in my courses, I have had students who were homeschooled, some who went to elite preparatory schools, others who attended large public schools, and everything in between. Additionally, there is a large population of international students and recent immigrants who studied in other countries prior to enrolling in a US college. Students' backgrounds and prior study habits will influence how they attempt to study in college and may help them understand who they are as learners, what their strengths are, and habits or strategies they could enhance.

The Reason Why You Don't Know "How to Learn in College"

At the beginning, you may feel intimidated and believe you don't know how to learn at a college level. That is true for most people, because there is not a single learning technique that works for all courses or for everyone. Which strategy will work for you depends on many factors, including the subject you are learning, the setting, your instructor's teaching style, and who your classmates are. Additionally, you need to consider your interest in the topic, its relevance for your future career, how much time you have, if you need accommodations due to a learning disability or other types of disability, your natural talent, and more.

Some students express shame or remorse when they realize that the study techniques used in high school are not enough for college-level material. These students feel they should have worked harder in high school, even though they graduated with high grades and were accepted into very competitive programs. However, it is likely that not investing excessive time or effort into their courses allowed them to participate in other enriching and formative experiences. Students learned in high school in the way that was needed then; now they need to find the strategies and tools that will help them learn in college.

In my experience, students feel motivated and persevere more to improve their learning strategies when they know the evidence behind recommended study methods and life habits. In this book, I will focus on the scientific basis of a variety of factors that you need to consider when creating a learning journey. This includes basic needs such as sleep, nutrition, and exercise, as well as communicating with faculty and staff and advocating for academic accommodations that can help you acquire and express knowledge.

The science of how people learn has been evolving for centuries. In recent times, contributions by neuroscience, behavioral science, psychology, and other fields of study have elucidated what helps people remember and apply their knowledge and skills. In some cases, the consensus has shifted. It is possible that a seemingly helpful strategy proves to be difficult to implement while offering only marginal benefits. Other well-known strategies have been disproved and some more have not even been peer-reviewed, meaning that there is no solid evidence that they are beneficial. You will not find them in this book.

What you'll find in this book is information about your physical, physiological, and emotional needs, and why they are relevant to your performance as a student. You can also read about habits, mindsets and biases that can help or hinder your engagement. The book also covers evidence-based learning strategies and techniques, including how to manage your time and effort, prioritize tasks, organize materials, plan your study time, self-test, and more. You will get some ideas and recommendations that you can adapt to your particular situation. I'm intentionally avoiding giving you strict parameters for any recommendation, as you are the only person that really knows what works for you.

Although all students can find the book helpful, it will be especially useful to those identifying as neurodivergent. Students who self-identify as being autistic or ADHDers, or as having mental health conditions, learning disabilities, and other neurodivergent identities can face challenges regarding their executive function and capacity for engagement, which translates into finding it difficult to organize, plan, and carry out different academic tasks.

The book is intended to be short and sweet, taking into consideration your time constraints. You will find references listed at the end of each chapter, in case you want to explore any particular topic in more detail.

In Brief

What is known about how to comprehend and apply newly acquired information is constantly evolving, as researchers find out more about how humans learn, new technologies are adopted, educators refine their teaching, and how students' interest in each topic and the time they have available to dedicate to each subject varies. It is unrealistic and unfeasible for anyone to really "know how to learn" in all settings and all topics. Self-compassion and understanding that college is a new environment requiring new study techniques will allow you to focus on finding your own best practices. That's what this book is all about!

References

Burdman, P., Heller, R., & Baker, M. (2024). Report: The limits of calculus: revisiting the role of math education in college admissions. *just equations*. Retrieved February 23, 2026, from https://justequations.org/resource/the-limits-of-calculus-revisiting-the-role-of-math-education-in-college-admissions

Cornell, E. (1868). Letter to Andrew Dickson White. "I would found an institution": The Ezra Cornell Bicentennial (2007). Retrieved on November 14, 2025, from https://rmc.library.cornell.edu/ezra/exhibition/anystudy/REX027_139_1_2.pdf

Diamond, D. M. (2005). Cognitive, endocrine and mechanistic perspectives on non-linear relationships between arousal and brain function. *Nonlinearity in Biology, Toxicology, Medicine*, *3*(1), nonlin.003.01.001. https://doi.org/10.2201/nonlin.003.01.001

Fitzpatrick, P. J. (1955). The early teaching of statistics in American colleges and universities. *The American Statistician*, *9*(5), 12–18. https://doi.org/10.1080/00031305.1955.10501125

Geiger, R. L. (2014). *The history of American higher education: Learning and culture from the founding to World War II*. Princeton University Press. https://doi.org/10.1515/9781400852055

Haake, M. (2017). The academy in Athenian politics and society – Between disintegration and integration: The first eighty years (387/6–306/5). In M. Haake (Ed.), *Plato and the Athenian academy*. Universität Münster. https://doi.org/10.1017/9781108554664.006.

Haake, M. (2020). the academy in athenian politics and society – between disintegration and integration: The first eighty years (387/6–306/5). In P. Kalligas, C. Balla, E. Baziotopoulou-Valavani, & V. Karasmanis (Eds.), *Plato's academy: Its workings and its history* (pp. 65–88). chapter, Cambridge: Cambridge University Press.

Jinek, M., Chylinski, K., Fonfara, I., Hauer, M., Doudna, J. A., & Charpentier, E. (2012). A programmable dual-RNA–guided DNA endonuclease in adaptive bacterial immunity. *Science, 337*(6096), 816–821. https://doi.org/10.1126/science.1225829

Kronzon, I. (2011). Carl Friedrich Gauss and Pravin Shah—A tribute to excellence. *Journal of the American Society of Echocardiography, 24*(10), 1168. https://doi.org/10.1016/j.echo.2011.07.001

National Center for Education Statistics (2023). *Undergraduate Enrollment*. Condition of Education. U.S. Department of Education, Institute of Education Sciences. Retrieved December 27th, 2025, from https://nces.ed.gov/programs/coe/indicator/cha

Sastry, S. S. (2006). The Newton-Leibniz controversy over the invention of the calculus. In E. J. Khamara (Ed.), *Space, time, and theology in the Leibniz-Newton controversy*. Ontos Verlag.

Yerkes, R. M., & Dodson, J. D. (1908). The relation of strength of stimulus to rapidity of habit-formation. *Journal of Comparative Neurology and Psychology, 18*(5), 459–482. https://doi.org/10.1002/cne.920180503

Zieffler, A., Garfield, J., & Fry, E. (2018). What is statistics education? In D. Ben-Zvi, K. Makar, & J. Garfield (Eds.), *International handbook of research in statistics education* (pp. 37–70). Springer International Publishing. https://doi.org/10.1007/978-3-319-66195-7_2

1 Sleep Enough, Eat Well and Move Your Body to Improve Your Learning

Learning requires access to sources of knowledge and someone to explain it or show a skill. It is crucial to be in an environment that is conducive to learning and to have the time to dedicate to studying or practicing new skills. You need to be ready to listen, read, imitate movements, discuss—that is, you need to be motivated. Your interest in a particular topic is important, as is not being distracted by worries, lack of sleep, hunger, or fear. In this chapter, you'll read about the importance of fulfilling your basic physiological needs in order to be able to focus on learning.

What Motivates Humans, According to Maslow

Abraham Maslow wrote in 1943 that human motivation depends on their needs being fulfilled. The most basic and important needs are *physiological*, which includes access to air, water, food, shelter, warmth, rest, sleep, and exercise. Until those are fulfilled, other needs are relegated. "A person who is lacking food, safety, love, and esteem will most probably hunger for food more strongly than for anything else" (Maslow, 1943).

Next come *safety* needs, which include a need for predictability, routine, order, and reliability, as well as a peaceful environment and having a sense of protection, knowing there are people that will defend you if necessary.

What follows is a need for *love, belonging, affection, and esteem*. Your feelings toward yourself and those expressed by people around you feed each other. You may feel more confident, prepared, and willing to take risks when people recognize and appreciate you. You need to be respected and to respect yourself; to feel cared for, included, valued, and confident in your abilities.

Finally, for a person to be completely happy and satisfied with life, there is a need for *self-actualization* and *self-transcendence*, which could mean a wide variety of things, such as being a parent, athlete, artist or inventor, and countless other professions or identities. This also includes having the *freedom* to speak, move, pursue one's own goals, and decide your own future, and to have access to *learning*, i.e., to acquire knowledge and skills.

DOI: 10.4324/9781003750246-2

Maslow (1943) did not propose a rigid hierarchy, acknowledging that, e.g., for some people, self-actualization is more important than love. You could also think that for some, painting may be more important than eating. Several studies, summarized by Bigelow and Williams (2020), have shown that human infants crave physical contact, and that caring touch between caregivers and infants exerts a positive effect on both the caregiver and the infant. Maslow (1943) also mentioned that the needs aren't required to be *fully* satisfied; partial fulfillment may be enough. Figure 1.1 shows Maslow's dimensions of human needs as a circle to emphasize the idea that all of those needs are valuable and crucial for human fulfillment. Love/belonging and esteem, are shown under "emotional" needs, as I find them difficult to tease out, due to their significant overlap in meaning.

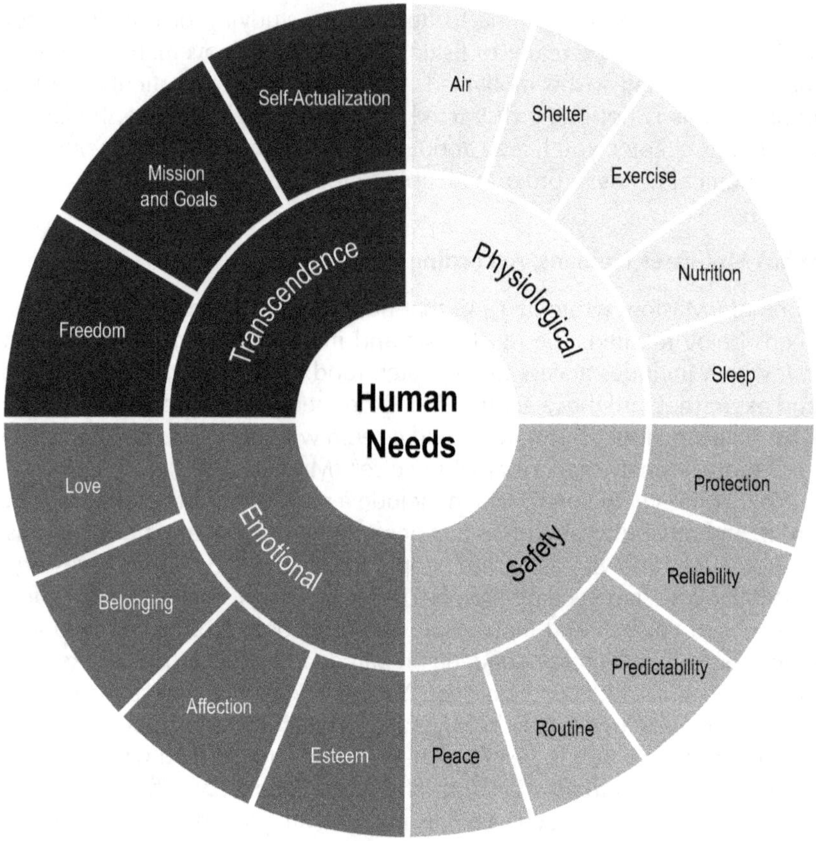

Figure 1.1 Dimensions of human needs. Concept by Florencia Ardon, PhD, based on Maslow (1943). Design by Dr. Julia Felice.

In my experience as academic advisor and lecturer in the topic of learning, many students pay insufficient attention to their physiological needs, with detrimental consequences to their academic achievement and/or their physical and psychological health. In this chapter, we'll discuss *sleep, nutrition, and exercise.*

You Learn While You Sleep

Why Do People Sleep?

Sleep is an imperative biological need, and the joint consensus of the American Academy of Sleep Medicine and the Sleep Research Society is that most people between the ages of 18 and 60 need to sleep *seven to nine hours per night on a regular basis.* For people who are sleep deprived, young adults, or those who are ill, sleeping more than nine hours may be appropriate (Watson et al., 2015).

Knowledge about sleep continues to evolve as technology gives researchers access to visualize different aspects of brain function, yet many aspects are still unknown (Lutz et al., 2026). It is known that sleep is not one state; sleep architecture is complex and includes four distinct stages of sleep, normally experienced in sequence. First, people go through three stages, all within the "non-Rapid Eye Movement" or NREM category, followed by an episode of "Rapid Eye Movement" or REM; then the cycle begins again. Altogether, people spend around 80% of their sleep time in NREM stages and the remaining 20% in REM sleep (Parrino et al., 2025).

NREM plays an important role for people's physical needs, such as muscle repair and growth; maintaining immune system function; successful reproduction; clearing the brain from toxic metabolic by-products, such as β-amyloid, which are linked to Alzheimer's disease; maintaining insulin sensitivity; and memory consolidation (Cordone et al., 2019; Lutz et al., 2026; Mahoney, 2010; Olarescu et al., 2000; Patel et al., 2024; Wong et al., 2015).

NREM Stages

a *N1* lasts between 1 and 5 minutes, around 5% of your time asleep, and is a very light sleep. You breathe regularly, your muscle tone is present, and you may experience some involuntary twitches. If you woke up during this stage, you could believe you were just "resting your eyes."
b *N2*, the next stage, lasts around 25 minutes in the first cycle, increasing in duration every time, and cumulatively amounts to around 45% of total sleep time. During N2, your heart and breathing rates slow down, your body temperature drops, and you are unlikely to react to "normal"

light or noise. This stage is also related to memory consolidation, specifically procedural or "muscle memory" and declarative memory, meaning general knowledge and facts, as well as your experiences.

c *N3* is the deepest sleep stage, and you spend around 25% of your sleep time in this stage. It is also known as slow-wave sleep (SWS). During N3, you are unlikely to wake up even with loud noises (>100 decibels, equivalent to the noise of a rock concert). If you wake up during this stage, you would be confused, feeling "brain fog" for up to one hour; this feeling is also called "sleep inertia." This stage is closely linked to bone, muscle, and tissue growth and repair, and to the strengthening of your immune system. It is also involved with emotional memory, both fear and reward-related memories (Parrino et al., 2025; Patel et al., 2024).

Characteristics of REM

Brain activity during REM sleep looks similar to that seen while you are awake; meanwhile, your body is mostly immotile except for your eyes and muscles needed to sustain life, such as the diaphragm. The first time you enter REM sleep is 90 minutes after falling asleep and lasts about 10 minutes, increasing in duration with each cycle so that your last REM stage may last up to 1 hour. The majority of your dreams happen during this stage, and most people tend to wake up during REM in the morning (Patel et al., 2024), which may explain why you remember your last dream somewhat vividly.

REM sleep seems to be deeply involved in maintaining and shaping new memories, integrating them with old memories. It is also linked to both negative and positive emotional memory, especially through the replaying and reactivation of your feelings, and gives shape to your emotional responses and your mood. People who experience longer REM stages and undergo a traumatic event are unlikely to develop post-traumatic stress disorder (Lutz et al., 2026; Parrino et al., 2025). Your body's need for REM sleep is evident in the so-called REM-rebound effect: When an individual is severely sleep deprived or for other reasons misses REM sleep, the body compensates for the missed REM sleep by entering REM stage earlier or experiencing longer REM stages (Parrino et al., 2025).

Effect of Sleep Duration on Memory Consolidation

Memory consolidation is the process used by your brain to transform what you experience into long-term memories you can later use. It involves *systems consolidations*, i.e., a reorganization of memories in different regions of the brain, as well as *synaptic consolidations*, i.e., adjustments to the connections between neurons. NREM and REM sleep complement each other and are crucial for memory consolidation: During *NREM* sleep, memories are *recalled* and *replayed*, which allows your brain to compress them for easier storage, and are transferred from the hippocampus to regions in the brain cortex, becoming more permanent. During *REM* sleep, memories are *integrated*, that is, memories are grouped with similar memories, creating networks that allow you to recall those memories to decide a course of action or to add a new experience to a given network. It is also during REM sleep that your memories are given an emotional "tag." REM sleep is crucial for spatial memories, abstract thinking, mental flexibility, creativity, and generalization of learning, which is how you can apply a skill, rule, or knowledge to new situations (Kim & Park, 2025; Lutz et al., 2026). When you don't sleep enough, e.g., six hours instead of eight, you don't give your brain the time required to conduct all of these processes, leading to suboptimal learning.

Regulation of the Sleep-Wake Cycle

Nighttime sleep is influenced by both your circadian rhythm and sleep homeostasis, and this is reflected in your sleep cycle. At the beginning of the night, your brain shows more periods of slow-wave activity, mostly because of homeostatic sleep pressure. During this time, non-REM sleep is predominant. In the early morning hours, you spend more time in REM sleep, under the influence of your circadian rhythm (Cajochen & Schmidt, 2025).

Sleep homeostasis balances the need to sleep with the need to be awake. During the time you are awake, your need to sleep (sleep pressure or drive) increases; conversely, as you sleep, your need to be awake increases. Sleep homeostasis greatly depends on ATP metabolism. While you are awake, the brain uses ATP for energy; ATP breaks down, and adenosine accumulates as a by-product. The accumulation of adenosine and other substances during wakefulness makes you sleepy (Deboer, 2018; Gangitano et al., 2023). Caffeine helps you stay awake by blocking adenosine receptors in the brain, preventing adenosine's promotion of sleepiness (Baranwal et al., 2023).

The circadian rhythm refers to your main or central clock, located in the Suprachiasmatic Nucleus (SCN) of the hypothalamus (Honma, 2018). This clock responds to environmental cues or "zeitgebers," such as physical activity, eating, and most importantly, light. The SCN promotes both your wakefulness, which is highest in the early evening, and sleepiness, which is highest at night. Your wakefulness is stimulated by dopamine, norepinephrine, histamines, and acetylcholine, while your sleepiness is induced mainly by melatonin, produced at night by the pineal gland, which is controlled by the SCN (Cajochen & Schmidt, 2025; Gangitano et al., 2023).

One of the most important zeitgebers is natural light, early in the day. Since your innate circadian clock is slightly longer than 24 hours, light helps align your circadian clock with solar time. Indeed, when graduate students were exposed to bright light early in the morning, they were able to fall asleep faster, slept most of the time they were in bed, and enjoyed a more restful sleep than when they were exposed to a regular office light. The beneficial effect of the bright light increased with each day of exposure (He et al., 2023). Natural daylight offers the most benefits (de Menezes-Júnior et al., 2025). You don't have to be outside to enjoy the benefits of natural light; simply being indoors near a sunny window in the morning is enough to lower the levels of sleep-inducing melatonin and help reset your circadian rhythm for earlier wake-up times.

Why Don't Students Sleep Enough?

In an anonymous survey I conducted for this book, I asked students whether they consider they sleep enough to feel refreshed and fully awake the next day. Of the 56 respondents, only 4% stated they *always* sleep enough, 64% answered they *sleep enough most days,* but sometimes wake up tired. But 32% replied they *wake up tired most days* and are sleepy during the day.

In addition to sleep duration, schedule regularity is crucial. In the same survey, students evaluated the regularity of their sleep schedule. Four percent stated they always follow a regular schedule, going to sleep and waking up at the same time every day. A further 55% answered that they have a sleep schedule that is mostly regular, but not very strict, or that they follow a regular schedule most days, except for holidays and special occasions. Another 14% responded they sleep little during the week and *catch up* on the weekend. Finally, 27% conceded that their sleep is all over the place, both in terms of when they go to sleep and wake up, and how many hours they sleep per night. *This is the group at most risk of suffering detrimental consequences of sleep deprivation*.

The need to sleep tends to be undervalued. It is not unusual to hear people say, "I don't really need to sleep that much" and "I have gotten used to not sleeping much." There is a very detrimental, competitive culture in college and some companies, where lack of sleep is viewed as proof of commitment and investment. It leads to "one upping": "You slept five hours? I only slept three!" and to students feeling guilty if they sleep "too long" even when "too long" means meeting the recommended seven to nine hours.

The truth is that you cannot escape your biological needs. It is likely that your perception of how well you function with little sleep may be impaired by your lack of sleep, as your cognition capabilities decline when you are sleep deprived. Similarly to how a person under the influence of alcohol can inaccurately claim to be completely fine and sober, students have told me they don't need more sleep, even when they are falling asleep during classes. When on a regular basis you have difficulty falling or staying asleep, or not feeling rested after sleeping, even in an optimal sleep environment and giving yourself enough time and opportunity to sleep, you are possibly experiencing insomnia (Patel et al., 2024; Roth et al., 2007).

Insomnia involves predisposing, precipitating, and perpetuating factors. Advanced age is a *predisposing* or risk factor. *Precipitating* factors are acute events or stressors, such as final exams or illness. *Perpetuating* factors relate to how you deal with insomnia; some of your coping mechanisms can exacerbate and prolong it, such as using your smartphone when you wake up in the middle of the night (Levenson et al., 2015).

Medical causes of insomnia include sleep apnea, restless leg syndrome, pain and some chronic health conditions, medications, genetic risk factors, and aging. If you believe you may be struggling to sleep because of a medical condition, it would be helpful to speak to a physician or other medical practitioner about your situation.

A person's neurological makeup can also make it hard for them to sleep. ADHDers (like me) tend to have a cacophony of thoughts as they try to go to sleep, finally remembering an assignment due soon, or simply having a great idea they want to act upon. Worrying about the future, and ruminating about the past, make it more difficult to fall asleep or to return to sleep after waking up during the night. While worrying and rumination are somewhat common in people with depression, most people will experience them on occasion. It is important to note that feeling distressed about your lack of sleep makes it harder to go to sleep, creating a vicious cycle (Levenson et al., 2015; Roth et al., 2007).

Environmental and lifestyle causes of insomnia include jetlag and nighttime or shift work, as well as college living situations. Some environmental causes of insomnia are prevalent in college residence halls or shared housing situations, including noise and bright lights. Class schedules and other commitments, as well as social life, can lead to eating heavy meals late at night or engaging in intense exercise in the evening, both of which interfere with sleep. Not engaging in academic work during the day, for a variety of reasons, may translate into needing to work on assignments or studying late at night, delaying sleep.

In the same way as busy parents, professionals, and even military servicemembers, some students engage in what is called "bedtime procrastination" or "revenge bedtime procrastination" (Barrow et al., 2025). It refers to delaying going to sleep when there are no valid reasons to stay awake, because those evening hours are a "need this me-time" (Hill et al., 2022). In a systematic review of studies looking at this issue, Hill et al. (2022) found that bedtime procrastination is associated with lower self-control, and that it increased stress, anxiety, and depression. Bedtime procrastinators tended to find bedtime routines unpleasant and to both wake up and eat dinner later. There is a correlation with screen use; often, people spend this time awake at night engaging in low-effort activities such as watching short videos or reels on the internet. And generally, this time does not bring more than a very momentary satisfaction, with detrimental consequences the next day.

College students tend to experience sleep deprivation. Students participating in two studies reported sleeping around six hours/night and going to sleep at 1:00 a.m. or later on a regular basis, even when they had early morning classes the next day (Creswell et al., 2023; Ng et al., 2023). UK college students participating in a 2019 survey were categorized as "poor sleepers" based on their self-evaluation of sleep quality, and 28% of them reported significant daytime sleepiness. Furthermore, 59% stated their sleep habits impacted their health and well-being, and 62% reported their learning was affected. The study found that sleep quality, daytime sleepiness, depression, anxiety, and general well-being all correlated with each other (Stores et al., 2023).

My students' comments about their own sleep deprivation include the following:

- I think I often don't sleep enough because I have some fear in the back of my mind that I haven't done enough work, or I've forgotten something, so I'd feel guilty going to bed at a reasonable hour. (Emily)
- I struggle with sleeping enough because nighttime is some of the only time I have to myself. Sleeping more means that I have less time to do the things that I want to do. It also becomes a vicious cycle where being tired means I am less productive during the day, which means I have to cut down on sleep to stay productive. (Alexandra)
- I always say I'll make up for the sleep I lost the next day, but the next day comes and I end up sleeping late again. It's like a never ending cycle. (Anthony)
- My sleep quality is often a direct reflection of my academic workload and my belief that I can "catch up" on rest over the weekend. (A student)

Detrimental Effects of Not Sleeping Well

The importance of sleep is most obvious when seen through the *detrimental effects of not sleeping well*. Chronic sleep deprivation, i.e., routinely sleeping less than seven hours a night, is associated with a variety of health conditions, including decreased insulin sensitivity and diabetes, high blood pressure, heart disease, stroke, more frequent illnesses, and weight gain. It is also associated with impaired cognition and slower reaction time, reflected in a greater risk of accidents, as well as having difficulty concentrating and performing work-related tasks. Chronic sleep deficit may cause moodiness, fatigue, irritability, depression, carbohydrate cravings, and generally a decrease in quality of life. (Levenson et al., 2015; Madan Jha, 2022; Roth et al., 2007; Watson et al., 2015). One of my students commented that lack of sleep caused "a sharp decline in my memory retention and cognitive processing during morning lectures."

Studies have shown the importance of *sleeping well*. Ng et al. (2023), evaluating college students who were relatively sleep deprived (sleeping 6:03 hours on average), found that when students slept longer than usual, they were in a better mood and less sleepy. They were also more motivated in the morning, although motivation decreased throughout the day. In another study (Creswell et al., 2023) with similarly sleep deprived first-year students (averaging 6:37 hours of sleep per night), students who slept more at the beginning of the academic term had a higher final grade point average (GPA). In contrast, students who slept fewer than six hours a night had a lower final GPA.

A study where adolescents were allowed to sleep only five hours a night for seven days found that as the sleep debt accumulated, their working memory, executive functioning, and especially their sustained attention and processing speed decreased. In contrast, the control group slept about eight hours a night and maintained their baseline level of performance, mood, and level of sleepiness, while improving their processing speed (Lo et al., 2016).

Regularity in sleep duration is crucial. Ng et al. (2023) reported that students whose nighttime sleep duration varied more than one hour from one night to the next were less motivated and in a more negative mood in comparison to students with more regular sleep durations. In addition to how long you sleep, your sleep schedule needs to be consistent. The more unpredictable your sleep schedule is, the harder it is for your body to regulate your sleep-wake cycle (Deboer, 2018).

Sleep deprivation is detrimental to your learning. It hinders your memory consolidation and organization, and decreases your capacity to balance your emotional responses, which happen during N2, N3, and REM stages, as explained earlier. Not sleeping enough affects your physical health, mood, and motivation and in turn your engagement with learning. You cannot learn from a class you don't attend, a lecture you don't hear, or a book you don't read (discussed in more detail in Chapters 4 and 5).

College students fall asleep later at night due to an age-related delayed circadian rhythm and to their social environment. It is important to recognize that enrollment in early morning classes doesn't mean students taking those classes go to sleep earlier the night before: In many cases, they wake up earlier than usual but go to sleep at their usual time. Those students sleep about one fewer hour when they have early classes, leading to daytime sleepiness and impaired attention.

A study by Yeo et al. (2023) found that college students who had an early morning class slept less and took naps during the day. They determined that

GPA was highest for students with no morning classes and decreased as the number of early morning classes increased. The researchers advocate for universities to avoid mandatory early morning classes, stating that while they understand the institution's need to maximize the use of classrooms and minimize scheduling conflicts, early morning classes are detrimental to students learning.

While you, as student, cannot dictate when the university schedules classes, you can take into consideration your sleep needs and, if you need to sleep later, try to enroll in classes offered in the afternoon. If you have courses that are mandatory and only offered in the morning, the recommendation is to set your regular bedtime based on the start time of your earliest class.

How Can You Recover from Sleep Deprivation?

The treatment for occasional sleep deprivation is simply sleeping longer as soon as the opportunity arises. Sleeping in on weekends is a type of compensatory sleep and is linked to lower risk of heart disease (Liu & Song, 2024).

Naps can partly compensate for sleep deprivation. For instance, Ng et al. (2023) found long daytime naps improved mood and motivation. After a long nap, college students felt less sleepy, both for the remainder of that day, as well as the following day. However, naps need to be timed very carefully, as a nap later in the day can decrease your homeostatic sleep pressure, making it hard to fall asleep. And, when someone wakes up during deep sleep (N3), they tend to feel groggy for a while (Goel, 2017). To avoid grogginess or disorientation after napping, limiting your naps to 20–30 min would be appropriate (Baranwal et al., 2023). You also need to consider that daytime naps are shorter than nighttime sleep, and have a different pattern of sleep stages. It seems that the function of naps is different from that of nighttime sleep, and napping could have implications in your capacity to learn (Cajochen & Schmidt, 2025).

The detrimental effects of *chronic sleep restriction* are hard to counteract. After a partial sleep deprivation period, high achieving adolescents were given the opportunity to sleep for up to nine hours for two nights. The compensatory sleep was not enough to recover their sustained attention capacity, processing speed, or alertness (Lo et al., 2016). In a study with college students, after five nights of not sleeping enough, sleeping for ten hours the following night did not restore their usual attentiveness level, and they still felt sleepy and fatigued. By continuing to sleep well for a total of five nights (nine hours in bed) after being sleep deprived, they no longer felt sleepy, but their attentiveness remained low (Goel, 2017).

Several of my students have mentioned that when they are sleep deprived and then one night sleep much longer than usual, they wake up feeling more tired than before. This has led some to incorrectly conclude that this means sleeping for longer (e.g., nine hours) is detrimental for them. In reality, as seen earlier, in situations of chronic sleep restriction, one night or two of compensatory sleep is not enough. It would be necessary to continue sleeping well (e.g., eight to nine hours/night) until sleep deprived people feel alert and rested the next day. My personal recommendation for those who don't quite believe they need to sleep that much would be to track their mood, alertness, short-term memory, and any other parameters they find easy to track. They would track them while sleep deprived and continue tracking during a recovery period, to evaluate the benefits sleeping more brings *them* more objectively.

My students have found sleeping better has helped them:

- By establishing a more consistent bedtime, I have found that my general well-being has stabilized; I feel more mentally resilient and am able to engage more deeply with complex learning materials without the constant interference of daytime fatigue. (A student)
- When I prioritize sleep, I feel more focused, less stressed, and more engaged in class. (Alfredo)
- After creating a constant sleep schedule, paired with a rigorous academic and extracurricular schedule, I am now able to be more present in my daily life. (DK)

What Can You Do If You Must Stay Awake While Sleep Deprived?

If for some reason you do need to be awake even though you are sleep deprived, you can use *caffeine*. Caffeine increases your alertness and vigilance, reaction time, problem-solving, and reasoning, as well as your ability to perform complex tasks. Its effect declines the longer you remain awake; at some point, it will cease to prevent sleepiness, and your performance will decrease (Murray & Traylor, 2025). Importantly, caffeine only blocks your body's ability to recognize that you're sleepy; it does not solve the core issues that are making you not being able to sleep enough.

If you are regularly sleep deprived because your schedule is truly very busy, it is worth examining what can wait or is not *needed*. This may require taking fewer classes, not taking a very challenging version of a course if a not-so-challenging version exists, joining fewer clubs, etc. Sleeping less is not a long-term, sensible solution.

Recommendations to Create a Good Sleeping Environment and Habits

Creating a good sleeping environment and habits, also called *sleep hygiene*, can be challenging in college, especially when living in a group setting (residence halls, fraternity/sororities, or other shared housing). It is also possible that if students are severely sleep deprived, achieving good sleep hygiene will seem overwhelming and impossible to achieve. This could lead to them losing the motivation to try, or the sleep deprivation could be so extreme as to prevent students' ability to plan or act. In those cases, it is important to reach out to healthcare professionals who could help them create a plan of action that allows them to sleep better and for longer.

There are many aspects of sleep hygiene that you can act upon, while other aspects are not under your control.

Good sleep hygiene includes the following (Baranwal et al., 2023; Goel, 2017; Levenson et al., 2015):

Environmental Conditions

a *Temperature*: Aim for ~60°F–68°F (~15–20°C) to allow your body's core temperature to drop, which is a physiological requirement for sleep. This may be tricky to achieve if you don't have a way to control your room temperature or if you have a roommate. Having a fan on, or covering yourself with lighter blankets, could help keep your immediate environment at the right temperature.

b *Light*: Your room should be dark; even low levels of light, e.g., from your phone, can delay sleep. This also depends on your living situation. Some people find it helpful to use blackout curtains or sleep masks to cover all sources of light.

c *Noise*: This is probably the most difficult aspect to control. Even if you have a good environment inside your room, you may not be able to control the noise created by your neighbors or coming in from the street. However, you can reach out to people who may be able to help, e.g., your residential staff or your neighbors, and take advantage of tools to block out noise, such as fans, noise makers, music, or wearing ear plugs.

d *Create a comfortable environment*: your mattress, pillow, and bedding should help you feel snug and cozy.

Actions that Lead to Good Habit Creation

a *Associating bed with sleep*. This involves associating the optimal environmental conditions mentioned earlier with sleep, meaning you'd only go to bed when you're planning to sleep, using your bed only to sleep or soothing activities that don't cause stress, as stress may interfere with sleep.

b *Setting a schedule*. Define consistent bed/wake-up times throughout the week, aiming to sleep between seven and nine hours. This has been seen as one of the most important steps in creating the conditions for restful sleep. It supports your circadian rhythm and sleep homeostasis and creates a strong association between the time of day and sleep. Except for some specific circumstances, this is under your control.

c *Relaxing before bed.* Maintain a soothing and calming environment that may make it easier for you to fall asleep. Some activities that help include meditation and relaxation exercises such as focusing on your breath or performing a body check, stretching, listening to a podcast crafted to induce sleep, writing on a to-do list or calendar any pending task you remember as you try to go to sleep, distracting yourself from your worries or writing them down. If you would like help learning how to manage intrusive thoughts and minimizing worrying and ruminating, consider reaching out to your student health center.

d *Early exposure to sunlight.* It helps you reset your biological clock, supporting your circadian rhythm.

e *If you cannot fall asleep* within 15 minutes, you can get up and engage in soothing activities, then try again. This will help to keep the connection between rest and bed intact. Staying in bed, worrying about not sleeping, can create "conditioned or learned arousal," by associating your bed with anxiety instead of with rest. The same happens if you wake up briefly and then engage in activities that may interfere with going back to sleep; you may teach your body to wake up at that time to watch videos, read the news, etc.

f *Avoid very long, late afternoon or evening naps,* if possible, to prevent interfering with your homeostatic sleep pressure.

g *Exercising regularly.* It is not very clear what the mechanism of action of exercise is, but it has been seen that 30 minutes of moderate aerobic exercise enhance sleep by increasing the amount of deep sleep and total hours of sleep a night. It has also been shown to lower anxiety near bedtime. However, intense exercise three to six hours before bedtime can interfere with sleep.

h *Avoid large meals near bedtime.* Avoid eating within two hours of planned bedtime. Eating close to bedtime is associated with going to sleep late and a shorter sleep duration.

Common Substances That Can Interfere with Sleep

a *Caffeine,* present in coffee, black tea, green tea, yerba mate, and chocolate, keeps you awake by interfering with the feeling of sleepiness by blocking adenosine receptors in the brain. It makes it harder to fall asleep and reduces sleep duration and quality. Caffeine effects on people vary considerably, but generally, it should be avoided in the late afternoon and evening: the half-life of coffee is six to seven hours.

b *Stimulants* including some medications for ADHD (e.g., Adderall) and other medications, if taken in the late afternoon or evening.

c *Nicotine* has been found to lead to light sleep and waking up too early due to nicotine withdrawal symptoms.
d *Alcohol* is a sedative but disrupts your sleep cycle by increasing the time you spend in deep sleep (N3) while decreasing the duration of your REM sleep, total sleep duration, and its general quality. Additionally, using alcohol as an aid to fall asleep is a risk factor for substance use disorder.

Eat Well to Learn Well

The National Institute of Environmental Health Sciences (n.d.) defines nutrition as "the process of consuming, absorbing, and using nutrients from food that are necessary for growth, development, and maintenance of life."

Ensuring proper nutrition is a crucial part of learning. Unfortunately, it is one of the first areas disregarded when workload increases, even though lack of nutrition decreases your cognitive capacity and affects your health. In college campuses, it is common for students to skip meals even when they have a meal plan that includes two or more full meals per day.

Proper nutrition means ingesting enough liquids, including water, coffee, tea, soup, for example, and enough calories to fuel your body. That is the highest priority and falls within Maslow's description of human needs (1943), mentioned at the beginning of this chapter.

Once the *eating enough* piece is covered, you can focus on *what* you eat. The USDA's Dietary Guidelines for Americans 2020–2025 (2020–2025 DGA; U.S. Department of Agriculture and U.S. Department of Health and Human Services, 2020) focuses on macronutrients, i.e., protein, fat, and carbohydrates, followed by micronutrients, that is, vitamins and minerals (more in the following sections).

Depending on your lifestyle or circumstances, you may need additional or more specific macro- and micronutrients. Athletes, pregnant people, young and older adults, and people who have diabetes or other health conditions will have very specific needs.

Finally, you should consider the *added psychological and cognitive benefits* of eating regularly and using mealtimes to enjoy a well-deserved break. Sharing meals with others brings many benefits: Studies by De Neve et al. (2025) and Dunbar (2017) found that people who eat with others feel happier, are more satisfied with life, have higher levels of positive feelings, are more trusting of others, engage more with their local communities, and have more friends they can rely on. It adds to your sense of belonging, discussed at the beginning of this chapter. You don't need to enjoy your meal in the same room; you can share dining experiences and connect with friends and loved ones across the globe through online resources such as virtual meetings, videocalls and similar tools. Ellie and her partner, both college students, live far away from each other but manage to enjoy meals together. She wrote about this:

> My partner and I have been doing long distance for 5 months. We call several times a day and go on virtual restaurant dates. While it's not the same as being in person, we are still able to feel connected and loved, and it adds joy and color to both our lives.

There are many diets, be it for weight management or for specific conditions. Some are focused on lowering or increasing your intake of one particular macronutrient or limiting the hours in which you can eat. If you are interested in trying one out, it is recommended to speak to your primary care physician or a specialist to see if a given diet is a good idea for you, considering your situation and lifestyle.

The Components of Your Diet

Water

Water is crucial for your organism's metabolism, adequate blood circulation, for regulating your body temperature, absorbing valuable micronutrients, and more. The specific amount of liquid that you need to ingest per day depends on your level of activity, the temperature around you, your body size, and the amount of water in the food you eat (Armstrong & Johnson, 2018). Water is the most consumed beverage in the US 2025 DGAC; U.S. Department of Health and Human Services, 2024), and you also ingest water through soda, coffee, tea, and milk, and food such as stews and soups. Some of the food you eat is rich in water, e.g., melons, berries, oranges, romaine lettuce, tomatoes, and cucumbers. All of these add up to your *total water intake*. A recent study recommends a total water intake of 3.4 liters/day for males and 2.6 liters/day for females to ensure optimal hydration (Seal et al., 2023). Coffee and other caffeine-containing beverages are mild diuretics, increasing urine production, meaning that they are not as hydrating as non-caffeinated drinks.

Macronutrients

Carbohydrates are your main source of glucose, which is the main substrate needed for your cells to create usable energy. Carbohydrates are divided into "simple," "complex," and "fiber." Simple carbohydrates, e.g., fructose, lactose, and glucose, are found in candy, soda, fruit juice, milk, honey, and table sugar. These are quickly digested and converted into glucose. Complex carbohydrates are found in plants, e.g., potatoes, apples, lentils, and rice, and foods like pasta and bread, and require a longer process and more time to be digested. Fiber helps your digestion and ability to maintain healthy blood glucose and cholesterol levels. Simple carbohydrates are not considered as healthy as complex carbohydrates or fiber, and excess consumption is a risk factor for type 2 diabetes (Holesh et al., 2023).

Proteins are composed of amino acids and are used to manufacture hormones, enzymes, antibodies, neurotransmitters, and other substances. Some amino acids are categorized as essential, meaning that your body cannot synthesize them, and they must be part of your diet. These amino acids are involved in muscle growth and repair, development, reproduction, lactation, immune function, metabolism, and other crucial processes (Lopez & Mohiuddin, 2024).

Not eating enough protein puts you at risk of anemia, cardiovascular dysfunction, decreased immunity, transport, and storage of nutrients. A diet low in protein can lead to physical fatigue, emotional disorders, loss of calcium and bone mass, hair loss and more (Wu, 2016). Proteins are abundant in animal products, e.g., meat, eggs, milk, cheese, and yogurt, and in some vegetables like beans, peas, lentils, nuts, popcorn, and soy (2025 DGAC).

Fats or lipids are essential to produce sex hormones, maintain the structure of your cells, store energy, regulate body temperature, and to absorb vitamins A, D, E, and K. Fats include triglycerides, phospholipids, cholesterol and other fatty acids, and are divided into unsaturated and saturated. Saturated fats are found in animal products like meat, butter, lard, cheese, and yogurt; excess consumption is a risk factor for cardiovascular disease (2025 DGAC).

Micronutrients

Vitamins and minerals are needed in very small amounts and are crucial for normal metabolism and tissue function. You need to eat food rich in *vitamins*, as your body cannot produce them. They are needed for your vision, cell growth and differentiation, bone metabolism, calcium regulation, neuromuscular function, absorbing iron, etc. You need *minerals* to sustain your body functions, such as muscle contraction, maintaining adequate blood pressure and fluid balance, nerve impulse transmission, energy metabolism, oxygen transport, and synthesizing DNA, RNA, cell membranes, bones, and teeth.

Some health conditions and living in certain places, such as far away from the Equator, are risk factors for *nutritional deficiencies*. Deficiencies in vitamin A, vitamin D, folate, iodine, iron, and zinc are common; milk and orange juice among other foods are fortified with vitamins and/or minerals. While it is preferred to obtain your proteins and minerals from food, supplementing with multivitamins may be appropriate, under professional guidance (Espinosa-Salas & Gonzalez-Arias, 2023).

Effect of Nutrition on Physical Health

The 2024 National College Health Assessment (NCHA) conducted by the American College Health Association (2024), found that 2.6% of college students surveyed had a cardiovascular disorder, 3.3% had hypertension, and 3.7% high blood cholesterol; both are risk factors for stroke and heart disease. Diabetes, insulin resistance, and metabolic syndrome, also of concern, were reported by 3.6% of respondents to the 2024 NCHA. This is similar to the prevalence reported by the 2025 DGAC for adults ages 20–39 years, which is 4%.

Food choices that lower the risk of developing type 2 diabetes and other health conditions include higher amounts of vegetables, fruit, legumes, nuts, whole grains and fish or seafood. In contrast, ultra-processed food, higher amounts of red and processed meats, refined grains, and fried, salty, or sweet snacks are associated with poor health outcomes (2025 DGAC).

Effect of Nutrition on Mood and Academic Performance

"Hangry" is defined as feeling bad-tempered or irritable as a result of hunger (Oxford English Dictionary, n.d.). In a study of daily life effects of feeling hungry in adults, Swami et al. (2022) found that feeling hungry is linked to negative emotions, as well as to experiencing less pleasure. The researchers believe it could be related to low blood glucose levels lowering people's emotional self-control, meaning that small daily hassles are enough to trigger anger and irritability. Similarly, Ackermans et al. (2022) found that women fasting for 14 hours reported more tension, anger, fatigue, and confusion than nonfasting women.

"Emotional" or "stress eating" was reported by students in a focus group, who used mostly snacks to improve their mood (Sogari et al., 2018). Similarly, college students under stress reported eating food with more fat and sugar content and stated there were many barriers that prevented them from eating healthy food (Dalton, 2024).

Reuter et al. (2021) found that students who reported higher GPAs tended to have healthier eating habits, including eating breakfast at least five days per week. In contrast, eating more fast food was linked to a lower GPA. Similarly, Cheng and Rebecca Yew (2025) found that skipping breakfast was associated with poor academic performance, memory, and attention. In another study, students who regularly ate a nutritious breakfast were able to concentrate better during morning classes (Abdullah et al., 2024).

What You Should Eat: USDA's Dietary Guidelines

The 2020–2025 DGA are relatively flexible, and focus on following a "healthy dietary pattern," i.e., what people habitually eat and drink, instead of dictating specific amounts by food group. They recommend choosing *nutrient-dense* food and drinks, ingesting the nutrients needed, and limiting foods and beverages high in added sugars, saturated fat, and sodium, as well as alcoholic drinks.

A common difficulty people face when planning their diet is determining their calorie needs. For college-age people, the 2020–2025 DGA estimate between 2,400 and 2,600 calories/day for sedentary males and 1,800–2,000 calories/day for females. For moderately active people, it increases to 2,800 calories/day for males and 2,000–2,200 calories/day for females. Finally, active males should eat 3,000–3,200 calories/day and females, 2,400 calories/day.

A "healthy dietary pattern" includes eating vegetables, fruits, grains, dairy, proteins, and oils. The 2020–2025 DGA recommend at least 3 cups of vegetables/day, 2 cups of fruits, 8 ounces of whole grains, 3 cups of dairy, 6 ounces of protein, and 31 grams/day of oils. Added sugars and saturated fats should be limited to less than 10% of all calories ingested per day, and sodium to less than 2,300 mg per day.

You can easily impact the *nutrient density* in food. For example, you may want to eat 1 cup (8 g) of air-popped popcorn, which contains 31 calories, 6.22 g of carbohydrates, 1.16 g of fiber, and 1.03 g of protein, as well as many vitamins and minerals (USDA, 2018, 2019). Then, you add 2 tablespoons (30 g) of butter. That butter adds 204 calories and 24.66 g of fat, 13.68 g of which are saturated (USDA, 2018, 2019). You transformed a *nutrient-dense* food into a not-so-healthy choice. Your popcorn went from 31 calories, mostly from carbohydrates, to 235 calories, mostly from fat, including saturated fat, which you should minimize.

The 2025 DGAC states that while water is the most consumed beverage in the US, people also ingest sugar-sweetened drinks, such as soda, coffee, and tea. The added sugar in drinks translates into 38.7% of the total daily added sugars in males, and 34.7% in females.

Students' Dietary Habits

In the 2024 NCHA, a majority (72.5%) of college students reported drinking at least one sweetened beverage per day during the previous week. Most did not eat the recommended amount of fruit and vegetables: only 17.9% of college students answered they had eaten three or more servings of fruits in the previous week and only 28.2% had eaten three or more servings of vegetables in the previous week.

While the 2025 DGAC reports that 77% of 20- to 39-year-olds in the US eat breakfast, this is not the case for college students. A majority (68.2%) of college students reported skipping breakfast at least once a week (Nagalingam et al., 2024); this was especially true in the case of students who were facing financial constraints, identified as male, ate their first meal after 11 a.m., and ate snacks instead of a meal. Skipping breakfast was also common in college students surveyed by Cheng and Rebecca Yew (2025), with 67.3% stating they didn't eat in the morning.

Most college students in a focus group associated snacking with unhealthy eating (Sogari et al., 2018). However, several students prefer eating several snacks throughout the day instead of the breakfast-lunch-dinner pattern typical of the US. A few students reported eating healthy snacks, including nuts or fruit (Sogari et al., 2018).

Snacks are eaten by 86% of adults aged 20 or older in the US and provide snack eaters with 27% of their daily calories, 42% of daily added sugars and 26% of daily saturated fat. The most frequently eaten snacks include crackers, snack bars, pastries and other bakery items, candy, and ice cream (2025 DGAC).

Timing of meals is also important: *late evening meals*, i.e., food or beverages consumed after 8 p.m., can lead to poor nutrition: 66% of people aged 20–59 reported eating on average 550 calories' worth of food after 8 p.m. This meal accounted for 26% of daily added sugars and saturated fat. Most of the meals eaten late were snacks or sweets (2025 DGAC).

Barriers to Eating Enough or Following a Healthy Dietary Pattern in College

There are many obstacles preventing students from fulfilling their dietary needs, including lack of secure access to food, which is related to the price of food on campus and nearby grocery stores, and to the type of food offered or available.

Food insecurity in college campuses is unfortunately not rare; 42.3% of students surveyed for the 2024 NCHA declared having low or very low food security. Similarly, 41% of respondents in a national survey conducted by the Hope Center for Student Basic Needs at Temple University (2025) reported they experienced food insecurity in the previous month. Food insecurity is associated with anxiety, depression, and lower academic performance (Ahmad et al., 2022).

Students who have a meal plan that includes unlimited meals can face challenges related to limited opening hours of on-campus eateries, inconvenient locations, sensory issues such as noise and crowds in dining halls, time needed to eat on campus or cook at home, and more.

Other important barriers are food allergies and intolerances. Of the students surveyed for the 2024 NCHA, 13.1% declared having food allergies, and 1.1% reported having celiac disease. Depending on the severity of the allergy and intolerance, it may be critical for their food not to contain even traces of certain ingredients.

Religious and lifestyle dietary needs also play a role. In a recent study (Salvia et al., 2025), 4.6% of students surveyed reported adopting a vegan or vegetarian diet since starting college, while in another study 6.2% of students declared following a vegetarian diet (Olfert et al., 2022). Additionally, some religious needs may limit the type of meat student can eat, or the way the food should be prepared, e.g., halal and kosher diets. Muslim students may need to adhere to a certain meal schedule (e.g., during Ramadan), and other students may eat only within a certain window of time (e.g., intermittent fasting).

Students with food allergies or intolerances, specific religious or lifestyle-related dietary needs, and those facing sensory issues are at risk of social isolation, having a very limited amount of "safe" food and food-related anxiety (Konstantinou et al., 2025).

Some common issues faced by my students include the following:

- When I am stressed with school and cold during the winter, I crave comfort meals and have no energy to do anything more than use the microwave. I don't end up eating the healthiest.
- In the past, my nutritional habits were often dictated by convenience, leading to a reliance on processed snacks during long study sessions. I was motivated to improve my diet after recognizing a pattern of energy crashes that hindered my productivity in the afternoons.

Factors That Support Eating Enough and Following a Healthy Dietary Pattern in College

Eighty-six percent of colleges surveyed by Swipe Out Hunger (2024) stated offering a food pantry on campus to fight food insecurity. Additionally, the "Swipe Out Hunger" program allows students to donate *bonus meals* to be distributed to students in need. Of colleges surveyed, 27.4% offered this option.

Some colleges support students with allergies and intolerances by minimizing the risk of cross-contamination or cross-contact, providing ample training to dining staff, and labeling all food. To help students with limited time, or who want to avoid the noise and crowds inside dining halls, many institutions offer reusable containers or "grab and go" dishes, and have microwave ovens in public areas that students can use. Colleges' protective actions, including on-campus availability of healthy food choices, and ensuring they are not expensive, can minimize the negative impact of students' dietary and environmental needs on their quality of life (Konstantinou et al., 2025; Sogari et al., 2018).

Students' own actions are also important. Enjoying food is an important motivator to eat, and students can pay attention to the quality, flavor, smell, color, and texture of food to create appetizing dishes. Their meal companions are also important; for instance, students in a focus group mentioned that seeing others eating healthily motivated them to choose healthy food as well (Sogari et al., 2018). It is crucial to take mental note of the change you feel when you start eating more nutritious food, as one of my students did: "Transitioning to more balanced, nutrient-dense meals has vastly improved my physical well-being."

College students with dietary accommodation needs can reach out to campus staff such as disability consultants, nutritionists and dieticians who can work with students, offering guidance regarding dietary or sensory accommodations, and to design meals and snack ideas that help students eat a balanced diet.

Two of my students found that learning to cook can lead to eating healthy meals that they fully enjoy:

- Learning to cook has helped me improve my nutrition. I learned ways to incorporate whole foods into my diet in ways that make me excited to eat. I follow the idea of "adding, not subtracting" from my meals. If I increase my water and vegetable intake, I find myself snacking less and not craving as many high-calorie, low-nutrition foods. I like to meal prep, so I have at least one nutritionally dense meal each day. This way, I can be more flexible when eating out with friends or celebrating and knowing I have met at least some of my nutrition and protein goals. (Alexandra)
- My mom is an amazing cook, so I try to learn from her and make the time to continue eating healthy. The food options at this school are incredible as well, so it is not difficult to find healthy foods on campus if I don't have time to make my own. (Hugo M)

Nutrition for Neurodivergent Students

Sensory differences in autism may mean that certain smells, taste, texture and colors cause repulsion and an aversive eating experience. These experiences may create or exacerbate eating-related anxiety, which can be further intensified if the dining hall environment is perceived as chaotic, loud, and crowded. Students' coping mechanisms, strategies to minimize sensory stimuli, and self-advocacy are crucial; however, it is also important that colleges take sensory needs into consideration when designing dining spaces and offerings. *Neurodivergent-inclusive* dining spaces are those that use soft or natural lightning, acoustic panels that dampen sound to create low-noise areas, clear signage, and a layout that clearly marks where different types of food are found, allowing students to take food outside and offering a variety of food that takes in consideration sensory and other dietary needs, such as enabling students to avoid or to add dressings and sauces to their food (Dwyer et al., 2023; Tola et al., 2021)

Neurodivergent people, especially autistic people and ADHDers, tend to have more food intolerances or sensitivities, meaning that their bodies have difficulty digesting certain foods, or they have food aversions due to heightened sensitivity to one or more food characteristics, e.g., texture. The reasons for this are very complex and have not been fully elucidated (Hunter et al., 2025).

There is an association between neurodivergence, especially autism and ADHD, and eating disorders. Heightened sensitivity to external stimuli and aversive eating experiences can lead to ARFID (Avoidant Restrictive Food Intake Disorder), while a decreased sensitivity may lead to craving more stimuli from food, which could lead to binge eating. Similarly, the satiety cues may be felt too early, leading to eating very little, or too late, leading to eating in excess (Cobbaert et al., 2024).

The challenges faced by neurodivergent people include the sensory input given by the food itself, as well as other sensory processing differences. For example, some neurodivergent people are less sensitive to internal stimuli such as hunger or thirst (i.e., have lower interoceptive awareness), increasing the risk of dehydration and undernutrition. Some food restrictions could be related to literal and binary thinking in autistic students and may translate into students avoiding eating anything they consider unhealthy or unethical (i.e., orthorexia), for example (Cobbaert et al., 2024).

Emily, one of my students, stated that sensory issues create difficulties, and sometimes she needs to make hard choices:

> It's difficult for me to eat things I don't like or don't feel like eating, and if I can't find something I want to eat, I will sometimes not eat anything at all. I've found that I don't feel very good if I eat mostly unhealthy foods, nor do I feel good if I don't eat anything at all. I try to identify foods and snacks which are both healthy and made of foods I like. If I can't find something healthy, I'll allow myself something unhealthy because it's generally better than not eating anything at all.

Neurodivergent people may also have executive function issues, which could make them forget to eat or to drink water (Cobbaert et al., 2024) and not notice the passage of time—they may remember they haven't eaten after the dining hall has already closed. Those intending to cook at home may forget to buy groceries. Even choosing what to eat may be a stressful and challenging situation, especially when academic demands are high.

It is crucial that college staff helping neurodivergent students fulfill their dietary requirements use a *neurodiversity-affirming* approach. That is, they need to believe and understand that sensory processing differences are not under the person's control; strategies and tools need to ensure adequate nutrition while minimizing stress and frustration.

Active Body, Active Mind

Physical activity exerts a significant effect on your physical and mental health, as well as on your cognitive capacity. However, the benefits of exercising on a regular basis are not as readily apparent as those of sleep or eating. By this I mean that, if you don't sleep at all one night, you'll very likely feel disoriented and tired the next day; if you don't eat for a long time, you'll feel famished. But if you don't exercise one day, you probably won't feel anything. However, if you spend most days sitting for long stretches of time, at some point, you will start feeling the detrimental effects of not exercising. Still, it may be challenging to parse out which effects are unique to exercise. In fact, physical activity is often evaluated in conjunction with sleep, eating behaviors, body weight, and physical and mental health, as they are all interconnected.

Practicing group sports offers additional psychological benefits given by a strong sense of belonging and support given by your teammates. Group sports also improve your cognition, as they require learning rules, adapting to changing conditions, strategizing with your teammates, and more.

ADHD is believed to be more common among athletes than in the general population. Many athletes who are ADHDers started practicing sports because their caregivers felt uneasy about stimulant medications and believed exercise was a good alternative (Pujalte et al., 2023). Ekman et al. (2021) suggested that some traits of ADHD may be advantageous to athletes, such as the ability to hyperfocus, having a lot of energy, and their persistence and endurance.

Ekman et al. (2021), in a study comparing athletes to nonathletes in high school, concluded that the athlete population had more ADHD traits than nonathletes. In their study, a trained psychotherapist evaluated all study participants for ADHD; none of them had a previous diagnosis. Athletes showed a significantly higher likelihood of being ADHDers than nonathletes. Athletes reported experiencing more ADHD-related challenges in the classroom than nonathletes, while during trainings, those challenges were minimized. This could point toward strategies to improve the classroom environment to support students with ADHD traits.

Another study compared the effects of cycling or Hatha yoga on ADHDers and non-ADHDers. Cycling decreased impulsivity for both groups, while yoga only benefited ADHDers. Exercise did not improve attention or impulsivity, and didn't reduce hyperactivity signs in ADHDers (Dinu et al., 2023). While exercise may decrease some ADHD-related challenges in ADHDers, it's not considered that exercise can or should replace medication. In fact, while the National Collegiate Athletic Association (2025) bans stimulant medications, they provide an exception for student athletes who are ADHDers and are prescribed stimulant medications as a component of their ADHD treatment.

World Health Organization (WHO) Guidelines on Physical Activity and Sedentary Behavior

The WHO guidelines (2020) are given for different ages; the recommendations that follow are for adults aged 18–64 years. As stated in the guidelines, *physical activity* is any movement done by skeletal muscles that require spending energy.

The term *aerobic* in relation to *exercise* is defined by the *Merriam-Webster* Medical Dictionary (n.d.) as an *activity that increases the body's demand for oxygen, thereby resulting in a marked increase in respiration and heart rate*. It improves the capacity of the cardiovascular system to uptake and transport energy (Millstein, 2013). For the purposes of the WHO guidelines, *aerobic physical activity* or *endurance activity* is an activity in which the body's large muscles move in a rhythmic manner for a sustained period of time (Bull et al., 2020). It includes active recreation and games, including sports, games, play, and transportation by wheeling, walking, and cycling (WHO, 2020).

Muscle strengthening refers to activities that increase muscular strength, power, endurance, and mass, and promote bone growth and strength; this includes running, jumping rope, and lifting weights (WHO, 2020).

There are many ways to be physically active, including fun activities like dancing, which are sometimes overlooked as exercise. Similarly, work or household chores that require effort—lifting, pushing heavy objects, gardening, etc.—are also valuable as physical activities, and some of those chores may fit into the aerobic or muscle-strengthening categories. In contrast, *sedentary behavior* is defined as sitting, reclining, or lying down; these are typical of desk work, studying, attending lectures, driving, and watching TV.

While the evidence is deemed as having "moderate certainty," WHO strongly recommends regular physical activity for adults aged 18–64 years. The minimum time per week recommended depends on the intensity: for moderate intensity, they recommend 150–300 minutes (2:15–5:00 hours); for vigorous intensity, at least 75–150 minutes (1:15–2:15 hours), or an equivalent mix of both. Additionally, WHO highly recommends practicing muscle-strengthening activities of moderate or greater intensity that involve all major muscle groups two or more days a week. However, WHO also states that doing some physical activity is better than doing none, and recommends sedentary adults to start by doing small amounts of exercise and gradually increase the frequency, intensity, and duration over time (WHO, 2020).

How Much Do College Students Exercise?

College students are in an environment that allows them to engage in as little or as much physical activity as they desire. Arguably, the student population with the highest level of physical activity are varsity athletes. For the

24–25 academic year, the National Collegiate Athletic Association (2024) registered a total of 554,298 student athletes for all divisions, constituting around 3% of the total student population (National Student Clearinghouse Research Center, 2025).

Many other students participate actively in sports, e.g., intramural sports, student organizations or clubs, and other recreational physical activities such as dance, which can take place on or off campus. The number of students involved in these activities cannot be accurately measured.

The fall 2024 NCHA Health Assessment of students across the US found that 70.4% of students engaged weekly in 150 minutes of moderate aerobic exercise, 75 minutes of vigorous aerobic exercise, or a combination of both; 41.2% reported participating in the recommended aerobic exercise in addition to muscle-strengthening activities. Finally, only 32.8% stated being *highly active*, defined as meeting the recommendations for muscle-strengthening activities and *twice* the amount of aerobic exercise (National Student Clearinghouse Research Center, 2025). This means that 29.6% of college students do not meet WHO's minimum recommendations of weekly aerobic exercise.

Many academic activities, research, and on-campus employment facilitate a sedentary lifestyle, e.g., sitting during lectures or studying. The physical activity of many students is limited to walking to class and to other activities. Their daily amount of exercise depends on the landscape and size of their college campus, location of the different courses and events they attend, and availability of public transportation or parking spaces. Engaging in an active lifestyle may not be needed or encouraged in college; in many ways, students need to desire and be given the opportunity to be physically active. Some colleges offer fun physical education courses, such as scuba diving, tree climbing, figure skating, martial arts, and more, and have increased the opportunity for students to remain active while having fun—for example, by building bowling alleys or climbing walls on campus.

My students mentioned some reasons they don't exercise as much as they think they need:

- I am in a demanding major and, as much as I like working out, expending the extra energy to do so seems more harmful than helpful when I'm already so exhausted from work, classes, homework, and extracurriculars. (Maddy)
- I have frequently struggled to exercise consistently due to the belief that physical activity is a secondary priority to my studies. (A student)
- I hardly exercise at all, partially because I feel like I'm not "qualified." I never did sports as a kid, so my endurance is really, really bad. I don't want to start and see that I'm not good enough to do it. (Madeline)

The Risks of a Sedentary Lifestyle

College students tend to spend a lot of time sitting. In a qualitative study, students mentioned that to feel productive, they needed to sit down to study and remain sitting for a long time, without breaks and much less getting up. They commented they often remained sitting, even during study breaks. Students also said they needed to be in the right mindset to engage in challenging academic work and that when they are in "the zone," i.e., intensely focused, they often forget to take breaks. Other students avoided taking breaks, fearing exiting "the zone" or getting distracted (Wood et al., 2024).

Not taking enough breaks and remaining in uncomfortable body postures for long periods of time can lead to musculoskeletal pain, as was the case for 87% of architecture students in a study. Neck pain was the most common type of pain, followed by lower back, elbow, and hand pain. Prolonged standing and sitting also caused pain. Up to 48.8% of the students said pain prevented them from participating in everyday activities (Algabbani, 2024).

Kuai et al. (2025) saw that sedentary behaviors correlated with sleep deprivation. This created a vicious cycle: sedentary behaviors induced mental fatigue and physical discomfort. Students tried to alleviate their mental fatigue by engaging online at night, consequently going to sleep later, and experiencing lower quality sleep. The next day, they felt tired and were less likely to be physically active, and the cycle began again.

Zhang et al. (2025) found that university students who usually sat for more than six hours a day had significantly higher levels of anxiety and depression, and poorer sleep quality. A sedentary lifestyle was linked to less healthy nutritional habits, more stress, and chronic health conditions.

Excessive and prolonged sedentary behaviors can lead to insulin resistance, which could lead to pre-diabetes and eventually type 2 diabetes. Other detrimental effects include decreased cardiorespiratory fitness, loss of muscular strength and mass, bone mass, an increase in body fat, blood lipid concentrations, and inflammation (Pinto et al., 2023).

Maddy, a student of mine, commented about the impact of sedentary behaviors: "I realized that prolonged sedentary behavior was leading to physical discomfort and persistent 'brain fog.'"

Exercise Improves Your Physical Health

According to WHO (2020), physical activity lowers the risks of hypertension, death due to cardiovascular disease, type 2 diabetes, colon and breast cancers, and developing anxiety and depression. They consider that physical activity supports weight management and improves sleep and health-related quality of life.

Pinto et al. (2023) reported that when mostly sedentary people incorporate more physical activity, there are health benefits that can be observed relatively soon, such as an improvement in insulin activity, blood glucose concentration, and blood pressure. In the long run, minimizing sedentary behaviors improves brain blood flow, cardiovascular fitness, and lipid composition in blood. Increasing physical activity also causes a decrease in risk factors for diabetes.

"Active commuting," that is, wheeling, walking, or cycling to work or classes, was seen as highly beneficial. Dinu et al. (2019) analyzed 23 studies and concluded that active commuting reduced the risk of mortality (−8%), cardiovascular disease (−9%), and diabetes (−30%). Cycling also reduced the risk of mortality for any cause (−24%) and mortality due to cancer (−25%). Similarly, Wu et al. (2021) found that active commuting decreased the risk of obesity (−12%) and diabetes (−18%).

My students stated that exercising more has made a positive difference in their lives:

- Since incorporating regular movement into my routine, I've experienced a significant boost in my mental clarity. This improvement in physical health has supported my learning by acting as a natural stress reliever, allowing me to return to my work with renewed focus and a more positive outlook. (A student)
- Exercise has always helped me feel better. It's easy to miss how important it is, but taking an hour to get myself moving makes me feel more alive and is also something I can feel good about doing. Even if classwork for the day was brutal, I can get a workout in and feel good about achieving something. (Pat O)
- I exercise a good amount due to my commitment to Division I Athletics. I notice that being on a team keeps me consistent with staying healthy and being disciplined to a schedule. (DK)
- Having a gym buddy to hold each other responsible has led me to exercise enough. I tend to sleep better and feel more energized if I exercise consistently, so that motivates me to exercise. (Dahlia)

Exercise Supports Well-Being

A review by Singh et al. (2023) summarized the results of multiple studies and found that increasing physical activity mitigated symptoms of mild-to-moderate depression, anxiety, and psychological distress. More intense exercise was linked to greater improvements for depression and anxiety. Yoga and similar practices were most beneficial for anxiety, and depression was most effectively managed through resistance exercise (i.e., muscle-strengthening activities, including weightlifting and exercises using resistance bands).

Exercise has been proven to raise levels of several "feel good" hormones and other neurotransmitters such as endocannabinoids, endorphins, serotonin, and dopamine, which reduce stress, lift your spirits, improve mood, help you regulate emotions, and produce a sensation of euphoria and well-being (Pujari, 2024). Indeed, Wang et al. (2022) determined that exercise improved college students' emotional intelligence, which enhanced participants' subjective well-being, i.e., students felt more positive emotions, less negative emotions, and more life satisfaction.

It is important to emphasize that mental health, in addition to supporting a person's well-being, is crucial for academic success. Zhao et al. (2024), based on their observations of physical activities in college students, concluded that high-level cognition is influenced and regulated by positive emotions.

Exercise Improves Executive Function and Cognition

It is believed that long-term training improves the physiological structure and function of the central nervous system and the brain. Sports practice include sport-specific learning, as well as development of a variety of skills, such as motor, decision-making, visual attention, and anticipation. Athletes demonstrate enhanced working memory—that is, the ability to hold information in their mind and use it appropriately. Athletes also show better decision-making, problem-solving, and inhibition, i.e., the capacity to ignore distractions and control one's actions and reactions. Elite athletes show better cognitive flexibility, i.e., switching their attention, responses, and perspectives, which is developed over a longer period of time (Doucette et al., 2025; Ren et al., 2025).

Similarly, college students high in aerobic fitness were more likely to use more efficient strategies to solve an arithmetic task than students with low aerobic fitness. They also showed cognitive flexibility, shifting their strategies as the tasks became more difficult (McGowan et al., 2025). Studying high schoolers, Jaimes Crispín and Sigales Ruiz (2025) found that students who engage in physical activity had a higher GPA.

Self-efficacy refers to a person's confidence and conviction in their ability to overcome challenges and accomplish specific goals, which can be shaped by their experiences of success and failure; it is an important component of academic success. Wang et al. (2022) determined that exercise improved self-efficacy in college students, enhancing their well-being. Similarly, Zhao et al. (2024) found a strong association between physical activity and self-efficacy in college students; they posit that exercise contributes to self-confidence and resilience, i.e., the ability to overcome setbacks.

In Brief

Sleeping seven to nine hours a night and eating enough nutritious food will help you think more clearly, and maintain your physical, emotional, and mental health. *Sleep deprivation* can produce behaviors similar to those experienced by ADHDers, such as not being able to pay attention during class. Lack of sleep also leads to poor retention of information during the day and insufficient consolidation of memories. Not eating enough can lead to feeling *"hangry"* and unable to pay attention, while becoming more impulsive and reactive. For students facing executive function challenges, exercise, and group sports in particular, may help improve attention span and reaction time, while decreasing impulsiveness. Acquiring good sleep, eating and physical activity habits can take time. It is recommended to start improving your habits in those three areas by establishing an attainable goal, rather than trying to fix everything at once.

References

Abdullah, M., Khurram, K., Asim, A., Naveed, E., Abbas, M., Raja, H. Z., Saleem, N., Alnaser, A. F., Aldhafeeri, Y. R., & Alnusayri, F. S. (2024). Impact of breakfast consumption and sleep habits on morning attention and concentration among health professional students. *Cureus*. https://doi.org/10.7759/cureus.69592

Ackermans, M. A., Jonker, N. C., Bennik, E. C., & De Jong, P. J. (2022). Hunger increases negative and decreases positive emotions in women with a healthy weight. *Appetite, 168*, 105746. https://doi.org/10.1016/j.appet.2021.105746

Ahmad, N. S. S., Sulaiman, N., & Sabri, M. F. (2022). Psychosocial factors as mediator to food security status and academic performance among university students. *International Journal of Environmental Research and Public Health, 19*(9), 5535. https://doi.org/10.3390/ijerph19095535

Algabbani, M. F. (2024). Prevalence of musculoskeletal pain among architecture undergraduates students: A cross-sectional study. *Work, 78*(3), 841–847. https://doi.org/10.3233/WOR-230459

American College Health Association (2024). *National college health assessment III: Reference group executive summary Fall 2024*. Retrieved November 26, 2025, from https://www.acha.org/ncha/data-results/survey-results/academic-year-2024-2025/

Armstrong, L. E., & Johnson, E. C. (2018). Water intake, water balance, and the elusive daily water requirement. *Nutrients, 10*(12), 1928. https://doi.org/10.3390/nu10121928

Baranwal, N., Yu, P. K., & Siegel, N. S. (2023). Sleep physiology, pathophysiology, and sleep hygiene. *Progress in Cardiovascular Diseases, 77*, 59–69. https://doi.org/10.1016/j.pcad.2023.02.005

Barrow, T. R., Cooper, C. R., Revell, L., Haugen, T., & Gregg, B. T. (2025). The characterization of revenge bedtime procrastination in military servicemembers. *Military Medicine*, usaf519. https://doi.org/10.1093/milmed/usaf519

Bigelow, A. E., & Williams, L. R. (2020). To have and to hold: Effects of physical contact on infants and their caregivers. *Infant Behavior and Development, 61,* 101494. https://doi.org/10.1016/j.infbeh.2020.101494

Bull, F. C., Al-Ansari, S. S., Biddle, S., Borodulin, K., Buman, M. P., Cardon, G., Carty, C., Chaput, J.-P., Chastin, S., Chou, R., Dempsey, P. C., DiPietro, L., Ekelund, U., Firth, J., Friedenreich, C. M., Garcia, L., Gichu, M., Jago, R., Katzmarzyk, P. T., … Willumsen, J. F. (2020). World Health Organization 2020 guidelines on physical activity and sedentary behaviour. *British Journal of Sports Medicine, 54*(24), 1451–1462. https://doi.org/10.1136/bjsports-2020-102955

Cajochen, C., & Schmidt, C. (2025). The circadian brain and cognition. *Annual Review of Psychology, 76*(1), 115–141. https://doi.org/10.1146/annurev-psych-022824-043825

Cheng, S.-H., & Rebecca Yew, L. Q. (2025). Breakfast skipping: Influencing factors and its impact on cognitive function and academic performance among Malaysian university students. *Perceptual and Motor Skills, 132*(5), 829–850. https://doi.org/10.1177/00315125251329999

Cobbaert, L., Millichamp, A. R., Elwyn, R., Silverstein, S., Schweizer, K., Thomas, E., & Miskovic-Wheatley, J. (2024). Neurodivergence, intersectionality, and eating disorders: A lived experience-led narrative review. *Journal of Eating Disorders, 12*(1), 187. https://doi.org/10.1186/s40337-024-01126-5

Cordone, S., Annarumma, L., Rossini, P. M., & De Gennaro, L. (2019). Sleep and β-amyloid deposition in Alzheimer disease: Insights on mechanisms and possible innovative treatments. *Frontiers in Pharmacology, 10,* 695. https://doi.org/10.3389/fphar.2019.00695

Creswell, J. D., Tumminia, M. J., Price, S., Sefidgar, Y., Cohen, S., Ren, Y., Brown, J., Dey, A. K., Dutcher, J. M., Villalba, D., Mankoff, J., Xu, X., Creswell, K., Doryab, A., Mattingly, S., Striegel, A., Hachen, D., Martinez, G., & Lovett, M. C. (2023). Nightly sleep duration predicts grade point average in the first year of college. *Proceedings of the National Academy of Sciences, 120*(8), e2209123120. https://doi.org/10.1073/pnas.2209123120

Dalton, E. D. (2024). Emotional eating in college students: Associations with coping and healthy eating motivators and barriers. *International Journal of Behavioral Medicine, 31*(4), 563–572. https://doi.org/10.1007/s12529-023-10193-y

de Menezes-Júnior, L. A. A., Sabião, T. D. S., Carraro, J. C. C., Machado-Coelho, G. L. L., & Meireles, A. L. (2025). The role of sunlight in sleep regulation: Analysis of morning, evening and late exposure. *BMC Public Health, 25*(1), 3362. https://doi.org/10.1186/s12889-025-24618-8

De Neve, J.-E., Dugan, A., Kaats, M., & Prati, A. (2025). Sharing meals with others: How sharing meals supports happiness and social connections. In S. Wang, J. F. Helliwell, R. Layard, J. D. Sachs, J.-E. De Neve, & L. B. Aknin (Eds.), *Wellbeing Research Centre* (1st ed., pp. 57–92). University of Oxford. https://www.worldhappiness.report/ed/2025/sharing-meals-with-others-how-sharing-meals-supports-happiness-and-social-connections

Deboer, T. (2018). Sleep homeostasis and the circadian clock: Do the circadian pacemaker and the sleep homeostat influence each other's functioning? *Neurobiology of Sleep and Circadian Rhythms, 5,* 68–77. https://doi.org/10.1016/j.nbscr.2018.02.003

Dinu, L. M., Singh, S. N., Baker, N. S., Georgescu, A. L., Singer, B. F., Overton, P. G., & Dommett, E. J. (2023). The effects of different exercise approaches on attention deficit hyperactivity disorder in adults: A randomised controlled trial. *Behavioral Sciences, 13*(2), 129. https://doi.org/10.3390/bs13020129

Dinu, M., Pagliai, G., Macchi, C., & Sofi, F. (2019). Active commuting and multiple health outcomes: A systematic review and meta-analysis. *Sports Medicine, 49*(3), 437–452. https://doi.org/10.1007/s40279-018-1023-0

Doucette, M. M., Sánchez Escudero, J. P., Rhodes, R. E., & Garcia-Barrera, M. A. (2025). Associations of physical activity and history of sports participation with subjective and objective measures of executive functioning in university students. *Journal of American College Health, 73*(6), 2433–2442. https://doi.org/10.1080/07448481.2023.2299414

Dunbar, R. I. M. (2017). Breaking bread: The functions of social eating. *Adaptive Human Behavior and Physiology, 3*(3), 198–211. https://doi.org/10.1007/s40750-017-0061-4

Dwyer, P., Mineo, E., Mifsud, K., Lindholm, C., Gurba, A., & Waisman, T. C. (2023). Building neurodiversity-inclusive postsecondary campuses: Recommendations for leaders in higher education. *Autism in Adulthood, 5*(1), 1–14. https://doi.org/10.1089/aut.2021.0042

Ekman, E., Hiltunen, A., & Gustafsson, H. (2021). Do athletes have more of a cognitive profile with ADHD criteria than non-athletes? *Sports, 9*(5), 61. https://doi.org/10.3390/sports9050061

Espinosa-Salas, S., & Gonzalez-Arias, M. (2023). Nutrition: Micronutrient intake, imbalances, and interventions. In *StatPearls*. StatPearls Publishing. Retrieved December 22nd, 2025, from https://www.ncbi.nlm.nih.gov/books/NBK597352/

Gangitano, E., Baxter, M., Voronkov, M., Lenzi, A., Gnessi, L., & Ray, D. (2023). The interplay between macronutrients and sleep: Focus on circadian and homeostatic processes. *Frontiers in Nutrition, 10*, 1166699. https://doi.org/10.3389/fnut.2023.1166699

Goel, N. (2017). Neurobehavioral effects and biomarkers of sleep loss in healthy adults. *Current Neurology and Neuroscience Reports, 17*(11), 89. https://doi.org/10.1007/s11910-017-0799-x

He, M., Ru, T., Li, S., Li, Y., & Zhou, G. (2023). Shine light on sleep: Morning bright light improves nocturnal sleep and next morning alertness among college students. *Journal of Sleep Research, 32*(2), e13724. https://doi.org/10.1111/jsr.13724

Hill, V. M., Rebar, A. L., Ferguson, S. A., Shriane, A. E., & Vincent, G. E. (2022). Go to bed! A systematic review and meta-analysis of bedtime procrastination correlates and sleep outcomes. *Sleep Medicine Reviews, 66*, 101697. https://doi.org/10.1016/j.smrv.2022.101697

Holesh, J. E., Aslam, S., & Martin, A. (2023). Physiology, carbohydrates. In *StatPearls*. StatPearls Publishing. Retrieved December 22nd, 2025, from http://www.ncbi.nlm.nih.gov/books/NBK459280/

Honma, S. (2018). The mammalian circadian system: A hierarchical multi-oscillator structure for generating circadian rhythm. *The Journal of Physiological Sciences, 68*(3), 207–219. https://doi.org/10.1007/s12576-018-0597-5

Hunter, C., Smith, C., Davies, E., Dyall, S. C., & Gow, R. V. (2025). A closer look at the role of nutrition in children and adults with ADHD and neurodivergence. *Frontiers in Nutrition, 12*, 1586925. https://doi.org/10.3389/fnut.2025.1586925

Jaimes Crispín, D. C., & Sigales Ruiz, S. R. (2025). Eating habits and academic performance in secondary school: A cross-sectional analysis in a public school. *Revista Cuidarte, 16*(3). https://pmc.ncbi.nlm.nih.gov/articles/PMC12654285

Kim, J., & Park, M. (2025). Systems memory consolidation during sleep: Oscillations, neuromodulators, and synaptic remodeling. *BMB Reports, 58*(10), 425–436. https://doi.org/10.5483/BMBRep.2025-0033

Konstantinou, G. N., Pampoukidou, O., Sergelidis, D., & Fotoulaki, M. (2025). Managing food allergies in dining establishments: Challenges and innovative solutions. *Nutrients, 17*(10), 1737. https://doi.org/10.3390/nu17101737

Kuai, F., Wu, X., Zhou, X., & Liu, W. (2025). Association and benefits of 24-h activity behavior and academic procrastination among Chinese college students based on the isotemporal substitution model. *Frontiers in Public Health, 13*, 1700750. https://doi.org/10.3389/fpubh.2025.1700750

Levenson, J. C., Kay, D. B., & Buysse, D. J. (2015). The pathophysiology of insomnia. *Chest, 147*(4), 1179–1192. https://doi.org/10.1378/chest.14-1617

Liu, Z., & Song, Y. J. (2024). Weekend compensatory sleep is associated with reduced risk of heart disease: A prospective UK biobank-based cohort study. *European Heart Journal, 45*(Suppl. 1), ehae666.3582. https://doi.org/10.1093/eurheartj/ehae666.3582

Lo, J. C., Ong, J. L., Leong, R. L. F., Gooley, J. J., & Chee, M. W. L. (2016). Cognitive performance, sleepiness, and mood in partially sleep deprived adolescents: The need for sleep study. *Sleep, 39*(3), 687–698. https://doi.org/10.5665/sleep.5552

Lopez, M. J., & Mohiuddin, S. S. (2024). Biochemistry, essential amino acids. In *StatPearls*. StatPearls Publishing. Retrieved January 11, 2026, from: https://www.ncbi.nlm.nih.gov/books/NBK557845/

Lutz, N. D., Harkotte, M., & Born, J. (2026). Sleep's contribution to memory formation. *Physiological Reviews, 106*(1), 363–483. https://doi.org/10.1152/physrev.00054.2024

Madan Jha, V. (2022). The prevalence of sleep loss and sleep disorders in young and old adults. *Aging Brain, 3*, 100057. https://doi.org/10.1016/j.nbas.2022.100057

Mahoney, M. M. (2010). Shift work, jet lag, and female reproduction. *International Journal of Endocrinology, 2010*, 1–9. https://doi.org/10.1155/2010/813764

Maslow, A. H. (1943). A theory of human motivation. *Psychological Review, 50*(4), 370–396. https://doi.org/10.1037/h0054346

McGowan, A. L., Ellison, O. K., Ham, M. S., Chandler, M. C., & Pontifex, M. B. (2025). Aerobic fitness modulates arithmetic strategy use in college-aged young adults. *Trends in Neuroscience and Education, 40*, 100258. https://doi.org/10.1016/j.tine.2025.100258

Merriam-Webster Medical Dictionary (n.d.) *Aerobic*. Retrieved February 17, 2026, from https://www.merriam-webster.com/dictionary/aerobic#medicalDictionary

Millstein, R. (2013). Aerobic exercise. In M. D. Gellman & J. R. Turner (Eds.), *Encyclopedia of Behavioral medicine*. New York: Springer. https://doi.org/10.1007/978-1-4419-1005-9_1087

Murray, A., & Traylor, J. (2025). Caffeine toxicity. In *StatPearls*. StatPearls Publishing. http://www.ncbi.nlm.nih.gov/books/NBK532910/

Nagalingam, L., Felicia, J. P., Aishwarya, P. M., & Nithya, V. (2024). A cross-sectional study on the prevalence of skipping breakfast among college-going students in a private university. *Cureus*. https://doi.org/10.7759/cureus.76700

National College Health Association (2024). *National college health assessment Fall 2024 Reference group data report*. Retrieved November 26, 2025, from https://www.acha.org/ncha/data-results/survey-results/academic-year-2024-2025/

National Collegiate Athletic Association (2025). Medical Exceptions Procedures. Retrieved May 29 2026, from https://www.ncaa.org/sports/2015/1/23/medical-exceptions-procedures.aspx

National Institute of Environmental Health Sciences (n.d.). *Nutrition, health, and your environment*. Retrieved December 6, 2025, from https://www.niehs.nih.gov/health/topics/nutrition

National Student Clearinghouse Research Center (2025). *Current term enrollment estimates*. Retrieved November 17, 2025, from https://nscresearchcenter.org/current-term-enrollment-estimates/

Ng, A. S. C., Massar, S. A. A., Bei, B., & Chee, M. W. L. (2023). Assessing 'readiness' by tracking fluctuations in daily sleep duration and their effects on daily mood, motivation, and sleepiness. *Sleep Medicine, 112*, 30–38. https://doi.org/10.1016/j.sleep.2023.09.028

Olarescu, N. C., Gunawardane, K., Hanson, T. K., Møller, N., & Jørgensen, J. O. L. (2000). Normal physiology of growth hormone in normal adults. In K. R. Feingold, R. A. Adler, S. F. Ahmed, B. Anawalt, M. R. Blackman, G. Chrousos, E. Corpas, W. W. de Herder, K. Dhatariya, K. Dungan, E. Hamilton, J. Hofland, S. Jan de Beur, S. Kalra, G. Kaltsas, N. Kapoor, M. Kim, C. Koch, P. Kopp, … D. P. Wilson (Eds.), *Endotext*. MDText.com, Inc. http://www.ncbi.nlm.nih.gov/books/NBK279056

Olfert, M. D., Barr, M. L., Mathews, A. E., Horacek, T. M., Riggsbee, K., Zhou, W., & Colby, S. E. (2022). Life of a vegetarian college student: Health, lifestyle, and environmental perceptions. *Journal of American College Health, 70*(1), 232–239. https://doi.org/10.1080/07448481.2020.1740231

Oxford English Dictionary (n.d.). *Hangry*. Retrieved December 6, 2025, from https://www.oed.com/search/dictionary/?scope=Entries&q=hangry

Parrino, L., Rausa, F., Balella, G., Bottignole, D., Rosenzweig, I., & Mutti, C. (2025). The 70 years since the discovery of rapid eye movement sleep: History, electroencephalographic features and unsolved issues. *Journal of Sleep Research, 34*(3), e14342. https://doi.org/10.1111/jsr.14342

Patel, A. K., Reddy, V., Shumway, K. R., & Araujo, J. F. (2024). Physiology, sleep stages. In *StatPearls*. StatPearls Publishing. http://www.ncbi.nlm.nih.gov/books/NBK526132/

Pinto, A. J., Bergouignan, A., Dempsey, P. C., Roschel, H., Owen, N., Gualano, B., & Dunstan, D. W. (2023). Physiology of sedentary behavior. *Physiological Reviews, 103*(4), 2561–2622. https://doi.org/10.1152/physrev.00022.2022

Pujalte, G. G. A., Narducci, D. M., Smith, M. S., King, R., Logan, K., Callender, S. S., Liebman, C. A., Kane, S. F., Israel, M. P., Wolf, S. F., Nuti, R., & Khodaee, M. (2023). Athletes with attention-deficit/hyperactivity disorder: Position statement of the American medical society for sports medicine. *Clinical Journal of Sport Medicine, 33*(3), 195–208. https://doi.org/10.1097/JSM.0000000000001152

Pujari, V. (2024). Moving to improve mental health - the role of exercise in cognitive function: A narrative review. *Journal of Pharmacy and Bioallied Sciences, 16*(Suppl 1), S26–S30. https://doi.org/10.4103/jpbs.jpbs_614_23

Ren, S., Shi, P., Feng, X., Zhang, K., & Wang, W. (2025). Executive function strengths in athletes: A systematic review and meta-analysis. *Brain and Behavior, 15*(1), e70212. https://doi.org/10.1002/brb3.70212

Reuter, P. R., Forster, B. L., & Brister, S. R. (2021). The influence of eating habits on the academic performance of university students. *Journal of American College Health, 69*(8), 921–927. https://doi.org/10.1080/07448481.2020.1715986

Roth, T., Franklin, M., & Bramley, T. J. (2007). The state of insomnia and emerging trends. *The American Journal of Managed Care, 13*(5 Suppl), S117–S120. https://www.ajmc.com/view/nov07-2643ps117-s120

Salvia, M. G., Onteeru, M., Lipson, S. K., & Quatromoni, P. A. (2025). Adopting vegetarian and vegan eating patterns: Associations with disordered eating behaviors among young adult college students. *Eating Behaviors, 57*, 101967. https://doi.org/10.1016/j.eatbeh.2025.101967

Seal, A. D., Colburn, A. T., Johnson, E. C., Péronnet, F., Jansen, L. T., Adams, J. D., Bardis, C. N., Guelinckx, I., Perrier, E. T., & Kavouras, S. A. (2023). Total water intake guidelines are sufficient for optimal hydration in United States adults. *European Journal of Nutrition, 62*(1), 221–226. https://doi.org/10.1007/s00394-022-02972-2

Singh, B., Olds, T., Curtis, R., Dumuid, D., Virgara, R., Watson, A., Szeto, K., O'Connor, E., Ferguson, T., Eglitis, E., Miatke, A., Simpson, C. E., & Maher, C. (2023). Effectiveness of physical activity interventions for improving depression, anxiety and distress: An overview of systematic reviews. *British Journal of Sports Medicine, 57*(18), 1203–1209. https://doi.org/10.1136/bjsports-2022-106195

Sogari, G., Velez-Argumedo, C., Gómez, M. I., & Mora, C. (2018). College students and eating habits: A study using an ecological model for healthy behavior. *Nutrients, 10*(12), 1823. https://doi.org/10.3390/nu10121823

Stores, R., Linceviciute, S., Pilkington, K., & Ridge, D. (2023). Sleep disturbance, mental health, wellbeing and educational impact in UK university students: A mixed methods study. *Journal of Further and Higher Education, 47*(8), 995–1008. https://doi.org/10.1080/0309877X.2023.2209777

Swami, V., Hochstöger, S., Kargl, E., & Stieger, S. (2022). Hangry in the field: An experience sampling study on the impact of hunger on anger, irritability, and affect. *PLoS One, 17*(7), e0269629. https://doi.org/10.1371/journal.pone.0269629

Swipe Out Hunger (2024). *Campus food pantries: Insights from a 2023 survey*. Retrieved on November 28, 2025, from https://swipehunger.org/wp-content/uploads/2024/03/Campus-Food-Pantries-Insights-From-a-2023-Survey.pdf

The Hope Center for Student Basic Needs at Temple University (2025). *The Hope Center 2023–2024 student basic needs report* (February 26, 2025). Retrieved November 28, 2025, from https://hope.temple.edu/sites/hope/files/media/document/Hope%20Student%20Basic%20Needs%20Survey%20Report%20202324.pdf

Tola, G., Talu, V., Congiu, T., Bain, P., & Lindert, J. (2021). Built environment design and people with autism spectrum disorder (ASD): A scoping review. *International Journal of Environmental Research and Public Health, 18*(6), 3203. https://doi.org/10.3390/ijerph18063203

U.S. Department of Agriculture and U.S. Department of Health and Human Services (2020). *Dietary guidelines for Americans, 2020–2025* (9th ed). Retrieved November 29, 2025, from https://www.dietaryguidelines.gov/sites/default/files/2020-12/Dietary_Guidelines_for_Americans_2020-2025.pdf

U.S. Department of Health and Human Services. (2024) Scientific Report of the 2025 Dietary Guidelines Advisory Committee: Advisory Report to the Secretary of Health and Human Services and Secretary of Agriculture. https://doi.org/10.52570/DGAC2025

USDA (2018). *Butter, salted*. USDA Foods. Retrieved November 29, 2025, from https://fns-prod.azureedge.us/sites/default/files/resource-files/Butter_Salted.pdf

USDA (2019). *Snacks, popcorn, air-popped*. FoodData Central Food Details. Retrieved November 29, 2025, from https://fdc.nal.usda.gov/food-details/167959/measures

Wang, K., Li, Y., Zhang, T., & Luo, J. (2022). The relationship among college students' physical exercise, self-efficacy, emotional intelligence, and subjective well-being. *International Journal of Environmental Research and Public Health, 19*(18), 11596. https://doi.org/10.3390/ijerph191811596

Watson, N. F., Badr, M. S., Belenky, G., Bliwise, D. L., Buxton, O. M., Buysse, D., Dinges, D. F., Gangwisch, J., Grandner, M. A., Kushida, C., Malhotra, R. K.,

Martin, J. L., Patel, S. R., Quan, S. F., & Tasali, E. (2015). Recommended amount of sleep for a healthy adult: A joint consensus statement of the American academy of sleep medicine and sleep research society. *Sleep, 38*(6), 843–844. https://doi.org/10.5665/sleep.4716

Wong, P. M., Manuck, S. B., DiNardo, M. M., Korytkowski, M., & Muldoon, M. F. (2015). Shorter sleep duration is associated with decreased insulin sensitivity in healthy white men. *Sleep, 38*(2), 223–231. https://doi.org/10.5665/sleep.4402

Wood, H. C., Prabhakar, S., Upsher, R., Duncan, M., Dommett, E. J., & Gardner, B. (2024). Understanding university students' experiences of sitting while studying at home: A qualitative study. *PLoS One, 19*(12), e0314768. https://doi.org/10.1371/journal.pone.0314768

World Health Organization (2020). *WHO guidelines on physical activity and sedentary behavior*. Geneva. Licence: CC BY-NC-SA 3.0 IGO. https://www.who.int/publications/i/item/9789240015128

Wu, G. (2016). Dietary protein intake and human health. *Food & Function, 7*(3), 1251–1265. https://doi.org/10.1039/C5FO01530H

Wu, J., Li, Q., Feng, Y., Bhuyan, S. S., Tarimo, C. S., Zeng, X., Wu, C., Chen, N., & Miao, Y. (2021). Active commuting and the risk of obesity, hypertension and diabetes: A systematic review and meta-analysis of observational studies. *BMJ Global Health, 6*(6), e005838. https://doi.org/10.1136/bmjgh-2021-005838

Yeo, S. C., Lai, C. K. Y., Tan, J., Lim, S., Chandramoghan, Y., Tan, T. K., & Gooley, J. J. (2023). Early morning university classes are associated with impaired sleep and academic performance. *Nature Human Behaviour, 7*(4), 502–514. https://doi.org/10.1038/s41562-023-01531-x

Zhang, L., Zhao, S., Zhao, S., Zheng, H., Ke, Y., Yang, W., & Lei, M. (2025). Sedentary behavior and its association with psychological well-being and sleep quality in adolescents: Evidence from a propensity score analysis. *Psychology Research and Behavior Management, 18*, 281–298. https://doi.org/10.2147/PRBM.S508382

Zhao, G., Sun, K., Fu, J., Li, Z., Liu, D., Tian, X., Yang, J., & Zhang, Q. (2024). Impact of physical activity on executive functions: A moderated mediation model. *Frontiers in Psychology, 14*, 1226667. https://doi.org/10.3389/fpsyg.2023.1226667

2 Taking Care of Your Mind Helps You Learn Better

You Belong

The sense of belonging is the feeling that you matter and are an important part of a group. That is, you feel accepted, included, respected, supported, and valued by that group (Pedler et al., 2022; Strayhorn, 2018). Students with a strong sense of belonging are more likely to continue their studies until graduation and ask for help when needed. They are more motivated, confident in their academic and social abilities, engaged, satisfied with their lives, and have better physical health (Duffy et al., 2020; Gopalan & Brady, 2020; Hansen et al., 2024; Pedler et al., 2022; Won et al., 2021; Wurster et al., 2021).

In the National College Health Assessment (NCHA), conducted by the American College Health Association (2024), the majority (67.8%) of students surveyed stated feeling like they belong at their college. Slightly more than half of them (57.3%) believed that people in their college look after each other.

Students' sense of belonging, motivation and confidence in their academic capabilities increases when they perceive *professors* as caring, supportive, friendly, and helpful, as well as when professors encourage participation in class, recognize their efforts, and create a positive environment in the *classroom*. As one of my students stated,

> I feel most at ease reaching out when faculty or staff foster an approachable environment that emphasizes the learning process over immediate mastery. Knowing that my peers are often navigating the same difficult material makes it much easier to initiate these helpful conversations.

Additionally, it is important for professors to offer structured lectures, allow students to learn the material using different modalities, make notes available to them, use objects and visual aids to enhance students' understanding of the topic, and offer support sessions, office hours, and one-on-one conversations (Kirby & Thomas, 2022; Strayhorn, 2018; Means & Pyne, 2017).

DOI: 10.4324/9781003750246-3

Your professors will feel *you are invested and care* for their course if you regularly attend class and participate in discussions, ask and answer questions, go to office hours, and communicate with them. As an instructor, I can say that if a student doesn't show up for class, doesn't submit assignments, or comes to class but is not paying attention, I will truly struggle to believe they are interested in the class. If at the end of the term they request an opportunity to increase their grade, I will most likely not grant it. On the contrary, if a student reaches out at the beginning of the term to let me know they may be late or absent or that they are facing personal issues, that's a whole different story! I will be more likely to provide them with supports they need, even without an official letter from the disability support office. Communication, not details, is what your instructor needs.

Community matters. Students experience a greater sense of belonging if they have access to people who share their background and experiences, feel that what they learn can be applied to their own communities, find service opportunities that can benefit people with identities similar to theirs, and when their identity is explicitly accepted (Museus, 2014). It is also important for institutions to offer academic advising, tutoring, mentoring, multicultural and identity-based resource centers, and student organizations where students can interact with those who share their identities and interests (Means & Pyne, 2017). As Emily, one of my students, has experienced,

> I think it's really important to have friends who can support you, e.g. take classes with you, help you rest, help you remember to eat, etc. I have an incredible network of friends through a Christian ministry on campus, and it's been the best thing for my college experience and mental health.

The institution's role is to offer programs and ensure access to positive experiences and communities. However, it is your responsibility to seek out and take advantage of opportunities offered by your college or your peers, as well as by religious, cultural, and social communities on and off campus. Your sense of belonging as well as your belief in your capabilities will grow when you participate in social and leadership activities (Strayhorn, 2018). Those activities can take place in your residence hall, college campus, local community, or other countries and involve as few or many people as you're comfortable interacting with simultaneously. You can play a team sport, participate in activities organized in your residence hall, travel as part of a course or a project team, attend club meetings or join its executive board (see more in the following sections).

As a student, you play a crucial role in enhancing your own sense of belonging and that of your classmates and other peers. You all have the same needs: to be noticed, for your opinion to be heard, to be seen as a source of support and information, to feel respected and appreciated, and to experience both good and bad situations together. You may need to be intentional about including others, especially those who don't share your ethnic, religious, gender, and other social identities (Strayhorn, 2018). It is worth it; both inside and outside the classroom: Creating belonging brings along a sense of trust and decreases stress for everyone.

Stress Motivates You to Learn

Any physical or psychological stimulus will act as a stressor or motivator and cause an emotional, physiological, or behavioral response. Kagan (2016) points out that at any point you are awake, you are under a certain level of arousal or stress. Stress and motivation are used interchangeably in the literature and can be used to clarify learning theory. After describing the different theories, I'll pull them together to show an overall view.

Types of Stress

In terms of duration, stress can be divided into *acute*, lasting hours or days, and *chronic*, lasting months or years. Regarding its effect on well-being, McEwen (2019) categorizes stress into three types. The first one is *good stress*. *Good stress* can mean an exciting challenge, such as applying to college or starting a new job, and good experiences, like exploring a new city or enjoying some time with friends.

The second type of stress described by McEwen (2019) is *tolerable stress*, i.e., when you suffer a loss or face a difficult situation (losing a loved one, failing a course). You can cope with this stress thanks to internal and external resources, such as emotional stability and having a strong support network, and strategies such as spending more time outdoors and less time on screens, exercising, and keeping in touch with loved ones (Deyo et al., 2024; Liu et al., 2024; Mickley Steinmetz et al., 2024).

If you go through the same difficult situation or loss but you don't have internal and external resources that help you cope, or the situation is so extreme that your resources are not sufficient, you would be facing *toxic stress*. *Toxic stress* can create feelings of anger, anxiety, guilt, sadness, etc., and lead to a decrease in performance and engagement (McEwen, 2019; Mickley Steinmetz et al., 2024).

You may have seen a "stress continuum" chart. It is based on a study by Yerkes and Dodson (1908) that describes the relationship between arousal and performance. They studied what level of "arousal," given by an electric shock, would be optimal for Japanese dancing mice to form the habit of entering a white rather than a black passageway or box. Mice were given an electric shock if they tried to enter the black area, and researchers considered mice had successfully learned this task when they consistently entered the white area. Researchers also tested different difficulty levels, making the difference between white versus black areas easy or hard to distinguish by using different lightning conditions.

When the task was *difficult* (i.e., it was hard to distinguish white and black), and the electric shock was very weak, mice learning was slow. Slightly stronger electric shocks led mice to learn quickly. After a certain point, increasing the strength of the electric shocks led to slower learning. In contrast, when the task was *easy*, weak electric shocks led to slow learning; mice learned faster as the electric shock grew stronger. There was no point at which a stronger shock would lead to slower learning. Rather, the researchers stopped at a certain level, as stronger shocks would have hurt the mice. Thus, when the task was difficult, stronger stimuli led to faster learning only up to a certain point, after which the stimulus led to mice seemingly giving up. And when the task was easy, stress was always needed to learn. In this experiment, mice need a source of stress given either by the task itself, i.e., internal or intrinsic, or to avoid an undesirable consequence, i.e., external or extrinsic.

It is worth noting that it has been hard to replicate this study or to apply it to the workplace or to human learning. However, it is seen that people do need motivation or stress to perform tasks and to learn. It may be being interested in the topic, or the desire to get a good grade, or the stress that comes with a looming deadline. What exactly will be the motivational or stress level needed for each person will naturally vary (Morsink et al., 2022). Learners have different natural talents, sensitivity to stress, background knowledge, and interests; each of them needs to find what gets them going. A framework that takes into consideration these factors is the Self-Determination Theory.

Self-Determination Theory

This theory, first posited by Ryan and Deci (2000), recognizes the importance of the psychological needs for autonomy, relatedness, and competence, and has been studied in relation to ADHDers.

Autonomy is supported by showing respect for the student's individuality, motives and perspectives, and by recognizing the student's goals, interests, and problem-solving strategies (Rajendran et al., 2016). *Relatedness* refers to the needs for love, belonging, affection, and esteem, which need to be at least partially satisfied before a person can focus on their self-actualization and transcendence, according to Maslow's theory of human motivation (Maslow, 1943). And *competence* refers to feeling satisfied with one's work, trusting one's capacity and ability.

Faculty, staff, and other people with authority over students who are facing executive function challenges, whether temporary or permanent, tend to offer incentives that would motivate *themselves*. This can lead to a mismatch between what a faculty member considers motivating, such as the threat of a low grade, and what would really motivate the student. The low grade alone may be insufficient, as the student may take into consideration the effort and time required to perform the task, the effect of that low grade on their final grade for that course, or on the grade point average for the academic term.

The capacity to decide how, when and for how long you will engage with a task relates to your need for *autonomy*. Some students who are ADHDers and perceive their classroom or home environment as too controlling and not supportive of their autonomy, feel low levels of relatedness with faculty and doubt their own competence (Rogers & Tannock, 2018). It is not surprising, then, that when a student feels guidelines are strict and restrictive, especially when the tasks are difficult, repetitive, and otherwise demanding, the student's academic performance could suffer, the student could become demotivated, and their well-being could decrease (Morsink et al., 2022).

Self-regulation, that is, setting one's own learning goals, strategies one will follow, monitoring one's progress and modify one's strategies as needed, is interconnected to autonomy and motivation. When students can conduct academic work on their own terms, that is, perform tasks according to their interest, enjoyment, and need for breaks, they become more motivated. Students mentioned feeling enjoyment, freedom, and a sense of ownership when autonomy was granted, leading to an increased likelihood of successfully completing tasks. In turn, this can foster a feeling of competence and self-efficacy, i.e., the person's confidence in their capacity to overcome challenging situations (Uthus & Løhre, 2025; Yang et al., 2025).

However, autonomy support needs to go hand in hand with guidance and accountability. If faculty gave you only autonomy, it is likely you would be unsure of what is expected of you, how you could achieve the objective of a given task, and what you'll learn from it. Effective guidance includes a clear structure where you can learn how to estimate the difficulty of each task, the workload it implies, and create an effective plan to tackle it. Then you would need to focus on completing that task, and after submission of an assignment, you would reflect on the factors that were effective or ineffective while working on the task (Uthus & Løhre, 2025). That is, the development of yourself as a self-regulating learner requires that you engage in metacognition (described in Chapter 3).

It is important, then, for you as a student to work together with your instructors to reach a happy medium that provides you with autonomy support, a feeling of relatedness and competence, while offering you the level of guidance and structure that you require.

"Good Learning": The Zone of Proximal Development

The psychologist Lev Vygotsky believed that learning and development go hand in hand. However, he cautioned that learning cannot be conceived simply as the "acquisition of the ability to think" or an "overall ability to focus attention." Rather, he proposed learning is "the acquisition of many specialized abilities for thinking about a variety of things" and "various abilities to focus attention on a variety of things" (Vygotsky, 1978). Vygotsky's model is based on the work of several psychologists and pedagogists, especially McCarthy (1930), who described the actual development level (ADL) and the zone of proximal development (ZPD) for language learning in children.

The first stage in learning and development is the *ADL*; that is, the learning and development already achieved and interiorized. Your ADL is what you've mastered: any action or process you carry out independently, problems you can solve by yourself, and any knowledge you can recall and apply on your own. It's a view toward the past (Vygotsky, 1978). A person would not be motivated to stay at this level; relearning or only doing what you already master leads to boredom and detachment.

The *ZPD*, the next level, looks toward the future: what can you do or learn next, what problem can you solve with support and instruction? Your capabilities "have not yet matured but are in the process of maturation," as Vygotsky (1978) described it. This is optimally your situation in any topic or process you're currently learning and will lead you to feel motivated and eager to master that process or knowledge. Here it is important to know what support you need, in addition to the instruction given by the professor or teaching assistants. You may need to study in collaboration with peers, as advocated by Vygotsky, as well as to read textbooks or online material, etc. For neurodivergent students, and those with certain disabilities, academic accommodations may be crucial and indispensable (see Chapter 6 for more information on accommodations). It is expected that what is *today* in your ZPD will become part of your ADL, through your effort and practice, thus enabling you to tackle more difficult topics or problems. See Figure 2.1 for a visual representation of Vygotsky's model.

Interestingly enough, Vygotsky didn't name the level after ZPD—that is, what you *cannot do, even with support or instruction*. He did mention that imitation is different from understanding, giving the example of a child learning arithmetic who can recall and understand the solution if they see a teacher solving it. This would mean that arithmetic is currently in their ZPD. But if the teacher solves a calculus or other higher math problem on the board, the child could rewrite the problem but will not understand it, as it is beyond their ZPD, and trying to understand it at this point would be ineffective and a source of frustration and demotivation.

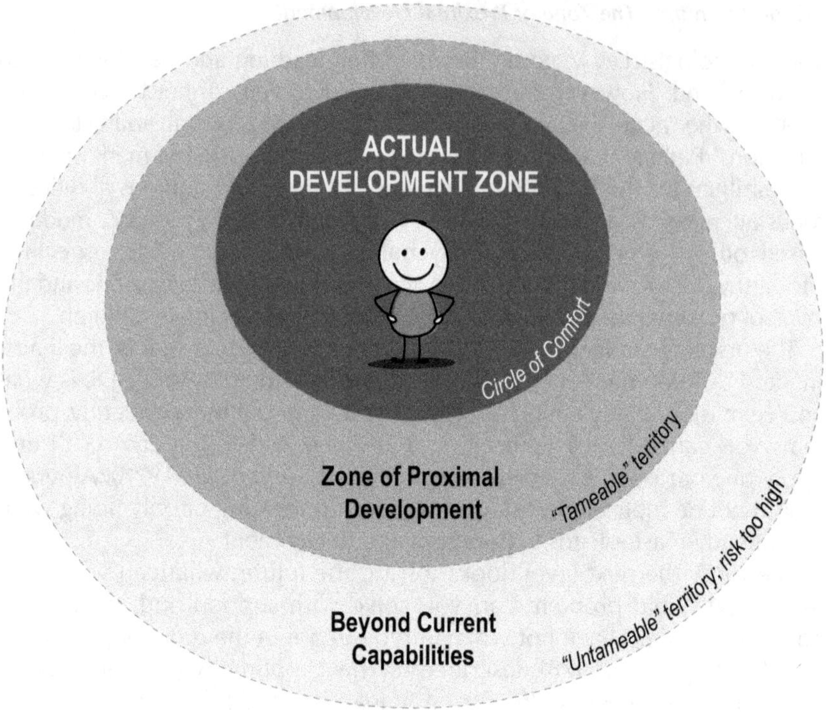

Figure 2.1 Professional and personal growth model. Concept by Florencia Ardon, PhD, based on Vygotsky's theory of learning and development (Vygotsky, 1978) and on Nadler's Edgework (Nadler, 1995). Design by Julia Felice, PhD.

Going back to Vygotsky's idea that learning and development varies by ability or concept you want to master, you need to keep in mind that your ADL and your ZPD vary considerably from one subject to another. You cannot assume how quickly or easily you will master a concept or process based on your performance on a different concept or process. Meaning, you cannot presume you'll master a certain level of physics as easily as you mastered biological concepts. Your ADL, your interest, and how your brain processes information will play a key role. This is not to say you cannot learn it, only that the learning process will likely differ. I want to emphasize this, because I've seen students become frustrated because they believed they should be able to quickly understand statistics, for example, based on their ease in learning algebra. And when that is not the case, students sometimes start losing trust in their abilities or intelligence, which can in turn become an obstacle to their learning.

From time to time, take a moment to recognize how far you've advanced in your learning. This will increase and maintain your motivation in the face of difficulties. Compare your current knowledge and understanding to what you knew and comprehended a year or two ago. You'll realize that much of what was in your ZPD is now firmly in your ADL, and that you are now ready and able to learn many skills, knowledge and understanding that were previously out of reach.

Edgework

In *Edgework* (Nadler, 1995), Reldan Nadler aimed at improving adventure-based experiences, such as those provided by a variety of camps and schools. Before embarking on such experiences, students are in a *Circle of Comfort*, that is, a condition where the people, space, and activities the student engages with feel familiar, safe, comfortable, and predictable.

Then, students are asked to enter the *Edge*, a somewhat unfamiliar, risky, uncomfortable, and unpredictable territory, where they'll encounter unfamiliar people and activities. However, this space is "tameable" and not too different or far away from their *Circle of Comfort*.

Taming the *Edge* enhances the students' self-esteem and expands their *Circle of Comfort*. This *tamed territory* is defined by growth, stretching the self, and by success, possibly immediately after a peak in frustration, confusion, or fear.

The area beyond the *Edge* is too different and far away from their *Circle of Comfort*. It can be frightening and make you scared and anxious. As a result, students may want to remain in or immediately return to their *Circle of Comfort*. Subsequently, Nadler's concept was illustrated with concentric circles or ovals (e.g., Van Gelderen, 2023). The innermost is the *Circle of Comfort* or "comfort zone," surrounded by the *Edge, "tameable" territory* or *"learning zone."* The outermost circle is the *"untameable" territory* or *"panic zone."* Figure 2.1 shows Edgework along the ZPD as a professional and personal growth model.

Applying Edgework to your life, you could think that your *Circle of Comfort* includes positive experiences, people that support you, and activities you feel at ease doing. The "tameable" *territory* represents courses in areas you have not explored yet, moving to a new city, and interacting with people whose beliefs, backgrounds and identities may be different from yours.

Having support and guidance from others, as well as useful resources, will help you *tame* the new territory. However, your beliefs are key, as they can limit you and make you afraid of trying, or can encourage you to experiment or learn something new. Nadler encourages you to accept valuable support from instructors, peers, and loved ones and to develop an "inner coach" (Nadler, 1995), or even an "inner champion," by talking to yourself as you would talk to someone you love.

To increase your confidence and self-esteem, you can show yourself evidence of everything you have accomplished and remind yourself about all the positive experiences you've had, especially those that seemed intimidating at the beginning. This can help increase your willingness to try; you can also tell yourself that if you try and it doesn't work, it's OK! It's better to know that the activity or course is not a good fit for you than not trying at all.

Putting It All Together

Translating these concepts to learning in college, you can think of the following conditions:

a *Too easy*. Corresponds to the Circle of Comfort and ADL. There is no or very little stress, motivation, or action. In this condition, no learning is needed, you are feeling cozy and have no immediate needs. During summer or winter academic breaks, for example, students would have no reason to study what they already mastered and would have no new academic tasks to do. During academic terms, if deadlines are too far into the future, or there is little learning to do, students may not be motivated to work on a project or assignment that is due in two weeks, or to review content they already know or find too easy. It could also be that the tasks are too simple in comparison to the planning or preparation needed. Staying too long in this condition can lead to boredom, decreased well-being, and unwillingness to re-engage in learning or new experiences.

b *Just right*. Corresponds to the Edge and ZPD. This condition can include various levels of stress. The motivation to engage in tasks or studying may be given by *proximity*, if the assignment is due soon; *difficulty*, if the project requires more time and/or effort; *relevance or extrinsic motivation*, if the result is very important for their grade or goals; or *intrinsic motivation*, if it is something the student finds enjoyable.

   a *Routine*. Characterized by good stress and motivation, where you take action. Students are attending classes; participating in projects; working on assignments; engaging in new experiences; taking care of themselves; provided with the right amount of academic, emotional, or physical challenges; receive emotional support from others; and engage in positive self-talk. As students master new material, effectively navigate personal difficulties, and expand their support network, they begin to flourish (Knoesen & Naudé, 2018).

   b *High stakes*. Characterized by good stress that is intense and acute, where you take action. This happens, for example, just before an exam or the deadline for an important essay. Stress can be *tolerable* if students have been taking care of themselves by sleeping enough, taking breaks, staying connected with loved ones, trusting themselves and being supported by others. Performance could be good or excellent; a good example would be an athlete running much faster during a competition than during training. The extrinsic reward—a good grade, positive feedback, winning a competition—will increase inner satisfaction and self-esteem.

c *Too hard*. Corresponding to a panic zone or "cannot do" level, where stress is intense, acute, or chronic, and toxic. In this condition, you are not physically, emotionally or academically prepared, e.g., if you take a high-level course for which you don't possess enough background knowledge, and you don't have enough support from others or you hold negative beliefs about your capacity. It could also be that you are not sleeping well, have very little time to study for multiple exams or work on projects, are going through a severely difficult situation, or the stakes are simply too high. Learning will be shallow, short-lived, or insufficient, your academic performance would likely be poor, and your mental health would suffer. If stress remains intense and becomes chronic, it can lead to severe burnout.

d *Some caveats*: It is possible for executive function to make it difficult for students to start a task, even if the task is within the "just right" zone. Additionally, some tasks may be "just right," but the rubrics or instructions are difficult to understand. It is not always a matter of motivation.

Table 2.1 Characteristics of conditions by difficulty level

Characteristics	*Conditions by Difficulty Level*			
	Too Easy	*Just Right Routine*	*Just Right High Stakes*	*Too Hard*
Stress level	Minimal or nonexistent	Good, tolerable, and chronic	Good, tolerable, intense, and acute	Excessive, toxic, intense, acute, or chronic
Task demand	Simple, requires very little or no effort or time	Interesting, attractive, challenging, relevant	Challenging, exciting	Excessive, unclear, confusing, requires too much effort or time
Motivation and rewards	Demotivated, no rewards expected	Motivated, intrinsic rewards	Highly motivated, extrinsic rewards	Demotivated, rewards are unattainable
Activity level	None or very little	Enough, constant, active	More intense than usual	None or very little
Performance	Unsatisfactory or nonexistent	Satisfactory or excellent	Satisfactory or excellent	Unsatisfactory or nonexistent

(*Continued*)

Table 2.1 (Continued)

Characteristics	*Conditions by Difficulty Level*			
	Too Easy	*Just Right Routine*	*Just Right High Stakes*	*Too Hard*
Associated emotions	Comfort, coziness, boredom, irrelevance	Excited, curious, ready, content, satisfied	Fearful, frustrated, anxious, eager, satisfaction, pride	Confused, fearful, anxious, depressed, hopeless, helpless
Self-determination theory	None or very little need for competence	Autonomy, relatedness, and competence are present, as well as guidance and structure	Autonomy, relatedness, and competence are present, as well as guidance and structure	Guidance structure, and relatedness are missing; competence is inadequate and relatedness is absent
Vygotsky's theory of learning	Actual development level	Zone of proximal development	Zone of proximal development	Beyond current capabilities
Nadler's Edgework	Circle of Comfort	Edge, territory to tame	Edge, "tameable" territory	Risk is too high, territory not "tameable"

Elaborated by Florencia Ardon, PhD, based on the theory of learning and development (Vygotsky, 1978), Edgework (Nadler, 1995), and Self-Determination Theory (Ryan & Deci, 2000).

Your Mindset Leads the Way

Mindset is defined by the *Cambridge Dictionary* (n.d.) as a person's way of thinking and their opinions. It defines how you see and face challenging situations. There are several interconnected ways to refer to your *mindset*, including the well-known *growth mindset* (Dweck & Yeager, 2019), which is the belief that your capacities are not fixed, and can be developed over time. Yanagisawa et al. (2025) propose a separate construct, a *positive mindset* or *positive thinking* that refers to an optimistic outlook on life, i.e., the ability to maintain positive expectations for the future, emphasizing possible positive outcomes.

Another view of mindset that is helpful to consider is the *stress mindset*, which refers to whether you see stress as intrinsically negative or positive. Interpreting stress under a positive light, i.e., "stress-is-enhancing" helps people show more willingness to accept challenges, view stress as an opportunity for growth and leads a person to adopt a solutions-finding attitude and use positive reframing. In the long term, cultivating a "stress-is-enhancing" mindset improves life satisfaction (Yang et al., 2025).

Finally, a more comprehensive theory, in my view, was written by Aron Antonovsky (1987), the "Sense of Coherence" (SOC). SOC requires that you hold three beliefs: (1) stressors resulting from one's internal or external environments in the course of living are structured, predictable, and explicable; (2) one has access to internal and external resources to face any demand given by those stressors; and (3) these demands are challenges, worthy of investment and engagement. He called these three beliefs comprehensibility, manageability, and meaningfulness.

Vinje et al. (2022) describe *comprehensibility* as the need for a person to understand the nature of a problem before being able to deal with it, and they explain that *manageability* depends on the person's access to internal and external resources. Internal resources include your intellect, problem-solving skills, optimism, and self-esteem, while external supports are given by your family, friends, college, workplace, and the community. Vinje et al. (2022) consider that, for Antonovsky, *meaningfulness* represents the belief that life is worth living.

SOC influences your response to current and future difficulties and enhances your resilience. It is correlated to self-efficacy—that is, confidence in your capacity to cope with challenges in diverse environments. It is based on your past experiences and influences your perception and evaluation of current and future challenges (Yang et al., 2025). Each positive outcome becomes evidence of your capability, feeding into your sense of agency and further strengthening your resilience.

Antonovsky created a SOC scale reflecting a person's view or attitude toward life; a higher SOC reflects a stronger belief in the world as comprehensible, manageable, and meaningful. SOC is not static; in highly stressful situations, one or more of SOC's components could be missing, and the SOC score would decrease. Yang et al. (2025) studied the effect of stress on college students and found that SOC decreased during periods of acute stress but improved once the stress faded away. However, SOC remained low when students were under chronic stress.

When assessing a challenging situation, it is necessary to evaluate how realistic it is for you or someone else to overcome it. I'm thinking of the words of Stella Young, an influential and fierce advocate for disability rights, who was a wheelchair user. She stated, "[N]o amount of smiling at a flight of stairs has ever made it turn into a ramp. Never." (Young, 2014).

Some situations cannot be solved by mindset, perseverance, or motivation alone, and some may be truly impossible to overcome. Limitations could be due to rules and regulations, systemic barriers, resources available at your institution or the place where you live, or by your own abilities or capabilities. For instance, even if I really want to become a gymnast and start training ten hours a day, I will never reach the level of an Olympic athlete. My innate flexibility and agility make it impossible, and my age is another unmovable barrier. Instead of dwelling on the impossibility of becoming an Olympic gold medalist, I can evaluate what my real goal is. Maybe my goal is to keep myself physically fit. Gymnastics is only one way among many to achieve that, and another activity may be much better suited for me.

Prioritize Your Well-being

Situations That Could Affect Your Well-Being

A student arriving at college is not a blank slate. Their academic, social, and family experiences have shaped their beliefs in and about themselves, how they interact with faculty, staff, and peers and how they solve problems in ways that may not be easy to see or understand. Negative experiences prior to entering college can include adverse childhood experiences (ACE), suffered by a person, typically in the family environment, before turning eighteen. ACEs can be a traumatic event or chronic stressful and/or traumatic situations. A recent study of college students (Colburn et al., 2021) found that, on average, respondents had suffered 2.14 ACEs. The consequences of the ACEs faced by these students included more stress, poor mental health, and lack of social support.

Neurodivergent and disabled students may have received accommodations and support in high school, which would increase the likelihood of asking for help in college. Many are familiar with different tools that enable them to succeed academically and in other aspects of college life, have a better idea of what accommodations exist and how to request them. However, students who have faced discrimination and lacked support in high school due to their disability, gender, ethnicity, race, and other marginalized identities may not disclose their accommodation needs.

Students who have suffered ACEs or discrimination in high school are under significant stress. While the institutions have a responsibility to support them, it's necessary that students disclose their situation to a trusted staff or faculty member and use strategies and tools that can mitigate the challenges they're facing (discussed in Chapter 6).

In college, students face a variety of challenges, including financial insecurity, difficulty finding food that fits their religious, cultural, or nutritional needs, issues with their roommates, getting sick, or the illness of a loved one, bullying, hazing, microaggressions, discrimination, anxiety, depression, adapting to an academically rigorous environment, sleep difficulties, and many others (American College Health Association, 2024). Many institutions offer programs and support to prevent those challenges and to deal with those experienced by students, and work to continually improve and expand their offerings. At the same time, students can use a variety of strategies to improve and/or sustain their well-being.

Strategies that Support Your Well-Being

Your well-being is enhanced by positive experiences and engagement, such as attending in-person or online counseling services, well-being or life coaching sessions, peer support programs, professional, identity and interest-based student organizations and clubs, and meditation or mindfulness sessions (Colburn et al., 2021; Wang & Jin, 2025). Establishing a good relationship with supportive and caring faculty and staff, especially early in your college career, is a crucial factor in building resilience in relation to academic struggles (Wang & Jin, 2025).

In a study, medical school students ranked factors that supported their well-being at the beginning, middle and end of an academic year. Overall, family was considered particularly important, followed by academic performance and friends. Students assigned less importance to sleep, physical fitness, alone time, hobbies, and financial stability. Their search for flourishing was also evident; they mentioned looking for inner peace, quietude, and purpose (Chatterjee et al., 2022).

While in this study medical students didn't rank them as highly, attending to your basic needs is important, e.g., having a safe place to live, sleeping enough, eating a nutritious diet, exercising, etc. (discussed in Chapter 1). In fact, in another study by Milne et al. (2025), medical students reported increased well-being when they had slept well, exercised in groups, were hydrated, and had eaten a nutritious meal.

On the other hand, you should also avoid overwhelming yourself, and engage in activities or learning within the *ZPD* or *Edge*, without venturing too far into the "cannot do" or "panic zone." This means avoiding, for example, taking too many credits or hard courses, working long hours, participating in too many extracurricular activities, enrolling in courses for which you don't have adequate preparation, etc., all of which can lead to burning out. At the same time, you can actively foster your well-being. Some strategies are described next.

Taking Advantage of Flow and Hyperfocus States

Flow

Csikszentmihalyi (2008) described flow in 1990 as an optimal experience when "there is no need to worry, no reason to question one's adequacy," situations in which "attention can be freely invested to achieve a person's goals, because there is no disorder to straighten out, no threat for the self to defend against."

Recent research describes several characteristics of flow in which a person (a) dedicates all mental effort to the activity; (b) is fully engrossed in the activity; (c) may engage minimally or not at all in self-reflection and is not worrying about being judged by others; (d) feels in control; (e) has a clear goal with a sense of direction and focus; (f) receives clear and encouraging feedback during the activity, feels the activity is pleasurable and intrinsically rewarding, and wants to experience it again; (g) loses track of time; the brain reward systems are very active, diminishing feelings of fatigue, pain, and other sources of discomfort; and (h) is doing something at a "just right" difficulty level and is neither bored nor anxious (van der Linden et al., 2021).

Since by definition the person is capable of performing the activity without much problem, success is highly likely; this accomplishment fosters satisfaction and self-efficacy. Academic work will frequently be somewhat too challenging to lead to a flow state. However, participating in non-academic activities that are flow-inducing can improve focus and coping abilities that will benefit students in their academic work. Csikszentmihalyi (2008) posited that people experiencing flow "as often as possible" would enjoy an enhanced quality of life.

A flow-inducing activity studied by Wang and Tang (2025) is Chinese calligraphy, an activity that is quiet, precise, and repetitive. They found that calligraphy fosters active focus, peace of mind, sustained attention, and that improves self-reflection skills. Activities with similar characteristics include many common hobbies, such as birding, hiking, photography, coloring, gardening, etc. All of these allow for flow to happen; when the person is alone, the activity itself provides encouraging feedback, e.g., observing how much of a jigsaw puzzle one has put together.

Musical performance is another flow-inducing activity, which can lead to a decrease in performance anxiety levels. A study of musicians determined that the factors most likely to promote flow were (a) ability and challenge being balanced, (b) understanding the task or having clear instructions, (c) receiving clear feedback that was immediate, unambiguous and directly related to the task, and (d) low stakes, e.g., absence of negative consequences regardless of outcome (Moral-Bofill et al., 2023).

Van der Linden et al. (2021) propose that flow can be associated to the brain's Default Mode Network activity when the task is effortless and relies on automatic processing (e.g., a long-distance runner while training), whereas if the person is engaged in cognitive activities such as playing a challenging game, flow is associated with Central Executive Network activity (both networks are described in Chapter 3). This latter flow state corresponds to hyperfocus, a state very well-known to many neurodivergent people (Ashinoff & Abu-Akel, 2021).

Hyperfocus

Ashinoff and Abu-Akel (2021) describe four criteria for hyperfocus: (1) It is a highly engaging task for the person performing it. (2) It involves an intense state of sustained or selective attention. (3) There is a decreased perception of other stimuli, even if relevant. (4) The task performance is higher while the person is in a hyperfocus state.

Hyperfocus is commonly seen in autistic people and ADHDers. Oroian et al. (2025) studied adults who are ADHDers, and found they hyperfocused frequently, for periods ranging from hours to days. Most commonly, hyperfocus was related to work activities (35%), followed by creative activities (25%) and gaming (20%). Like Ashinoff and Abu-Akel (2021), Oroian et al. (2025) found that work-related hyperfocus increased productivity, as reported by 30% of study participants. However, respondents reported that hyperfocus was a double-edged sword; for 30% of them, it was also linked to neglecting responsibilities, missed deadlines and, for 55% of participants, hyperfocus impacted their social lives. Self-care was another area neglected.

One difference in connotations between hyperfocus and flow is that flow only considers pleasant, "optimal" situations, while hyperfocus also includes unpleasant states, as reported by Oroian et al. (2025). Hupfeld et al. (2019) acknowledge this difference; in their study, researchers asked participants about hyperfocus during their favorite activities and were able to detect a relationship between hyperfocus and enjoyment. In this study, Hupfeld et al. (2019) evaluated hyperfocus and flow using separate questionnaires. They found that people who reported experiencing hyperfocus more frequently were also more likely to experience flow more often. Hyperfocus was correlated with having a diagnosis or traits of ADHD, but flow was not; the researchers propose that hyperfocus is a deeper state of flow and that ADHDers may be uniquely able to experience a deep flow, i.e., hyperfocus, that creates detachment from the surrounding environment. Similarly, Ashinoff and Abu-Akel (2021) argue that hyperfocus and flow refer to the same mental state.

Neurodivergent people are starting to speak about their positive experiences with hyperfocus. For example, ADHDers deemed hyperfocus beneficial during school exams or at work (Nordby et al., 2023). A similar view was expressed by children diagnosed with ADHD, interviewed by Ling and Diamond (2025). In a recent essay, Wheatcraft (2025) mentions that "intelligence, ambition and autistic hyperfocus brought me professional success of unimaginable heights."

Mindfulness and Meditation

Meditation is a practice aimed at creating a state of relaxation and inner peace, fostering awareness and control over the person's thoughts and emotions. It trains the person to focus on one thought, sensation, or feeling, and helps develop self-regulation and resilience. While meditating, the person practices watching their own thoughts and feelings without engaging with them, creating detachment and calm (Calderone et al., 2024). Mindfulness is a meditation technique that focuses on the present and encourages acceptance of thoughts, emotions, or physical sensations as they are, without judging or trying to control them (González-Martín et al., 2023).

Both practices are increasingly offered by colleges, with positive results. A systematic review by González-Martín et al. (2023) found compelling evidence that mindfulness practices decrease stress, depression, anxiety, and distress, while improving attention and cognitive awareness in college students. A study by Glena et al. (2024) found that after four 15-minute sessions of mindfulness in the classroom, students demonstrated increased awareness and acceptance of their feelings, thoughts, and physical sensations (i.e., their state of mindfulness). While the researchers didn't find a significant improvement in students' distress level, participants' feedback was positive, stating they would recommend mindfulness to friends and that it helped them relax, focus, and stay present in the moment.

After participating in a few meditation activities myself, I introduced some mindfulness activities in my classroom. The first term or two we only practiced a few times, as an introduction and example of this practice. Some students found it relaxing but others thought it was a waste of time or found it stressful. I then decided to try out practicing mindfulness for a few minutes every single class. The contrast is outstanding, as mindfulness is now consistently praised by students at the end of the term, and many continue practicing some type of mindfulness activity afterward.

Not all types of mindfulness activities work for everyone. I found it very difficult to engage with imagery-based scripts ("imagine yourself turning into a mountain"), and some gratitude-based scripts can induce distress if it reminds the person of their own lack of positive experiences or relationships, as unfortunately happened to a couple of my students. I quickly learned to stay away from those types of scripts! Instead, we engage in a few minutes of mindfulness-related activities such as deep and slow breathing, watching nature videos, or body scans (i.e., focusing on the sensations of a specific part of your body at a time). If you want to start practicing mindfulness, you could start by doing deep and slow breathing exercises. There are also many nature videos online, as well as meditation, breathing and mindfulness apps you can use on your smartphone or tablet. If you feel inclined to practice mindfulness with others, you could join a group that makes you feel safe. In any case, it is a good idea to start with short sessions (3–5 minutes) and increase the duration very slowly, as long sessions when you're starting practicing meditation or mindfulness can be somewhat stressful. You may need to develop a certain openness and acceptance of the experience, as well as finding the right type(s) for you.

Nature Prescription or Nature Rx

Spending time in nature is associated with improved social, emotional and physical health, and increasing numbers of colleges are "prescribing" students to go outdoors. Settings used include parks and botanical gardens, greenhouses, forests, rivers, waterfalls, lakes and more. Among the activities commonly used are meditating, reading, walking, hiking, biking, arts and crafts, farming or gardening, and bird watching. As reported in two reviews and meta-analyses (Menhas et al., 2024; Nguyen et al., 2023), participation in Nature Rx activities improved the physical and mental health of people across a wide range of age groups. Among the benefits of spending time in green or blue spaces were a reduction in stress, anxiety, and depression; decreased blood pressure; increase in daily step count; and time spent in moderate physical activity. Offerings in parks, lakeshores, and other public spaces benefit the community and encourage the strengthening of social connections and widening of social networks. Similarly, working or volunteering in community gardens and spaces also enhances people's well-being. At-home gardening, although providing fewer social benefits, supports people's physical and mental health (Menhas et al., 2024; Nguyen et al., 2023).

Collect Happy Moments: Glimmers

"Glimmers" is a term coined by Deb Dana (2018) as opposite to "triggers." It truly is important to enjoy life while you are a student; your college life comprises four or more years of your life that you'll never get back. This is something I tell my students every semester, because I see many of them focusing not just on their current studies, but on what they need to do in order to get into a desired career, graduate school, etc., leaving joy for "later." A study of university students showed that engaging with glimmers daily, *prioritizing positivity and well-being,* increased participants' overall well-being, happiness, and satisfaction with life. Students who routinely prioritized positivity felt more intense positive emotions from a wider variety of pleasant events (Catalino & Tov, 2022).

A *glimmer* is anything that brings you a moment of joy, pleasure, or happiness. Examples of glimmers include connecting with your family and friends, taking a "well-being day," exercising, attending a book club meeting, petting a dog, contact with nature (i.e., "Nature Rx"), eating lunch outdoors, playing a musical instrument, singing, being intentionally kind, enjoying a cup of coffee, savoring ice cream, reading a book... the options are endless (Catalino & Tov, 2022; Chatterjee et al., 2022; Schmitz et al., 2025).

Because evolution's goal is to ensure your survival before anything else, humans tend to put more weight on negative information, e.g., not being able to enroll in a desired class, not being offered a coveted internship, financial struggles, relationship challenges, and much more. This is called "negativity bias" and affects your relationships and trust in others (Xie et al., 2023). You can minimize their effect by engaging with your *glimmers,* thereby increasing your positive emotions. When enjoyed in company of your friends, glimmers will strengthen your relationships (Kringelbach & Berridge, 2010); when those moments happen in the classroom, your engagement in that course will increase and you will learn more.

You may need to intentionally change your focus when you start engaging with *glimmers*, and slowly your brain will adapt to not dwell so much on the negative situations, or at least to give equal weight to the negative and positive situations or feedback. In my case, I noticed I was focusing too much on cars cutting off in front of me, stopping for too long on a stop sign, going too slowly, etc. So, my short drive home was relatively unpleasant. I made a commitment to myself that anytime I realized I was feeling frustrated or annoyed while driving home, I would look at something pretty, like autumn leaves, small animals on the side of the road, a creek, etc. It did take some time, but now I am much calmer and happier on my home. If there's something similar in your day, I'd very much recommend testing this out!

In Brief

Your well-being is a key component of your capacity to learn. It will influence how you view challenges and stress, whether you notice and use available resources, and if you are willing to pursue meaningful goals. You can choose courses and programs that are interesting and fulfilling, ensuring you will have time and energy to engage deeply by not enrolling in too many courses or joining too many extracurricular activities. You will benefit from prioritizing sleeping well, eating nutritious meals, being physically active, and enjoying moments of calm and relaxation, both alone and in the company of friends and loved ones. Life is meant to be enjoyed all along, not *after* you graduate or are accepted to graduate school or get that promotion. It may just be that enjoying life is what makes it possible for you to achieve all your goals!

References

American College Health Association (2024). *National college health assessment III: Reference group executive summary Fall 2024*. Retrieved on November 26, 2025, from https://www.acha.org/ncha/data-results/survey-results/academic-year-2024-2025/

Antonovsky, A. (1987). *Unraveling the mystery of health: How people manage stress and stay well*. Jossey-Bass. https://doi.org/10.4135/9781446221129.n9

Ashinoff, B. K., & Abu-Akel, A. (2021). Hyperfocus: The forgotten frontier of attention. *Psychological Research, 85*(1), 1–19. https://doi.org/10.1007/s00426-019-01245-8

Calderone, A., Latella, D., Impellizzeri, F., De Pasquale, P., Famà, F., Quartarone, A., & Calabrò, R. S. (2024). Neurobiological changes induced by mindfulness and meditation: A systematic review. *Biomedicine, 12*(11), 2613. https://doi.org/10.3390/biomedicines12112613

Cambridge Dictionary (n.d.) *Mindset*. Retrieved December 15, 2025, from https://dictionary.cambridge.org/us/dictionary/english/mindset

Catalino, L. I., & Tov, W. (2022). Daily variation in prioritizing positivity and well-being. *Emotion, 22*(5), 874–879. https://doi.org/10.1037/emo0001070

Chatterjee, K., Edmonds, V. S., Girardo, M. E., Vickers, K. S., Hathaway, J. C., & Stonnington, C. M. (2022). Medical students describe their wellness and how to preserve it. *BMC Medical Education, 22*(1), 510. https://doi.org/10.1186/s12909-022-03552-y

Colburn, A. R., Kremer, K. P., & Jackson, D. B. (2021). Early trauma and psychosocial outcomes among college students. *Children and Youth Services Review, 126*, 106052. https://doi.org/10.1016/j.childyouth.2021.106052

Csikszentmihalyi, M. (2008). Flow: The psychology of optimal experience. In *1st Harper perennial modern classics ed.* Harper: Perennial.

Dana, D. (2018). *The polyvagal theory in Therapy: Engaging the rhythm of regulation* (1st ed.). W.W. Norton & Company.

Deyo, A., Wallace, J., & Kidwell, K. M. (2024). Screen time and mental health in college students: Time in nature as a protective factor. *Journal of American College Health, 72*(8), 3025–3032. https://doi.org/10.1080/07448481.2022.2151843

Duffy, R. D., Kim, H. J., Gensmer, N. P., Pendleton, L. H., Boren, S., & Garriott, P. O. (2020). Testing a critical cultural wealth model of well-being among first-generation students. *Journal of Counseling Psychology, 67*(2), 171–183. https://doi.org/10.1037/cou0000388

Dweck, C. S., & Yeager, D. S. (2019). Mindsets: A view from two eras. *Perspectives on Psychological Science, 14*(3), 481–496. https://doi.org/10.1177/1745691618804166

Glena, V. S., Mushquash, A. R., Gotwals, J. K., Sinden, K. E., & Pearson, E. S. (2024). "Staying in the present moment is important": Examining the impact of a short-term classroom-based mindfulness intervention among first-year students. *Journal of American College Health, 72*(9), 3186–3195. https://doi.org/10.1080/07448481.2022.2155057

González-Martín, A. M., Aibar-Almazán, A., Rivas-Campo, Y., Castellote-Caballero, Y., & Carcelén-Fraile, M. D. C. (2023). Mindfulness to improve the mental health of university students. A systematic review and meta-analysis. *Frontiers in Public Health, 11*, 1284632. https://doi.org/10.3389/fpubh.2023.1284632

Gopalan, M., & Brady, S. T. (2020). College students' sense of belonging: A national perspective. *Educational Researcher, 49*(2), 134–137. https://doi.org/10.3102/0013189X19897622

Hansen, M. J., Palakal, M. J., & White, L. (2024). The importance of STEM sense of belonging and academic hope in enhancing persistence for low-income, underrepresented STEM students. *Journal for STEM Education Research, 7*(2), 155–180. https://doi.org/10.1007/s41979-023-00096-8

Hupfeld, K. E., Abagis, T. R., & Shah, P. (2019). Living "in the zone": Hyperfocus in adult ADHD. *ADHD Attention Deficit and Hyperactivity Disorders, 11*(2), 191–208. https://doi.org/10.1007/s12402-018-0272-y

Kagan, J. (2016). An overly permissive extension. *Perspectives on Psychological Science, 11*(4), 442–450. https://doi.org/10.1177/1745691616635593

Kirby, L. A. J., & Thomas, C. L. (2022). High-impact teaching practices foster a greater sense of belonging in the college classroom. *Journal of Further and Higher Education, 46*(3), 368–381. https://doi.org/10.1080/0309877X.2021.1950659

Knoesen, R., & Naudé, L. (2018). Experiences of flourishing and languishing during the first year at university. *Journal of Mental Health, 27*(3), 269–278. https://doi.org/10.1080/09638237.2017.1370635

Kringelbach, M. L., & Berridge, K. C. (2010). The neuroscience of happiness and pleasure. *Social Research: An International Quarterly, 77*(2), 659–678. https://doi.org/10.1353/sor.2010.0049.

Ling, D. S., & Diamond, A. (2025). A qualitative study of the lived experience of children with ADHD. *Behavioral Sciences, 15*(12), 1698. https://doi.org/10.3390/bs15121698

Liu, M., Shi, B., & Gao, X. (2024). The way to relieve college students' academic stress: The influence mechanism of sports interest and sports atmosphere. *BMC Psychology, 12*(1), 327. https://doi.org/10.1186/s40359-024-01819-1

Maslow, A. H. (1943). A theory of human motivation. *Psychological Review, 50*(4), 370–396. https://doi.org/10.1037/h0054346

McCarthy, D. (1930). *The language development of the preschool child*. University of Minnesota Press.

McEwen, B. S. (2019). The good side of "stress". *Stress, 22*(5), 524–525. https://doi.org/10.1080/10253890.2019.1631794

Means, D. R., & Pyne, K. B. (2017). Finding my way: Perceptions of institutional support and belonging in low-income, first-generation, first-year college students. *Journal of College Student Development, 58*(6), 907–924. https://doi.org/10.1353/csd.2017.0071

Menhas, R., Yang, L., Saqib, Z. A., Younas, M., & Saeed, M. M. (2024). Does nature-based social prescription improve mental health outcomes? A systematic review and meta-analysis. *Frontiers in Public Health, 12*, 1228271. https://doi.org/10.3389/fpubh.2024.1228271

Mickley Steinmetz, K. R., Gaudier-Diaz, M. M., Huber, E. C., Edwards, B. H., & Muscatell, K. A. (2024). Investigating social connection as a protective factor against exam stress in college students. *Journal of American College Health, 72*(7), 1974–1977. https://doi.org/10.1080/07448481.2022.2109037

Milne, A., Novelli, A., Watson, C., Yousef, H., Copeland, W. E., Holterman, L. A., Rosen, L., Bai, Y., Curl, A., Pasqualoni, S., Kirby, S., Halvorson-Phelan, X. X., & Hudziak, J. (2025). Associations between daily wellness behaviours and outcomes among medical students: A longitudinal nightly survey study. *Medical Education, 59*(8), 862–870. https://doi.org/10.1111/medu.15724

Moral-Bofill, L., López De La Llave, A., & Pérez-Llantada, M. C. (2023). Predictors of flow state in performing musicians: An analysis with the logistic regression method. *Frontiers in Psychology, 14*, 1271829. https://doi.org/10.3389/fpsyg.2023.1271829

Morsink, S., Van Der Oord, S., Antrop, I., Danckaerts, M., & Scheres, A. (2022). Studying motivation in ADHD: The role of internal motives and the relevance of self determination theory. *Journal of Attention Disorders, 26*(8), 1139–1158. https://doi.org/10.1177/10870547211050948

Museus, S. D. (2014). The culturally engaging campus environments (CECE) model: A new theory of success among racially diverse college student populations. In M. B. Paulsen (Ed.), *Higher education: Handbook of theory and research* (Vol. 29, pp. 189–227). Netherlands: Springer. https://doi.org/10.1007/978-94-017-8005-6_5

Nadler, R. S. (1995). Edgework: Stretching boundaries and generalizing experiences. *The Journal of Experimental Education, 18*(1), 52–55. https://doi.org/10.1177/105382599501800110

Nguyen, P.-Y., Astell-Burt, T., Rahimi-Ardabili, H., & Feng, X. (2023). Effect of nature prescriptions on cardiometabolic and mental health, and physical activity: A systematic review. *The Lancet Planetary Health, 7*(4), e313–e328. https://doi.org/10.1016/S2542-5196(23)00025-6

Nordby, E. S., Guribye, F., Nordgreen, T., & Lundervold, A. J. (2023). Silver linings of ADHD: A thematic analysis of adults' positive experiences with living with ADHD. *BMJ Open, 13*(10), e072052. https://doi.org/10.1136/bmjopen-2023-072052

Oroian, B. A., Nechita, P., & Szalontay, A. (2025). Hyperfocus in ADHD: A misunderstood cognitive phenomenon. *European Psychiatry, 68*(S1), S306–S306. https://doi.org/10.1192/j.eurpsy.2025.662

Pedler, M. L., Willis, R., & Nieuwoudt, J. E. (2022). A sense of belonging at university: Student retention, motivation and enjoyment. *Journal of Further and Higher Education, 46*(3), 397–408. https://doi.org/10.1080/0309877X.2021.1955844

Rajendran, K., Kruszewski, E., & Halperin, J. M. (2016). Parenting style influences bullying: A longitudinal study comparing children with and without behavioral problems. *Journal of Child Psychology and Psychiatry, 57*(2), 188–195. https://doi.org/10.1111/jcpp.12433

Rogers, M., & Tannock, R. (2018). Are classrooms meeting the basic psychological needs of children with ADHD symptoms? A self-determination theory perspective. *Journal of Attention Disorders, 22*(14), 1354–1360. https://doi.org/10.1177/1087054713508926

Ryan, R. M., & Deci, E. L. (2000). Self-determination theory and the facilitation of intrinsic motivation, social development, and well-being. *The American Psychologist, 55*(1), 68–78. https://doi.org/10.1037//0003-066x.55.1.68

Schmitz, R. M., Gomez, G., Sainz Sujet, P., Schachle-Gordon, J., Hunger, K., Cost, K., & Chung, R. (2025). INTEGRATED PET THERAPY ON CAMPUS. A case study exploration of campus community members' perceptions of the well-being benefits associated with a canine-assisted intervention. *Journal of American College Health*, 1–10. https://doi.org/10.1080/07448481.2025.2583202

Strayhorn, T. L. (2018). *College students' sense of belonging* (2nd ed.). Routledge. https://doi.org/10.4324/9781315297293

Uthus, M., & Løhre, A. (2025). Students with inattention and their experiences of autonomy in learning activities: An interview study with two students and their teachers. *Frontiers in Psychology, 16*, 1624279. https://doi.org/10.3389/fpsyg.2025.1624279

Van Der Linden, D., Tops, M., & Bakker, A. B. (2021). Go with the flow: A neuroscientific view on being fully engaged. *European Journal of Neuroscience, 53*(4), 947–963. https://doi.org/10.1111/ejn.15014

Van Gelderen, M. (2023). Using a comfort zone model and daily life situations to develop entrepreneurial competencies and an entrepreneurial mindset. *Frontiers in Psychology, 14*, 1136707. https://doi.org/10.3389/fpsyg.2023.1136707

Vinje, H. F., Langeland, E., & Bull, T. (2022). Aaron Antonovsky's Development of Salutogenesis, 1979–1994. In M. B. Mittelmark (Eds.) et. al., *The Handbook of Salutogenesis. (2nd ed., pp. 29–45)*. Springer. https://doi.org/10.1007/978-3-030-79515-3_5

Vygotsky, L. S. (1978). Interaction between learning and development. In M. Cole, V. John-Steiner, S. Scribner, & E. Souberman (Eds.), *Mind and society: The development of higher psychological processes* (pp. 79–91). Cambridge, MA: Harvard University Press.

Wang, J., & Tang, K. (2025). Understanding the association of calligraphy activities with flow experience, peace of mind, and self-focused attention among university students. *Frontiers in Psychology, 16*, 1525503. https://doi.org/10.3389/fpsyg.2025.1525503

Wang, S., & Jin, C. (2025). Supportive teachers, thriving students: Mindfulness, self-efficacy, and media engagement as pathways to well-being. *Acta Psychologica, 259*, 105300. https://doi.org/10.1016/j.actpsy.2025.105300

Wheatcraft, L. B. (2025). Stigma, narrative fallacy, and expert thinking heuristics: The three pillars of epistemic injustice. *Narrative Inquiry in Bioethics, 15*(2), 108–110. https://doi.org/10.1353/nib.2025.a974078

Won, S., Hensley, L. C., & Wolters, C. A. (2021). Brief research report: Sense of belonging and academic help-seeking as self-regulated learning. *The Journal of Experimental Education, 89*(1), 112–124. https://doi.org/10.1080/00220973.2019.1703095

Wurster, K. G., Kivlighan, D. M., & Foley-Nicpon, M. (2021). Does person-group fit matter? A further examination of hope and belongingness in academic enhancement groups. *Journal of Counseling Psychology, 68*(1), 67–76. https://doi.org/10.1037/cou0000437

Xie, D., Chen, S., & Wu, Y. (2023). Focusing on the positive or the negative: Self-construal moderates negativity bias in impression updating. *PsyCh Journal, 12*(4), 547–560. https://doi.org/10.1002/pchj.651

Yanagisawa, K., Nakai, R., Asano, K., Kashima, E. S., Sugiura, H., & Abe, N. (2025). Optimistic people are all alike: Shared neural representations supporting episodic future thinking among optimistic individuals. *Proceedings of the National Academy of Sciences, 122*(30), e2511101122. https://doi.org/10.1073/pnas.2511101122

Yang, S., Ma, H., & Zhan, X. (2025). Stressful life events and sense of coherence in college students: Roles of coping, self-efficacy, and stress mindset. *Behavioral Sciences, 15*(6), 762. https://doi.org/10.3390/bs15060762

Yerkes, R. M., & Dodson, J. D. (1908). The relation of strength of stimulus to rapidity of habit-formation. *Journal of Comparative Neurology and Psychology, 18*, 459–482. https://doi.org/10.1002/cne.920180503

Young, S. (2014). I'm not your inspiration, thank you very much [Video]. Ted Conferences. https://www.ted.com/talks/stella_young_i_m_not_your_inspiration_thank_you_very_much

3 Mental Processes That Make Learning Possible

The Concept of Learning

Seifert and Sutton (2009) define learning as "relatively permanent changes in behavior, skills, knowledge, or attitudes resulting from identifiable psychological or social experiences." A key aspect of learning is *permanence*; something remembered for only a brief period of time was *not really learned*.

Depth of learning is categorized in several levels based on the "Taxonomy of Educational Objectives" (Bloom et al., 1956), created by a committee of faculty from several colleges, convocated by Benjamin Bloom. It is now commonly referred to as "Bloom's Taxonomy," and was revised in 2001 by Anderson and Krathwohl.

The taxonomy was created to help faculty organize educational goals and learning objectives according to their cognitive complexity. For learners, it is useful to be aware that this taxonomy exists and that faculty use it to create rubrics and exam questions; learners can also use it to determine how deeply they have learned a topic or subject and whether they are prepared to have the level of expertise required at the end of the academic term.

In the 2001 revision (Anderson & Krathwohl, 2001), the taxonomy is separated into *two dimensions*: knowledge and cognition.

The *Knowledge Dimension* refers to *what* you need to remember, divided into four categories: (a) *Facts*: technical vocabulary and jargon, as well as additional details, such as being able to state that cows are mammals and that means they give birth to living calves; (b) *Relationships*: classifications, categories, theories, structures, principles; (c) *Processes*: techniques and methods, criteria used to determine what procedure to use; and (d) *Metacognition*: how a particular professor grades, what notetaking techniques are appropriate to different courses, being aware of what you know and what you don't, knowing that to study psychology you need to be in a quiet space.

DOI: 10.4324/9781003750246-4

The *Cognition Dimension* refers to the cognitive processes you use in order to learn. It is divided into six categories. The first category is *Remember*, which includes *recognizing* and *recalling*. Recognizing is when, for example, you hear a phrase in Spanish: "buenos días" and know it means "good morning." What you're doing is hearing the phrase, searching in your long-term memory, and comparing the phrase you heard with the translation you already know. Recalling means being able to come up with the phrase on your own, searching into your long-term memory for the phrase that you need to say when you greet a Spanish-speaking friend.

The next step, *Understand*, requires you to connect information with each other, be it new or old. It involves a variety of skills, such as being able to convert salaries into income categories, or classify expenses (housing, transportation) and determine the percentage of earnings spent on each type of expense. If you also learned how a family's economic health is estimated, you could also determine (infer) if a family is under financial distress based on how much of their salary they spend in, say, housing. Understanding also implies the ability to summarize that information and explain it with your own words or without jargon, i.e., paraphrase it.

Apply, the third level, relates to carrying out a procedure, like math or chemistry problems, even when the situation or math problem is unfamiliar to us, which is a common situation students face in exams. Self-testing early in the term and reaching out to instructors can help you develop a deeper understanding of the reasoning behind the use of certain formulas or methods, which would help you apply that reasoning to unfamiliar problems. Applying requires generalizing, explained below in more detail.

Analyze comes next, and refers to being able to clarify how one or more situations, procedures, and problems relate to each other. This would include explaining the pros and cons of a war, determining which pandemic was the most devastating for humanity, explaining why two political pundits describe an incident in vastly different manners, etc. When answering a math problem, you would be able to distinguish the information you need to solve the problem and what is superfluous.

We then have *Evaluate*, which is judging whether a conclusion is valid, based on the evidence, or if its results are contradictory. You could also compare two solutions and determine which one applies better to a given situation. *Evaluating* relies on critical thinking, e.g., when you ask yourself, *can this be true? Is this the best explanation? Was the solution adequate to the problem, considering the different aspects needed to be considered?*

The uppermost and most complex level of learning is *Create*. Creating requires all other levels of learning and includes coming up with hypotheses, possible answers, or solutions, foreseeing the consequences of different procedures, crafting a plan, and carrying it out.

Creating can mean designing a house, painting a work of art, or developing a dissertation. In the workplace, a doctor could *create* a treatment plan for someone with diabetes. The doctor needs to *recall* many facts, such as what type of food is more likely to rapidly raise blood sugar levels, what medications are currently available, what their side effects are, and some facts about the patient. The doctor also needs to *understand, evaluate,* and *judge* how likely a patient is to follow the treatment, depending on the patient's lifestyle, age, other medical conditions, as well as if the medication they're prescribing can be taken along with the patient's current medications, etc. Finally, the doctor needs to write the treatment plan clearly and concisely to make sure the patient has all the information needed to follow the treatment at home.

Next, we'll explore some of the cognitive processes and systems required for learning: memory, attention directed either internally (Default Mode Network) or externally (Executive Control Network), metacognition, social cognition, and, finally, mental fatigue.

How Memory Works

Memory is the ability to retain information based on the mental processes of encoding (transforming the information into a format that can be stored in your brain), retaining that information across time, and retrieving it as needed from mental storage (American Psychological Association, n.d.).

Classification of Memories

Memories Are Categorized Into

Implicit, nondeclarative, or procedural memory. This type of memory is mostly unconscious, doesn't require effort or intentional recalling, and is guided by motivation, as valuable information will naturally attract your attention (Li et al., 2025). Implicit memory is related to performance and behavior, e.g., skills and habits. Interestingly, this is a type of memory that is difficult to explain, as if you tried to teach someone to tie their shoelaces without showing them (Dharani, 2015). This type of memory makes it possible to ride a bike without having to consciously balance yourself or drive home using your regular route without paying attention to street names or landmarks.

Explicit or declarative memory. This type of memory is conscious and requires mental effort and resources. It is divided into episodic and semantic.

Episodic memories are about events and experiences. In many cases, you only need to experience an event once to be able to remember it much later. This is especially true for unique, important, and emotional events, like a wedding. However, you need to have a certain background knowledge, e.g., the meaning of a wedding and who the couple is, as well as where and when it happened in relation to other events (Buzsáki et al., 2022; Paller, 2024). The process requires effort even if you unconsciously recall it whenever the memory is triggered, e.g., when you see the couple that got married, or you talk with others about the wedding (Paller, 2024).

Semantic memory deals with "what": facts, concepts, and general knowledge; it doesn't relate to a particular time or place (Buzsáki et al., 2022). Some memories need to be remembered "as is" or "verbatim," e.g., dates, names, and relationships, or "gist," e.g., concepts, meanings, patterns (Ahmad et al., 2024). A "verbatim" memory would be remembering your favorite beach, while the "gist" would be knowing that a beach has sand, water, waves, etc.

Steps for Memory Formation, Based on Atkinson and Shiffrin (1968)

Sensing the World

You are constantly sensing the world: you hear, see, touch, smell, taste, feel cold or warmth, etc. You only process or perceive a tiny portion of what you sense. What you perceive remains in your mind for 1–3 seconds and you forget it, unless you consider it crucial or relevant. If you were texting during class, your brain would be paying attention to what you are reading and processing the text, so you can write your answer. You may hear that the instructor is speaking, but would not process what they're saying, and would not remember it afterward.

Our brain doesn't pay equal attention to all senses. Visual input creates the strongest memories, followed by olfactory and then auditory. This is called the "visual dominance hypothesis." The reason for this dominance is believed to be the fact that images and videos are more distinct, offer more context, remain in front of you for longer, and allow people to go back and forth between different components, whereas something you hear is rapidly gone (Ahmad et al., 2024; Alhamdan et al., 2025; Lopis et al., 2021).

However, humans evolved to interact with inputs from multiple senses at the same time. The simultaneous reception of visual and auditory input seems to be crucial for transferring information from your sensory to your working memory. Other senses also play a role, enriching the information and adding memory cues. People can pay better attention, engage more, and get distracted less often when receiving both auditory and visual input (Alhamdan et al., 2025).

Storing and Using Information in Your Short-Term Memory

Relevant or crucial information received through your senses or retrieved from long-term memory is stored in your *short-term memory*, your mental sticky note. *Working memory* is a related concept, which includes keeping the information *and* manipulating or using it to plan, calculate, write, etc. (Draheim et al., 2022). Working memory allows you to keep in mind math rules and instructions while answering problems, understand what you read, evaluate different solutions, keep in mind what you want to say if you need to wait a few minutes to express it (Badre, 2025; Perone et al., 2018). To add something to your working memory, you create a representation of the information, i.e., *encode it*, and keep it at hand, i.e., *consolidate it* (see the following).

Our working memory is limited, only keeping around five to nine pieces of information for about 30 seconds (Asuncion & Khalili, 2024). This limited capacity helps you not crowd your brain with irrelevant memories and keep it ready to process essential information (Asuncion & Khalili, 2024; Barrouillet et al., 2024). Strategies used by your brain to efficiently use working memory include constant updating, i.e., removing data that is no longer relevant and adding any needed information. To both organize and increase memory capacity, your brain creates "chunks" of related memories, e.g., the image and the meaning of a text are grouped together. The number of chunks kept in working memory are limited to around four, but chunks can be grouped with other chunks (Asuncion & Khalili, 2024; Barrouillet et al., 2024; Thalmann et al., 2019).

Keeping items in your working memory requires effort, as you may need to set aside a piece of information, not forget it while you're dealing with another, and noticing what is happening around you without getting distracted (Barrouillet et al., 2024; Diamond, 2013). For instance, if you're working on a problem that requires several equations, you may need to remember the rule for that formula, do the calculations, *and* not pay attention to what other people are doing. This means that working memory requires *inhibition*, an executive function (explained next).

Your working memory is supported by the *prefrontal parietal system* to allow you to remain focused on a thought without getting distracted by the environment. However, when you move to another space, the support disappears, and it is difficult to sustain your focus (Diamond, 2013). This can explain why you may feel thirsty, go to the kitchen to get water, and forget what you wanted once you entered the kitchen. During your study sessions, it may be necessary to remain in one environment until you finish manipulating a piece of information.

Working memory issues affect long-term memory. As Cotton and Ricker (2022) stated, "[S]lowed or ineffective working memory consolidation may impact later long-term memory consolidation by failing to create a durable representation while awake, leaving sleep-related processes nothing to consolidate."

Storing Information for Future Use: Long-Term Memory

Long-term memory allows us, theoretically, to permanently store an unlimited amount of information. It is considered that only about 20% of what you hold in your short-term memory will be placed into long-term memory. For this to happen, the information needs to remain in your short-term memory, something you achieve by recalling ("maintenance rehearsal") and engaging with it ("elaborative rehearsal"). Once the information has been handled by your working memory, it needs to be processed via *encoding* and *consolidating* during sleep.

Encoding is the process by which you receive information and transform it into a specific mental format or representation, and it gives your brain a certain number of items to remember (Cotton & Ricker, 2022).

Consolidation of memories refers to establishing relationships between different pieces of information, adding context and nuance, and storing the information. Consolidation efficiency is evaluated by determining how much a person remembers after a certain period has elapsed between learning and recalling (Cotton & Ricker, 2022; Paller, 2024). For consolidation to happen, memories are recalled, selected, edited as needed, grouped with similar information, re-encoded, and re-stored; this process happens mostly during your deepest sleep and REM phases. There are several models of how and where memories are stored; most of them agree that the hippocampus and the prefrontal cortex are crucial, with other areas of the brain such as the amygdala playing a lesser role (Cotton & Ricker, 2022).

Intentionally Remembering

When you speak about learning, you are commonly talking about the knowledge and skills you have stored in long-term memory *that you can voluntarily and easily recall*. When you recall a memory, your brain rapidly scans different areas, collecting any pieces of information you need and placing them in an easily accessible location, i.e., your working memory. Once in your working memory, the information is re-activated, re-encoded and re-consolidated as needed, and later it is re-encoded and re-consolidated into your long-term memory. Memories remain easier to access and recall if you consciously retrieve the information or practice skills over several sessions, becoming part of your general knowledge (Cotton & Ricker, 2022; Paller, 2024).

The more times you recall an experience, the stronger the episodic memory will be (Paller, 2024), and the same is true for semantic memory. You will remember what you recall *more* frequently, while *the time* spent recalling a particular memory is not as important (Li et al., 2025). While you will spontaneously recall information that is of high personal value, you can also consciously recall memories, which is what happens when you study. Sievers et al. (2019) propose that reactivating a memory strengthens and stabilizes it, and that you re-encode the memory, in a way creating several memories related to the same information.

As Atkinson and Shiffrin (1968) stated, "[I]f one wishes to remember a telephone number permanently, one will often rehearse the number several times." The rehearsal maintains the information in short-term memory for a longer time and gives time for encoding and consolidation to happen, resulting in a stronger long-term memory (Atkinson & Shiffrin, 1968).

Relatedly, you need to distinguish between *recognition*, e.g., being aware that you have seen a person before, and *recall*, e.g., being able to describe that person to someone else, providing their name, occupation, and relationship to you (Li et al., 2025). When you cannot remember a fact, like the name of an aunt you haven't seen in many years, you can think of that memory as faded, and you can attempt to retrieve it using cues. If after seeing pictures of your aunt, being told who her parents are or when you saw her last, you still cannot remember after a while, you could think of that memory as irretrievable or forgotten (whether it's one or the other is a topic of debate among memory researchers).

Factors Affecting Memory

Memory performance is not a fixed characteristic. Your capacity to remember changes depending on several factors, including your mood, certain medications, and sleep deprivation. Improvements in those areas will likely improve your memory performance. However, there are certain limits that are difficult to modify. There are several techniques and methods aimed at improving memory, but so far, they have not proven to be successful or transferable across different types of information, tasks, or skills (Cotton & Ricker, 2022; Draheim et al., 2022).

Memory impairments can happen while encoding or consolidating information in working or long-term memory, as well as during its retrieval. They are related to several executive function issues and your behaviors, including the following: (a) Attention issues, such as short attention span or "Attentional blinks," i.e., a lapse of awareness. (b) Distractions, e.g., paying attention to unrelated thoughts or to other sources of information, like a smartphone. (c) Working memory not being updated, especially not discarding information no longer needed. (d) Needing more time than others to encode and/or consolidate information in working and/or long-term memory (Cotton & Ricker, 2022).

The relationship between memory performance and *stress* is very complex. Acute stress seems to increase attention, but chronic stress deceases attention and memory in general; mild stress enhances consolidation, but

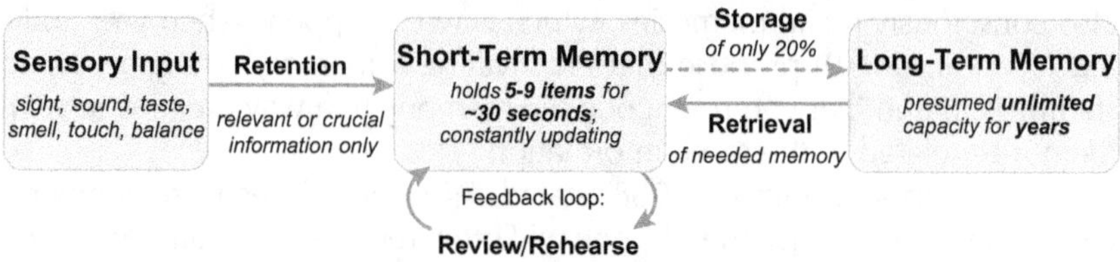

Figure 3.1 Creation of memories. Concept by Florencia Ardon, PhD, based on Atkinson and Shiffrin's memory system model (Atkinson & Shiffrin, 1968). Design by Julia Felice, PhD.

large amounts hinder it (Cotton & Ricker, 2022). In addition to stress, certain circumstances, conditions, and neurotypes have been linked to memory impairments. *Physical health conditions* include multiple sclerosis, hypothyroidism, caffeine and tobacco withdrawal, and a history of concussions. *Adverse experiences*, i.e., experiencing trauma, stigma, and/or discrimination, causes psychological distress, which decreases working memory capacity and leads to a lower ability to form memories. *Neurotypes* that have been linked to memory issues include attention-deficit hyperactivity disorder (ADHD), autism, bipolar, and schizophrenia due to attentional lapses; anxiety, as it can cause difficulty concentrating or recalling ("mind going blank"); depression, as difficulty concentrating and making decisions may be present; while learning disabilities, post-traumatic stress disorder (PTSD), and acute stress can decrease concentration capacity (Cotton & Ricker, 2022; Draheim et al., 2022).

Memory issues are for the most part related to temporal or permanent neurological differences, and may lead to missing appointments or events, forgetting conversations or names, having to re-read a paragraph immediately after reading it, etc. People who experience memory issues could benefit from freeing working memory capacity by using calendars, to-do lists, and other such tools, reviewing the material more times, or answering more practice problems, among other strategies. Figure 3.1 summarizes the memory formation process.

Interacting with Yourself and with the World

We pay attention to the world intermittently, fluctuating between perceiving and interacting with others and the environment, and directing our attention inward. The Default Mode Network (DMN) manages internal attention while the Executive Control Network (ECN) is in charge of external attention. Depending on what you need to pay attention to, the activity of one or the other will be suppressed. The "switch" that turns them on or off is the salience network, which detects important, i.e., salient, events or situations (Azarias et al., 2025; Menon, 2023).

You can maintain your attention on your environment to the point of intensely focusing on just one stimulus, blocking everything else, creating the "hyperfocus" or "in the zone" state. This is especially true of highly motivating and not very difficult tasks. However, your brain tends to go back to the "default," i.e., internal focus, leading to mind wandering or daydreaming, controlled by the DMN. When you are working on a task and the DMN activates, your attention lapses, decreasing performance and reaction times (Esterman & Rothlein, 2019; Menon, 2023).

After detecting a salient stimulus, the salience network may turn off the DMN and activate the ECN or vice versa (Azarias et al., 2025). Impaired functioning of the salience network can be responsible for unintentional disengagement from the world, i.e., involuntarily daydreaming and "zoning out."

The Default Mode Network: Daydreaming and Internal Communication

Humans depend on physiological and cognitive automatic processes, which save you a lot of time and energy, and allow your brain to focus on important actions and behaviors. This automatic processing is managed by the DMN and includes your *physical reactions* to your environment, like moving your hand away from a hot stove; *actions*, e.g., driving to your workplace; *habits* like preparing coffee in the morning; and *thoughts*, as seen with daydreaming, all of which you can do without having to intentionally think about your movements, route, or your surroundings.

When you're in silence and while resting, you give opportunity to your mind to wander. Mind wandering is something most people do and is a key characteristic of ADHD. During mind wandering, you are focused on your internal thoughts, which are flowing freely, while not paying attention to anything around you. Mind wandering can improve your long-term memory, as it allows your brain to recall and reprocess facts, events, and concepts, leading to longer lasting memory consolidation. While your mind is wandering, it also focuses on activities you need to perform and on your future goals, making it more likely that you'll achieve them (Girardeau et al., 2022).

The neurological characteristics of the DMN were discovered in 1997 and are believed to be involved in the following functions:

a *Sensing the world* around us, functioning in the background or "offline," allowing you to remain in a state of vigilance, to detect opportunities and threats (e.g., water, wolves). The DMN seems to be involved in processing and integrating your sensory experiences (Azarias et al., 2025; Menon, 2023).

b *Creating a sense of identity* by remembering, re-interpreting and re-evaluating personal experiences and engaging in introspection and reflection, thereby creating a personal narrative. Thus, the DMN is crucial for episodic memory and allows you to understand your mood, feelings, and motivation, as well as who you are, your likes and dislikes, and anything else related to distinguishing yourself from others (Azarias et al., 2025; Menon, 2023).

c *Envisioning the future*, e.g., creating different scenarios and planning your reactions to those scenarios. This allows you to create goals and plans to achieve them, as well as alternatives and coping strategies, according to opportunities or challenges you may face. The DMN also allows you to learn from past and current experiences, applying those lessons to future circumstances (Azarias et al., 2025; Menon, 2023).

d *Social cognition and communication*, i.e., perceiving and understanding other people's perspectives, beliefs, intentions, and motivation through their speech, facial expressions, body language, etc., allowing you, for instance, to anticipate what a person will say next, to infer the content and meaning of a conversation or lecture. Ultimately, this helps you determine your relationships with other people and whether they are close or casual friends, or acquaintances (Azarias et al., 2025; Menon, 2023).

e *Creative thinking*. Envisioning multiple possible scenarios, associating concepts that are apparently different, leads to new ideas, problem-solving, and innovation (Azarias et al., 2025; Menon, 2023).

Factors Influencing DMN Activity

DMN activity evolves through life, and is influenced by genetics, brain development, family and educational environment, and by personality traits. It is also modulated by your mental health and neurotypes, e.g., ADHD, anxiety, autism, depression, PTSD, and schizophrenia (Azarias et al., 2025; Menon, 2023).

Positive experiences, e.g., being surrounded by a supportive environment where you find social affection, connection, and support, benefit the DMN activity (Azarias et al., 2025). In contrast, difficult or negative experiences and conditions, including insomnia, sleep deprivation, sleep irregularity, chronic stress, childhood stress and adverse experiences, conflicts, social isolation and rejection, are detrimental to the DMN functioning, impairing your capacity to self-reflect and to understand others (Azarias et al., 2025; Lunsford-Avery et al., 2020).

Interestingly, *sleep* leads to a decrease in activity and connectivity of DMN, possibly because this allows your brain to restore different neurological processes during NREM sleep. During REM sleep, the DMN is disengaged, similar to what happens while you are awake and receiving visual input. This may allow you to process your dreams without interference of introspection and reflection (Hong et al., 2021).

While practicing *mindfulness meditation*, i.e., attending to the present moment without judgment, DMN activity decreases. Mindfulness meditation allows you to quiet your mind and seems to reduce rumination, i.e., a loop of negative thinking and self-talk, dwelling on negative experiences and feelings, that harms well-being. Mindfulness meditation is believed to lead to improved emotional regulation, capacity to focus, and mental health (Azarias et al., 2025; Devaney et al., 2021). For ADHDers (like me) and related neurotypes, mindfulness practice helps us have more control over when we allow our brain to turn on or off our DMN.

Executive Control Network: Your Interaction with the World

The ECN, also called executive function (EF), includes a variety of very complex cognitive processes and skills that allow you to set goals, plan, organize and initiate tasks, evaluate your progress, and complete those tasks, as well as to modify your strategies or even change goals as needed (Badre, 2025; Friedman & Robbins, 2022; Perone et al., 2018).

EFs are governed by the *prefrontal cortex* in the brain, and can be affected by a myriad of situations, as well as by mental and physical health conditions. EFs influence your decision-making and following through, including whether to suppress an impulse, or avoid or seek out a stimulus (Friedman & Robbins, 2022; Perone et al., 2018).

The three core EF categories are *inhibition*, *flexibility*, and *working memory*. These core EFs are required for "higher level" EFs, such as reasoning, problem-solving and planning (Diamond & Ling, 2016). Depending on the amount of emotion involved, EFs can range from "cool" to "hot," where "cool" only involves reasoning, and "hot," involves highly emotional situations (Friedman & Robbins, 2022; Perone et al., 2018).

Inhibitory control includes the following:

a *Attention control*, i.e., the ability to choose what you want to focus on and to block out other stimuli, such as paying attention to a conversation rather than to the music, television, or other conversations around you. Attention control helps you remain focused and "on task," and is influenced by your innate inhibitory control ability, interest in the topic, relevance of that topic for your future career, and your belief in yourself (Diamond, 2013; Friedman & Robbins, 2022; Perone et al., 2018).

b *Thought control,* also called *response inhibition* and *cognitive inhibition,* is the capacity to intentionally forget, suppress, or not pay attention to unnecessary or unwanted thoughts, information or memories, and disregard tasks that are complete or no longer relevant (Diamond, 2013; Friedman & Robbins, 2022).

c *Self-control,* i.e., the control you exert over your actions and behaviors, can be seen as the opposite of impulsiveness. Self-control gives you the capacity to remain sitting when formal or informal rules require it, to allow others to speak, to listen, wait for your turn, not change the topic or interrupt yourself, and to "think before you speak." Thinking before you speak means being aware of the consequences of saying everything you're thinking, waiting until you have all the facts to reach a conclusion, and, when questioned, evaluating several possibilities before answering (Friedman & Robbins, 2022; Zelazo, 2015).

Self-control enables you to wait for a *desirable reward* in the future instead of indulging in an immediate pleasure, i.e., the ability to "delay gratification" and persevere. A very long-term example is preparing and writing a dissertation. A dissertation typically requires many hours a day for reading, writing, and researching, even when the due date is months away. It is not as immediately gratifying as spending time with friends, traveling, etc. While those good experiences are also important for your well-being, giving in to immediate gratification too often would mean never finishing the dissertation.

People with suboptimal *hot* self-control are also less likely to learn from failure, and could be more willing to take unnecessary risks, especially if peers are doing so (Friedman & Robbins, 2022; Perone et al., 2018; Zelazo, 2015).

Cognitive Flexibility Refers to the Capacity to Change

a *Perspectives,* be it spatially, e.g., visualizing what an object would look like from another viewpoint, or socially, e.g., guessing how another person thinks or feels about a situation (Diamond, 2013; Zelazo, 2015).

b *Strategies,* finding new ways to solve problems or improve a product or process, which requires creativity and innovation. In class, a potential problem could be being able to write notes as fast as you need to; a potential solution would be using speech to text software, using a different notetaking method, annotating slides, etc., instead of trying to increase your handwriting skills (Diamond, 2013).

c *Plans,* according to different contexts or situations, such as changing travel destinations because flight or hotel prices increase. In college, this could be your ability and willingness to add, drop, or change a course depending on your academic load or because there is a new course that sounds very interesting (Diamond, 2013).

d *Attention*, as needed to achieve your goal. This includes coordinating multiple tasks to make progress in all your projects, focusing on different activities as needed, for example focusing on a lecture, writing notes, focusing again on the lecture, and so on. It also means updating your working memory, replacing information you no longer need with new and needed information, as well as monitoring what you're doing, and planning next steps depending on your advance toward your goals, or if the situation changes. A situation change would be for example if you were walking to class and received a message saying the class will take place online instead of in person. Your goal is still to attend class, but you need to change your behavior, as you may prefer to go to a quiet space instead of to the regular classroom (Badre, 2025; Friedman & Robbins, 2022; Perone et al., 2018).

Generalizing vs. Task-Specific Skills

Generalizing skills requires understanding how rules apply to different scenarios and the ability to break down relatively larger tasks into smaller ones (Badre, 2025). For instance, some of the actions involved in baking a cake, like pre-heating the oven, also apply to baking lasagna.

You will learn or apply your knowledge to a new situation more rapidly if the connection between old and new rules, policies, processes, etc. is clear. You may need to receive additional instruction and training (also referred to as *scaffolding*), and/or be given explanations in a very concrete and explicit way. An example of this would be upgrading from an older, gasoline-powered car to a much newer, electric car. While some general rules and processes are the same for both cars, some would be new or very different. In contrast, if you changed your car for another of similar age that uses the same type of fuel, the features may be only slightly different, and you would rapidly and easily get used to them.

The capacity to *generalize* makes learning easier but has disadvantages. When you are trying to pay attention to two unrelated tasks at once (i.e., multitasking or task-switching), the *generalizing* feature could cause errors. For example, if you were writing to one person and talking to another, you may say a word you meant to write or write a word you hear instead of the word you were thinking of (Badre, 2025).

On the opposite side, there are some *task-specific skills* that are heavily reliant on context and don't become *generalized*. They are protected from multitasking-related mistakes, but your learning slows down. Autistic people, in particular, tend to learn processes and tasks in a *task-specific* way, experiencing relative difficulty *generalizing* (de Marchena et al., 2015). At the same time, this may give them great advantages in tasks requiring precision and accuracy.

Self-Monitoring

This skill is crucial, as there are many situations that require you to immediately change your behavior. Self-monitoring allows you to notice you're about to make a mistake, like adding orange juice to cereal instead of milk. If you foresee the consequence on time, you can correct course. Immediately after, you will be more careful. If you were solving a complex formula on an exam and failed to monitor yourself, you could add instead of subtract a number, not notice, and get a lower grade as a result. Suboptimal self-monitoring is one of the EF issues common in ADHD (Shiels & Hawk, 2010).

Improving Executive Functioning

How well your EFs work depends on your innate brain anatomy and connectivity. Some functions or subfunctions may be affected or absent due to, for example, physical damage to the prefrontal cortex.

It is important to note that EFs require mental effort and tax your brain; performing several EFs in a fast sequence or simultaneously makes it more difficult to successfully execute all of them (Diamond, 2013). That is, if you're trying to pay attention to a difficult conversation in a loud space, the effort required to block distractions may impact self control, making it more difficult for you to resist eating that piece of cake.

Several neurotypes are linked to EF issues. ADHDers can face issues with a broad range of EF skills, such as emotional regulation and impulsivity, inhibitory control, organization, planning, time management, working memory, and attentional control. Autistic people can find it difficult to transition between activities or to adapt to change due to issues with cognitive flexibility and working memory (Pozo-Rodríguez et al., 2026). People with learning disabilities can face challenges with organization, planning and time management, working memory, cognitive flexibility, and inhibitory control, among other EF skills (Khouri et al., 2025). People with depression can face difficulties with decision-making and concentration, while people with schizophrenia can face difficulties in progressing toward a goal and in conducting effective "reality monitoring," that is, distinguishing between real and imaginary events (Friedman & Robbins, 2022). People with anxiety and depression can find it difficult to transition from one activity or thought to another, and to persevere working toward a goal (Warren et al., 2021).

Everyone is at risk of suboptimal or poor executive functioning: under stress, excess dopamine and cortisol are released, which disrupts the communication between the prefrontal cortex and other areas of the brain. *Stress* and *lack of sleep* affect EF similarly to ADHD, decreasing inhibitory control and cognitive flexibility. *Sadness and depression* decrease attentional control and cognitive flexibility. *Loneliness* affects selective attention and reasoning. Being *sick*, likely due to the immune response, affects EF in general (Diamond & Ling, 2016).

A common belief is that you can improve your EF if you want to do so; that EF is under control of your will and motivation. I've heard students justify not taking advantage of widely used tools, like to-do lists or calendars, stating, "I just need to pay more attention," "I'll be more careful next time," "I'll remember *this*, for sure." However, to pay more attention, concentrate on the task and remember, you need your EF to be working properly.

There is a vast variety of cognitive training strategies claiming to improve EFs, such as "brain training" programs aimed at improving memory and protecting from cognitive decline. A systematic review and meta-analysis of 43 studies of commercial "brain training" programs found no evidence of an effect on everyday functioning and other cognitive skills (Nguyen et al., 2022). Furthermore, as is the case with memory, there is little evidence that the training is generalizable; it appears to create task-specific skills (Cotton & Ricker, 2022; Draheim et al., 2022). This is especially true when training is repetitive and predictable; the person hones the ability to do that specific task correctly and will be able to apply the same strategies only to very similar tasks. Furthermore, any improvements in EFs decrease over time (Diamond & Ling, 2016), meaning that the brain connectivity may have improved for a while, but the underlying EF capacity of the person remains unchanged.

Longer lasting and more effective EFs improvements for everyone may be possible by decreasing stress, providing a supportive community that enhances your sense of belonging and social inclusion, improving or maintaining physical health, having ample opportunity to sleep, and feeling joy. (Diamond, 2013; Diamond & Ling, 2016).

Metacognition: Understanding How You Think

The *Merriam-Webster Dictionary* (n.d.) defines metacognition as the "awareness or analysis of one's own learning or thinking process." Metacognition interacts and somewhat overlaps with EF and social cognition skills (Fraiwan et al., 2025).

It can be divided into three areas (Friedman & Robbins, 2022):

a *Metacognitive knowledge*: awareness of available processes and tools, where to find the information, the demands of the task, objectives, what you need to know, etc.
b *Procedural metacognition*: planning, monitoring, and evaluating your experiences and actions.
c *Metacognitive control*: choosing the correct materials to study, dedicating enough time, pursuing the most appropriate course of action, etc.

Effective learning requires metacognition. Strong metacognitive skills are linked to superior time management, problem-solving skills and study strategies, while people who find it challenging to practice metacognition can have difficulties setting goals, solving problems, and changing strategies when they're under stress (Fraiwan et al., 2025). Poor metacognitive skills can be seen when students underestimate the difficulty of an exam or overestimate their ability to learn quickly, as happens with "unskilled but unaware" students (Serra & DeMarree, 2016). An environment that fosters task-switching and provides a constant overload of information depletes the metacognitive skills of students, who in consequence find it difficult to prioritize, organize and critically assess information (Fraiwan et al., 2025).

Metacognition empowers you to become a self-regulated, life-long learner, as metacognitive skills are instrumental in your learning at any stage in life and any subject. You receive feedback about the effectiveness of your learning strategies in numerous ways, which can range from not remembering someone's name, to a professor's comments about an essay. This feedback should be incorporated into your learning structure, making changes to the tools you use and strategies you employ (Roebers, 2017).

A key component of metacognition is reflection, that is, the deliberate evaluation of the effectiveness of a process, tool, or strategy *in relation to a goal* (Zelazo, 2015). A strategy may be highly effective, but upon reflection, you may recognize it will not help you reach your goals and needs to be discarded or modified. Reflection includes monitoring your thoughts and emotions through self-interrogation, e.g., "What do I need to know for the exam? Is the way I'm studying the best way to learn this topic?", and carrying out activities that help you learn, e.g., selecting the topics and material you need to study, and reviewing a graded exam to determine what your mistakes were and plan how to learn that material more effectively (Roebers, 2017).

To enable reflection, you need to momentarily stop receiving information and doing academic work, and to distance yourself from your experiences to look at the "big picture" (Zelazo, 2015). I encourage my students to evaluate the different components of their learning strategies, i.e., time allocation, prioritization, notetaking, etc., independently from who they are as learners. This allows for a more objective evaluation and helps avoid negative self-talk or rumination.

Reflection can be done individually or as a team, in the case of group projects. Reflection should allow a group to discuss previous experiences and current expectations and, as the project progresses, make sense of any issue that arises and identify what modifications should be made (Hartmann et al., 2023). As part of my course's curriculum, students participate in a group project that has the goal of crafting an effective team and is based on group and individual reflections. In many cases, the group reflections as they carried out the project led to improvements in their communication and work strategies.

Reflection is best done in several steps, where you initially evaluate a situation or process based on the most salient or important aspect. Then, as you continue to reprocess and reevaluate, you will notice more features and nuance, as well as relationships with other situations or processes in the past, allowing you to foresee different scenarios in the future, and create plans to achieve the most desirable results (Hartmann et al., 2023; Zelazo, 2015).

By reflecting on your own thinking process, evaluating your learning strategies, changing them as needed, and evaluating the benefits of the changes you made, you will continuously grow as a learner and refine your techniques, time management, problem-solving skills, mindset, and resilience (Fraiwan et al., 2025).

In *Edgework*, Nadler (1995) presents a process that is similar to metacognitive reflection. According to Nadler, personal growth resulting from an activity or process requires that you consciously process and interiorize the experience. Nadler proposes four steps, the first of which is *Awareness*, paying attention to what you feel, believe, or think when you are about to undertake a challenge (the "edge"). The next level is *Responsibility*, determining if your reaction and emotions are typical for you. Then comes *Experimentation*, trying something different the next time you face an *edge*, and evaluating if the change was beneficial. Finally, during *Generalization and Transfer*, you determine how your actions and reactions to one *edge* experience can apply to others (see Chapter 2 for a more in-depth description of *Edgework*).

Social Cognition: Understanding Other People

You don't learn as well in isolation. Learning is easier when done alongside peers and with support from someone with expertise or who has more knowledge than you do, e.g., an instructor (Vygotsky, 1978). This includes working in groups, participating in study groups and class discussions, or simply attending a lecture.

Neurological and cultural differences in facial expression and body language; use of eye contact (i.e., nonverbal social cues); voice intonation, rhythm, and volume, i.e., prosody of language; and differences in expressing sympathy and empathy can cause communication issues among people.

Recent research has shown that, for example, autistic people can easily understand the nonverbal social cues and prosody of other autistic people and have difficulties understanding those of non-autistic people. In the same way, non-autistic people can easily understand social cues from other non-autistic people but have difficulty understanding those of autistic people. This phenomenon is called the "double empathy problem" (Bollen & Van Grunsven, 2025; Cheang et al., 2025; Ren et al., 2023).

In addition to autism, ADHD, schizophrenia, anxiety, and depression are among the neurotypes that may be at a disadvantage when working in groups where a majority of the members are neurotypical. Barriers are similar for students whose first language is not English, or those whose cultural use of body language, facial expression, and eye contact, differ from those of the majority (Nestor & Woodhull, 2024; Ren et al., 2023).

Colleges can help improve students' experience and academic performance by minimizing sources of stress and miscommunication related to social interactions. This can be achieved through the creation of neurodiversity and culturally aware communities that foster collaboration and emotional support (Fraiwan et al., 2025), and by using neurodiversity-aware compassionate pedagogy and universal design for learning, where instruction is clear and concise, with explicit academic and social expectations (Hamilton & Petty, 2023).

Your Brain Needs to Take Breaks

Regulation of Motivation and Attention in the Brain

Motivation, which incentivizes you to start a task, requires the involvement of several neurotransmitters. *Dopamine* plays a key role in motivation and the capacity to focus on the task at hand. When the demands of the task and the level of performance become unbalanced, your motivation decreases and more mental effort is required to stay on task (Kok, 2022). However, when engaged in highly motivating or pleasurable tasks, you can sustain attention for longer (Kunasegaran et al., 2023). This could be involved in the state of "hyperfocus," "flow" and being "in the zone," and may explain why, even when exhausted, students report being able to "lock in" or keep studying when they find the topic very interesting, while being unable to focus for more than a few minutes when the topic is not as attractive to them. Other neurotransmitters involved in motivation and attention include *norepinephrine*, *noradrenalin*, and *serotonin*, which is additionally involved in mood regulation (Faraone et al., 2025; Kok, 2022).

Glutamate is another key neurotransmitter necessary for thinking, remembering, and learning. It also influences your mood and is crucial to sustain neuroplasticity. Glutamate is stored in brain cells, where it is needed for the cells' activity, and, when you engage in cognitive tasks or physical activities, it is released into the extracellular space, where it is needed for neuronal communication. A clearance mechanism transports glutamate back into cells, because if the concentration of glutamate in the extracellular space is excessive, it can cause cell death (Pal, 2021; Wiehler et al., 2022).

Reaching Mental Fatigue

When extracellular glutamate increases, it helps people feel energized and focused, but as it continues to accumulate, people's energy and focus decrease, leading to mental fatigue. Mental fatigue is a feeling of tiredness and stress that slows down brain activity, decreases the capacity to pay attention and EF in general, and can affect physical performance such as balance or strength. It can be accompanied by anxiety about unfinished tasks. Mental fatigue can be very dangerous, as it decreases a person's alertness and reaction time, making it more likely to be injured or involved in an accident. If not addressed, mental fatigue can lead to burnout and depression (Kunasegaran et al., 2023).

An early sign of mental fatigue is feeling more tempted to give in to distractors that require less cognitive effort, such as checking your cell phone. Tasks that require more mental effort are avoided even if there is a high-value reward attached to it; additionally, people start overestimating the difficulty of tasks (Steward et al., 2025). Once people reach mental fatigue, their executive functioning decreases, their motivation to continue working on a task drops, as does their ability to focus, remember properly, or process information (Kok, 2022). It is important to note that, at that point, people won't be able to accurately determine that they're mentally depleted (Kunasegaran et al., 2023; Wiehler et al., 2022).

Factors that Accelerate Mental Fatigue Include

a Performing difficult tasks requiring deep concentration or strenuous physical activity, which lead to a faster accumulation of extracellular glutamate (Wiehler et al., 2022).
b Decreased motivation when the tasks are too demanding, which increases the mental effort needed to continue dealing with those tasks (Kok, 2022).
c Receiving too much information, without having time to process it (Kunasegaran et al., 2023).
d Dealing with multiple EF demands that accumulated during the day, regardless of whether they are caused by work or learning tasks, or daily living needs such as cooking, cleaning, driving, etc. (Kunasegaran et al., 2023).
e Chronic stress created by difficult jobs or a high academic load, long working hours, and sleep deprivation (Kok, 2022; Kunasegaran et al., 2023; Wiehler et al., 2022).

Resting and Taking Breaks

Glutamate decreases during NREM sleep, as your body and brain rest (Wiehler et al., 2022). While you are awake, resting gives your brain time to remove excessive glutamate from the extracellular space in your brain. If you rest before you reach mental fatigue, you may be able to go back to work or study after a short break. Taking breaks throughout the day, as well as avoiding excessive demands on your EF, may help you avoid mental fatigue altogether.

Testing how long people should study before taking a break, Biwer et al. (2023) compared three conditions: (a) study sessions of 24 minutes followed by 6 minutes rest, (b) 12-minute sessions followed by 3-minute breaks, or (c) self-regulated, meaning students would take a break when they felt they needed it. Students in the self-regulated condition studied for longer, needed longer breaks afterward, and felt more fatigued, distracted, and less motivated to continue studying. This was likely due to students not being able to efficiently detect when they had reached mental fatigue, in the same way as participants in studies by Wiehler et al. (2022).

Another study by Ginns et al. (2023) requested students to answer a 20-minute math test, followed by 5 minutes of rest, a brief math lesson, and a second math test. During the 5-minute break, students either remained in silence or watched a nature video; a control group didn't rest. Students who rested performed better in the second math test than those who didn't rest. And students who remained sitting quietly reported feeling better able to focus on the lesson than those who didn't rest or students who watched the nature video. This is likely due to the DMN not being able to properly activate while they were receiving sensory input, in this case from the video, leading to only partial rest. Similarly, engaging with social media, texting and other such activities will reduce the effectiveness of the rest; appropriate rest requires disengagement from sensory inputs.

In an interview, Gabriel Garcia Marquez (2018), who won the 1982 Nobel Prize in Literature, mentioned he worked from 9 a.m. to about 2:30 p.m., explaining he had to set a strict work schedule for himself: "If you get carried away and don't stop on time, the last pages are written by a tired man.... You need rigor: start at one time and stop at another."

To study efficiently, then, you need to assume you *will* reach mental fatigue from either studying difficult topics or strenuous physical activity. Some of my students are student-athletes and a few have planned to work on assignments after afternoon practice, only to discover they cannot properly focus anymore. Trying to study while exhausted would further increase your mental fatigue, leaving you unable to fully understand or remember what you study, or to solve problems efficiently. Therefore, plan to study for set amounts of time, taking scheduled breaks that allow for real rest, disengaging from your senses as much as possible. Meditation, by the by, seems to improve glutamate metabolism, which is one more reason to practice it (Pal, 2021).

In Brief

Learning is a very complex process and, for the most part, requires effort. To learn anything, you need to remember, and to remember you need to pay attention to what you're hearing, reading, seeing, or doing. The capacity to focus on a lecture, for example, requires you to utilize your EF skills, which will allow you to dismiss external and internal interruptions, and have a method to capture the most important aspects of the lecture. Taking breaks is as important as being *present* in class or during study sessions. Rest allows your brain to clear itself from neurotransmitters and other substances which, when accumulated, interact with your capacity to process new information. Effective breaks require that you stop the flow of information from the environment, allowing your brain to process the information it has received. Your study sessions will be more useful by setting both focusing and resting periods. To determine when to take a break and generally optimize your learning practices, you can make use of metacognition, that is, using an outsider perspective to determine which learning strategies work for you, and whether they need to be modified in some way.

References

Ahmad, F. N., Tremblay, S., Karkuszewski, M. D., Alvi, M., & Hockley, W. E. (2024). A conceptual–perceptual distinctiveness processing account of the superior recognition memory of pictures over environmental sounds. *Quarterly Journal of Experimental Psychology, 77*(7), 1555–1580. https://doi.org/10.1177/17470218231202986

Alhamdan, A., Pickering, H., Murphy, M., & Crewther, S. (2025). From senses to memory during childhood: A systematic review and bayesian meta-analysis exploring multisensory processing and working memory development. *European Journal of Investigation in Hh, Psychology and Education, 15*(8), 157. https://doi.org/10.3390/ejihpe15080157

American Psychological Association (n.d.) Memory. In *APA dictionary of psychology*. Retrieved December 24, 2025, from https://dictionary.apa.org/memory

Anderson, L. W., & Krathwohl, D. R. (2001). *A taxonomy for learning, teaching, and assessing: A revision of Bloom's taxonomy of educational objectives*. Longman.

Asuncion, R. M. D., & Khalili, Y. Al. (2024). Short-term memory impairment. *StatPearls* [Internet]. Treasure Island (FL): StatPearls Publishing. https://www.ncbi.nlm.nih.gov/books/NBK545136

Atkinson, R. C., & Shiffrin, R. M. (1968). Human memory: A proposed system and its control processes. In K. W. Spence & J. T. Spence (Eds.), *The psychology of learning and motivation: Advances in research and theory* (Vol. 2, pp. 89–195). Academic Press.

Azarias, F. R., Almeida, G. H. D. R., De Melo, L. F., Rici, R. E. G., & Maria, D. A. (2025). The journey of the default mode network: Development, function, and impact on mental health. *Biology, 14*(4), 395. https://doi.org/10.3390/biology14040395

Badre, D. (2025). Cognitive control. *Annual Review of Psychology, 76*(1), 167–195. https://doi.org/10.1146/annurev-psych-022024-103901

Barrouillet, P., Camos, V., Pougeon, J., Beaudet, J., Croizet, P., & Belletier, C. (2024). Human cognitive system privileges processing over short-term storage: Asymmetry in working memory limitations. *Journal of Experimental Psychology: Learning, Memory, and Cognition, 50*(10), 1550–1578. https://doi.org/10.1037/xlm0001371

Biwer, F., Wiradhany, W., Oude Egbrink, M. G. A., & De Bruin, A. B. H. (2023). Understanding effort regulation: Comparing 'Pomodoro' breaks and self-regulated breaks. *British Journal of Educational Psychology, 93*(S2), 353–367. https://doi.org/10.1111/bjep.12593

Bloom, B. S., Engelhart, M. D., Furst, E. J., Hill, W. H., & Krathwohl, D. R. (1956). *Taxonomy of educational objectives: The classification of educational goals*. Longmans, Green and Co.

Bollen, C., & Van Grunsven, J. (2025). In defense of the double empathy problem hypothesis: An urgently needed alternative to fallacies and injustices in mainstream autism research. *Psychological Review*. https://doi.org/10.1037/rev0000605

Buzsáki, G., McKenzie, S., & Davachi, L. (2022). Neurophysiology of remembering. *Annual Review of Psychology, 73*(1), 187–215. https://doi.org/10.1146/annurev-psych-021721-110002

Cheang, R. T., Skjevling, M., Blakemore, A. I., Kumari, V., & Puzzo, I. (2025). Do you feel me? Autism, empathic accuracy and the double empathy problem. *Autism, 29*(9), 2315–2327. https://doi.org/10.1177/13623613241252320

Cotton, K., & Ricker, T. J. (2022). Examining the relationship between working memory consolidation and long-term consolidation. *Psychonomic Bulletin & Review, 29*(5), 1625–1648. https://doi.org/10.3758/s13423-022-02084-2

De Marchena, A. B., Eigsti, I.-M., & Yerys, B. E. (2015). Brief report: Generalization weaknesses in verbally fluent children and adolescents with autism spectrum disorder. *Journal of Autism and Developmental Disorders, 45*(10), 3370–3376. https://doi.org/10.1007/s10803-015-2478-6

Devaney, K., Levin, E., Tripathi, V., Higgins, J., Lazar, S., & Somers, D. (2021). Attention and default mode network assessments of meditation experience during active cognition and rest. *Brain Sciences, 11*(5), 566. https://doi.org/10.3390/brainsci11050566

Dharani, K. (2015). Memory. In *The biology of thought*. Academic Press.

Diamond, A. (2013). Executive functions. *Annual Review of Psychology, 64*(1), 135–168. https://doi.org/10.1146/annurev-psych-113011-143750

Diamond, A., & Ling, D. S. (2016). Conclusions about interventions, programs, and approaches for improving executive functions that appear justified and those that, despite much hype, do not. *Developmental Cognitive Neuroscience, 18*, 34–48. https://doi.org/10.1016/j.dcn.2015.11.005

Draheim, C., Pak, R., Draheim, A. A., & Engle, R. W. (2022). The role of attention control in complex real-world tasks. *Psychonomic Bulletin & Review, 29*(4), 1143–1197. https://doi.org/10.3758/s13423-021-02052-2

Esterman, M., & Rothlein, D. (2019). Models of sustained attention. *Current Opinion in Psychology, 29*, 174–180. https://doi.org/10.1016/j.copsyc.2019.03.005

Faraone, S. V., Ward, C. L., Boucher, M., Elbekai, R., & Brunner, E. (2025). Role of serotonin in the neurobiology of attention-deficit/hyperactivity disorder: A systematic literature review. *Expert Opinion on Therapeutic Targets, 29*(9), 637–654. https://doi.org/10.1080/14728222.2025.2552324

Fraiwan, M., Almomani, F., & Hammouri, H. (2025). Metacognition and social cognition dysfunction symptoms in university students: Prevalence and correlation with demographic and personal factors. *International Journal of Educational Research Open, 9,* 100514. https://doi.org/10.1016/j.ijedro.2025.100514

Friedman, N. P., & Robbins, T. W. (2022). The role of prefrontal cortex in cognitive control and executive function. *Neuropsychopharmacology, 47*(1), 72–89. https://doi.org/10.1038/s41386-021-01132-0

Garcia Marquez, G.. (2018). The writer's trade (interview). In *El Correo de la UNESCO*. Retrieved November 23, 2026, from https://courier.unesco.org/es/articles/gabriel-garcia-marquez-el-oficio-de-escritor-entrevista

Ginns, P., Muscat, K., & Naylor, R. (2023). Rest breaks aid directed attention and learning. *Educational and Developmental Psychologist, 40*(2), 141–150. https://doi.org/10.1080/20590776.2023.2225700

Girardeau, J.-C., Sperduti, M., Blondé, P., & Piolino, P. (2022). Where is my mind…? The link between mind wandering and prospective memory. *Brain Sciences, 12*(9), 1139. https://doi.org/10.3390/brainsci12091139

Hamilton, L. G., & Petty, S. (2023). Compassionate pedagogy for neurodiversity in higher education: A conceptual analysis. *Frontiers in Psychology, 14,* 1093290. https://doi.org/10.3389/fpsyg.2023.1093290

Hartmann, A., Vinke-de Kruijf, J., & Van Weesep, R. (2023). Asking the right questions: The role of reflection for learning in and between projects. *International Journal of Project Management, 41*(5), 102494. https://doi.org/10.1016/j.ijproman.2023.102494

Hong, C., Fallon, J., & Friston, K. (2021). FMRI evidence for default mode network deactivation associated with rapid eye movements in sleep. *Brain Sciences, 11*(11), 1528. https://doi.org/10.3390/brainsci11111528

Khouri, M., Massarwe, A., & Cohen, N. (2025). Challenges in higher education: Differences between students with and without specific learning disorder and the moderating role of executive functions. *PLoS One, 20*(9), e0331375. https://doi.org/10.1371/journal.pone.0331375

Kok, A. (2022). Cognitive control, motivation and fatigue: A cognitive neuroscience perspective. *Brain and Cognition, 160,* 105880. https://doi.org/10.1016/j.bandc.2022.105880

Kunasegaran, K., Ismail, A. M. H., Ramasamy, S., Gnanou, J. V., Caszo, B. A., & Chen, P. L. (2023). Understanding mental fatigue and its detection: A comparative analysis of assessments and tools. *PeerJ, 11,* e15744. https://doi.org/10.7717/peerj.15744

Li, Q., Tang, W., & Liu, X. (2025). Value-directed remembering: A dual-process perspective. *Behavioral Sciences, 15*(8), 1113. https://doi.org/10.3390/bs15081113

Lopis, D., Le Pape, T., Manetta, C., & Conty, L. (2021). Sensory cueing of autobiographical memories in normal aging and Alzheimer's disease: A comparison between visual, auditory, and olfactory information. *Journal of Alzheimer's Disease, 80*(3), 1169–1183. https://doi.org/10.3233/JAD-200841

Lunsford-Avery, J. R., Damme, K. S. F., Engelhard, M. M., Kollins, S. H., & Mittal, V. A. (2020). Sleep/wake regularity associated with default mode network structure among healthy adolescents and young adults. *Scientific Reports, 10*(1), 509. https://doi.org/10.1038/s41598-019-57024-3

Menon, V. (2023). 20 years of the default mode network: A review and synthesis. *Neuron, 111*(16), 2469–2487. https://doi.org/10.1016/j.neuron.2023.04.023

Merriam-Webster (n.d.) Metacognition. In *Merriam-Webster.com dictionary*. Retrieved December 23, 2025, from https://www.merriam-webster.com/dictionary/metacognition

Nadler, R. S. (1995). Edgework: Stretching boundaries and generalizing experiences. *The Journal of Experimental Education, 18*(1), 52–55. https://doi.org/10.1177/105382599501800110

Nestor, P. G., & Woodhull, A.-A. (2024). Neuropsychology of social cognition: Culture, display rules, and emotional expressivity. *Journal of Clinical and Experimental Neuropsychology, 46*(9), 811–827. https://doi.org/10.1080/13803395.2024.2428728

Nguyen, L., Murphy, K., & Andrews, G. (2022). A game a day keeps cognitive decline away? A systematic review and meta-analysis of commercially-available brain training programs in healthy and cognitively impaired older adults. *Neuropsychology Review, 32*(3), 601–630. https://doi.org/10.1007/s11065-021-09515-2

Pal, M. M. (2021). Glutamate: The master neurotransmitter and its implications in chronic stress and mood disorders. *Frontiers in Human Neuroscience, 15*, 722323. https://doi.org/10.3389/fnhum.2021.722323

Paller, K. A. (2024). Recurring memory reactivation: The offline component of learning. *Neuropsychologia, 196*, 108840. https://doi.org/10.1016/j.neuropsychologia.2024.108840

Perone, S., Almy, B., & Zelazo, P. D. (2018). Toward an understanding of the neural basis of executive function development. In *The neurobiology of brain and behavioral development* (pp. 291–314). Elsevier. https://doi.org/10.1016/B978-0-12-804036-2.00011-X

Pozo-Rodríguez, M., Cruz, S., Conde-Pumpido-Zubizarreta, S., Carracedo, A., Tubío-Fungueiriño, M., & Fernández-Prieto, M. (2026). A systematic review on the association between executive function and emotional regulation in autism, ADHD, and autism/ADHD. *Neuroscience & Biobehavioral Reviews, 183*, 106570. https://doi.org/10.1016/j.neubiorev.2026.106570

Ren, W., Guo, X., Huang, J., Liu, Q., & Zhang, Z. (2023). The influence of gaze direction on time perception: From the perspective of social perception. *Frontiers in Psychology, 13*, 967603. https://doi.org/10.3389/fpsyg.2022.967603

Roebers, C. M. (2017). Executive function and metacognition: Towards a unifying framework of cognitive self-regulation. *Developmental Review, 45*, 31–51. https://doi.org/10.1016/j.dr.2017.04.001

Seifert, K., & Sutton, R. (2009). The learning process. In *Educational psychology* (3rd ed.). Retrieved on December 29, 2025, from https://pressbooks.pub/uwgedpsych/chapter/the-learning-process/

Serra, M. J., & DeMarree, K. G. (2016). Unskilled and unaware in the classroom: College students' desired grades predict their biased grade predictions. *Memory & Cognition, 44*(7), 1127–1137. https://doi.org/10.3758/s13421-016-0624-9

Shiels, K., & Hawk, L. W. (2010). Self-regulation in ADHD: The role of error processing. *Clinical Psychology Review, 30*(8), 951–961. https://doi.org/10.1016/j.cpr.2010.06.010

Sievers, C., Bird, C. M., & Renoult, L. (2019). Predicting memory formation over multiple study episodes. *Learning & Memory, 26*(12), 465–472. https://doi.org/10.1101/lm.049791.119

Steward, G., Looi, V., & Chib, V. S. (2025). The neurobiology of cognitive fatigue and its influence on effort-based choice. *The Journal of Neuroscience, 45*(24), e1612242025. https://doi.org/10.1523/JNEUROSCI.1612-24.2025

Thalmann, M., Souza, A. S., & Oberauer, K. (2019). How does chunking help working memory? *Journal of Experimental Psychology: Learning, Memory, and Cognition*, *45*(1), 37–55. https://doi.org/10.1037/xlm0000578

Vygotsky, L. S. (1978). Interaction between learning and development. In *Mind in society: The development of higher psychological processes*. Trans. M. Cole, V. John-Steiner, S. Scribner, & E. Souberman. Harvard University Press.

Warren, S. L., Heller, W., & Miller, G. A. (2021). The structure of executive dysfunction in depression and anxiety. *Journal of Affective Disorders*, *279*, 208–216. https://doi.org/10.1016/j.jad.2020.09.132

Wiehler, A., Branzoli, F., Adanyeguh, I., Mochel, F., & Pessiglione, M. (2022). A neuro-metabolic account of why daylong cognitive work alters the control of economic decisions. *Current Biology*, *32*(16), 3564–3575.e5. https://doi.org/10.1016/j.cub.2022.07.010

Zelazo, P. D. (2015). Executive function: Reflection, iterative reprocessing, complexity, and the developing brain. *Developmental Review*, *38*, 55–68. https://doi.org/10.1016/j.dr.2015.07.001

4 Strategies That Lead to Effective Learning

Effective learning includes much more than what you normally think of as "studying." Studying encompasses the activities you perform in order to learn. The *American Psychological Association's Dictionary of Psychology* (n.d.) defines studying as "any attempt to acquire and remember information," and the *Merriam-Webster Dictionary* (n.d.-a) adds that it requires "application of the mental faculties." This encompasses going to class, listening to the lecture and taking notes, reading the textbook and your notes, reviewing the material and practicing what you know. In a course, you may be evaluated according to the facts you remember and how you apply the knowledge you have.

However, if you study only thinking of the grade, your learning will be shallow. As explained in Chapter 3, learning means "relatively permanent changes in behavior, skills, knowledge, or attitudes resulting from identifiable psychological or social experiences." (Seifert & Sutton, 2009). If you only remember a piece of information for a brief period of time, it was not really *learned*.

You will be motivated to learn what you find interesting and what you foresee will be useful to you in the future. This implies being aware of how a course you take will help you understand a higher level course, and what aspects of each course are the most crucial to deeply learn. Based on your previous experience, you may know what strategies have helped you master the diverse material and skills, as well as how much time you may need to dedicate to each course. This can give you a reasonable idea of what the academic term will look like, in terms of time and effort needed for your academic work.

Creating a reasonable and fulfilling schedule throughout your academic journey will ensure you have enough time and energy for optimal learning, while allowing you to balance your time and energy between academics and other components of your life, such as your career development and personal life.

DOI: 10.4324/9781003750246-5

To achieve this balance, *time management* is key. It encompasses a wide range of skills, including the following:

a *Budgeting time* or knowing how much time to dedicate to each activity or task. This includes your non-work time needs, including sleep, socializing, eating, commuting, and rest. Based on your finite time, you can then see how many tasks you can do after fulfilling your basic needs, and optimally, you use this evaluation to determine how many courses you should realistically enroll in, how many extracurricular activities you should join, how much time you have for socializing, and so on.
b *Task/activity management*. Sometimes you do have the time, BUT didn't plan what to do with that time. You may then resort to low-effort activities such as social media. OR you know what you want to do but cannot focus on it at that moment. OR you don't have the materials you need, you have questions about the rubrics, didn't know you had to watch a movie before writing an essay, etc. Task/activity management also includes prioritization, goal setting, planning, monitoring yourself to stay on task, remembering all your tasks and activities, and more.

This chapter is organized to go from long-term planning to organizing your study sessions.

Setting Useful Goals

Before starting planning what you'll do, you need to have certain goals. Some are long-term, like becoming a neurosurgeon, or they may be short term, like finishing this assignment before midnight.

Having goals that are too vague prevents you from making them a reality. Many times, students tell me, "I want a higher GPA," but for some students that means a 3.75, while for others it can be a 2.5. And as long as it only lives in your head, it is difficult to connect that goal with the actions you need to take.

A common model for goal setting is "SMART," which stands for *S*pecific-*M*easurable-*A*chievable-*R*elevant and *T*ime bound. A SMART goal includes *who* is involved, *what* exactly you desire to accomplish, *where* and *how* you will conduct the activity and for *how long*, materials needed, possible challenges, and, importantly, *why* you are doing it (Bahrami et al., 2022). While it may feel unnecessary and a waste of time at the beginning, setting SMART goals really helps define your objectives and how to achieve them. With practice, it will become less time-consuming and more helpful. One key piece that is not in the acronym is planning, which is, however, critical and should be written out as well.

You can transform a wish into a SMART goal, e.g., "I want to live in Paris for a semester." It is somewhat specific, as you're naming the city. A complete goal and plan could be:

> I want to study abroad in Paris *[S]* next fall *[T]*, studying art exhibited at the Louvre *[S]*, through the fine arts collaboration between my school and the Sorbonne *[A]*. I know I can thrive in that program because I have lived abroad before, and I'm doing really well in my history of art course; the professor actually recommended me to do this *[A]*. This will not only fulfill my childhood dream but will allow me to network with renowned art historians and restorers *[R]*.

Measurable is embedded—you will know if you achieved it if you do go to Paris in the fall and study the Louvre's art at the Sorbonne. This is still undoable unless you add a plan:

> The program is partially covered by financial aid; I need to work during all academic breaks at my old high school job, and I'll deposit my paychecks in my savings account to avoid spending them by mistake. I will also look for guidance from Emma Smith, the study abroad advisor, and keep meeting with her to make sure I am fulfilling all requirements.

Even when you face obstacles, having a goal and a plan helps you make changes as needed. One of my advisees had the longtime goal of going to the Galapagos Islands for a semester; the courses would count for her major. The program changed shortly before she was planning to go and no longer counted for her major. The study abroad advisor gave her other options; she ultimately enrolled in a similar program in Australia. Since she'd been planning courses, saving money, and knew the required paperwork, she was able to quickly pivot, fulfill a slightly different goal, and enjoy it.

In a study of the SMART model, Bahrami et al. (2022) determined that creating SMART goals significantly increased the likelihood of achieving them. Students who created SMART goals felt increased autonomy, competence, and relatedness (feeling connected and cared for by others), and felt good (interested, determined, and inspired). The researchers concluded that it is important to have autonomy to choose your goals, and for your goals to be aligned with your values and interests. Another crucial component mentioned is knowing what techniques are most likely to help you achieve your goals.

Not all objectives need to be framed as a SMART goal. Some objectives, like maintaining your room clean or a 4.0 GPA are possibly more easily achieved through that lens. Others, especially enjoying extracurricular activities and honing your skills in a sport or art, may need less constraints. A study of the emotions of professional golfers (Swann et al., 2016) showed that two different mindsets are important: "letting it happen" *and* "making it happen."

"Letting it happen" is related to a "flow" state that allows you to explore without a fixed desired outcome. In professional golfers, the "flow" was seen more frequently at the beginning of a tournament. "Keeping an open mind" is another way to think about it.

In "making it happen," the person is aware of the circumstances. For golfers, it's their current score; for a student, their current grade, how many assignments they need to submit, etc. They can then concentrate on improving their performance and know how to do it. This is similar to a SMART goal.

Pietsch et al. (2024) advocate for a "letting it happen" attitude for goals that are not specific and that allow exploration, such as when you start learning a new topic or a complex task, and you are not given specific guidance. If you translate this to an academic setting, the different stages could involve evaluating different possibilities for an honor's thesis. Within reason, you could explore a variety of topics and research methods. Once you have chosen a topic and research method, you can work toward a SMART goal.

This sequence can help you choose meaningful goals where you will enjoy not just the outcome but the activity itself, and it will give you more freedom to choose from a broad variety of topics or tools you can use. Exploring before setting a specific goal can also prevent negative feelings, such as frustration, which could affect your learning, and could make it more likely that you will be engaging with an activity or topic that is interesting, meaningful, and satisfactory (Pietsch et al., 2024). Additionally, since you will be intrinsically motivated, you will be more likely to stick to your plans and achieve your goals.

Knowing How Much Time You Really Have

Each week, there are a total of 168 hours (24 h/d × 7 days), in which you need to squeeze everything from sleep to learning and watching a movie. In my personal experience and that of my students, it is difficult to conceptualize how much that really is. When I ask in class how many hours there are in a week, responses vary from 50 to 500.

Maybe the difficulty of visualizing your available time is the reason students tend to overfill their academic schedules and end up *literally* not having enough time for it all. An activity we've found useful in my class is this: Grab 168 pieces of anything you want. Maybe candy, or pebbles, or marbles. Then, start distributing them to, first, your physical and physiological needs.

Crucially, you need to *sleep seven to nine hours a night*. This should be non-negotiable. For simplicity's sake, let's multiply 8 hours × 7 days = 56 hours. 168 – 56 = *112 hours left*.

Every day, you get dressed, shower, comb your hair and do other hygiene and physical self-care activities. That accounts for at least 2 hours a day, 14 hours in a week. 112 – 14 = *98 hours available*.

You eat and exercise daily. You may eat while you study and exercise on your way to class. But other times should be dedicated only to those activities. Assuming also only 2 hours a day, 14 hours a week, you have 98 – 14 = *84 hours available*. You'll get back to this, so keep it in mind.

Now, engagement in other activities depends on a multitude of factors: your financial situation, whether you participate actively in religious activities, enjoy volunteering, have a hobby, a significant other, caretaking duties, etc. The hours that you dedicate to those activities are a very important part of your life and should not be left for *after graduation*.

Focusing on academics, the basic measure system used in the US is "credit hours." As reviewed by Pardos et al. (2023), the concept of credit hours has been in use in the US since the early 1900s. The Office of Postsecondary Education, US Department of Education (2010) defines a credit hour as no less than one hour of direct instruction and a minimum of two additional hours of out-of-class student work. Credit hours are certainly imperfect, as the load varies in real life; a 3-credit course may require 12 or maybe 6 hours of additional study, instead of the calculated 9. However, it is a good starting point.

Most bachelor's degrees require 120 credits, taken over four years, and most associate's degrees require 60 credits over two years. Both correspond to 30 credits per year, or 15 credits per semester. While courses' credit hour assignations can vary widely, major or specialization courses are commonly worth between three and four credits.

You had *84 hours* available after satisfying some basic needs. If you take the average 15 credits and you consider 15 hours of class and 30 hours of work outside of the classroom, we're talking about 45 hours. 84 – 45 = *39 hours available*.

What do you do with those 39 hours? Well, that depends. Maybe you have a part-time job, requiring 15–20 hours a week, or caretaking duties that translate into 20 hours a week. If you play a varsity sport, you may spend 29–34 hours a week on athletics, which was the median reported in the NCAA GOALS Study (2025).

Don't forget to consider the time you need for transportation. Walking, taking the bus, riding a bike, doing your laundry, going to the grocery store—all those activities eat away your time.

Try to avoid overloading yourself with coursework. If you end up having some time on your hands, you can always engage in extracurricular or professional development activities, volunteering, and, most important of all, taking breaks, socializing, and enjoying life. Your use of time requires being aware of the time you have, as explained earlier, and prioritizing activities, described next.

Prioritizing and Saying No

The Eisenhower Matrix

In a speech given in 1954, President Dwight Eisenhower quoted an unnamed former college president: "I have two kinds of problems, the urgent and the important. The urgent are not important, and the important are never urgent." (Eisenhower, 1954)

"Urgent" refers to something that calls for immediate attention (*Merriam-Webster*, n.d.-b), while "important" is something necessary or of great value (*Cambridge Dictionary*, n.d.). Both definitions are in relation to yourself. It is urgent or important *to you*. "Urgent" would then be anything that you must do immediately. An urgent and very annoying (but necessary) event in college is a fire drill. It doesn't matter what you're doing, you must evacuate the area where you are. "Important" is what matters to you: learning a topic, mastering a skill, updating your resume, writing an application essay for graduate school, helping your friends, or keeping in touch with your loved ones.

Using the urgent and important categories, Stephen Covey (2009) created a time management matrix with four quadrants: "important and urgent," "important, not urgent," "urgent, not important," and "not important, not urgent." His son, Sean Covey, adapted it for college students (Covey, 2014). This matrix is known by several names, including the Eisenhower Matrix, which is the name I'm using here.

Using the urgent-important dimensions, you can evaluate any number of tasks and activities, whether they are menial and can be done in minutes, or crucial and requiring years. However, tasks and activities that deserve your attention are those that in addition to them being urgent and important *to you*, they need to be done *by you*.

Only you can do your own sleeping, eating, exercising, or learning. The fire drill is in the next building? Not your problem, you can continue working. Your friend has an exam? They need to study, not you. However, in the latter case, helping them study may be important to you, because you care about them. Helping them study would be important but not urgent; if you also had an exam, it would be important and urgent *for you* to study for *your* exam. Your friend could find someone else to study with; nobody can study *for you*.

You still have the same 168 hours per week mentioned about before. Optimally, your time should be spent on only two areas: "important and

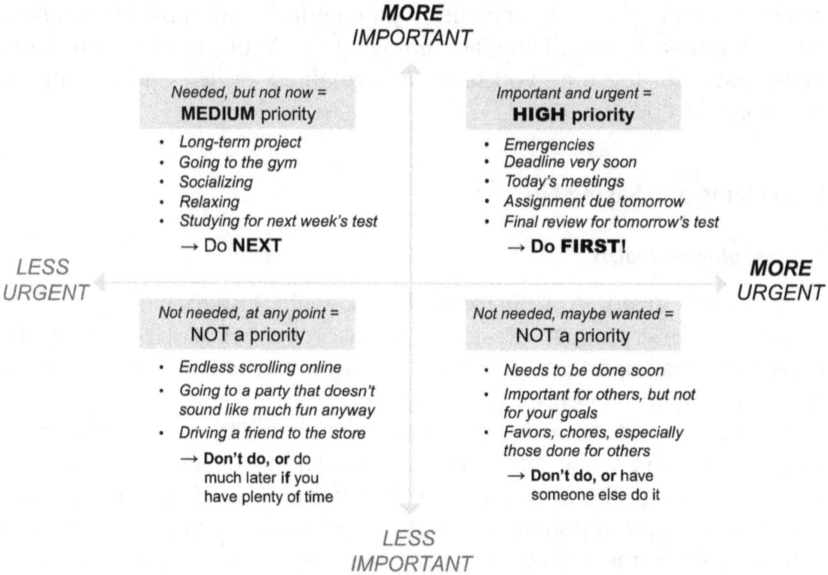

Figure 4.1 Eisenhower matrix. Concept by Florencia Ardon, PhD, based on Sean Covey's Time Matrix (Covey, 2014). Design by Julia Felice, PhD.

urgent," followed by "important, less urgent." You should not neglect them to engage in the low and null priority areas: "urgent, less important" and "less urgent and less important." Lastly, keep in mind that the matrix is dynamic; as mentioned earlier, helping a friend study may be in the "urgent, less important" category, or "important, less urgent" category, depending on whether it is important for you that your friend does well in that class and you don't have anything else requiring your attention. The matrix is shown in Figure 4.1.

Saying No

To be able to dedicate your time to what matters *to you* and can only be done *by you*, saying *NO* becomes crucial. For the areas of "urgent, less important" and "less important and less urgent," I recommend you to say *YES* only when these requirements are met: (a) You are doing fine: sleeping enough, doing well in your academics, fulfilling your obligations and taking care of yourself. (b) The person requesting a favor is someone you care for and helps you out. (c) What is asked from you aligns with your values. (d) It is something you have expertise on, or always wanted to learn or try or do. (e) You have more than enough time (estimate twice the time you're told it requires).

Setting boundaries is difficult, and you possibly need to practice how to say no in a way you're satisfied with. You don't need to flatly say no. It is possible that you cannot help *now* but *could next week*. Or you cannot commit to doing *everything* they request but can help with a little part of it. Or you know of someone who is better suited to perform that task and would be willing to help them. Saying no, however, is a crucial skill to learn. It will safeguard your capacity to achieve your goals, avoid overloading yourself, and will even help you keep long-term, healthy relationships with people you care for.

Finally, it is important to keep in mind that if you say no, you allow the person asking for the favor to find someone who *can* help them. If you say yes, and then you see it is impossible to finish it or you find you cannot do it well enough, you will have done that person a disservice. Only say yes when you can commit to doing it correctly and completely.

Setting goals, prioritizing, being able to say no, and being aware of the time you have, allows you to plan your academic load and extracurricular activities, which is what we'll speak about next.

Crafting Your Two- or Four-Year Plan of Studies

Selecting courses each term depends on several factors, including general graduation requirements and those of your major, concentration, specialization, or track, as well as your own wishes, which could include additional majors or minors. It can be overwhelming to choose between courses that fulfill the same requirement, especially if you have many to select from. In that way, I was fortunate that my major's curriculum was very rigid and didn't give me the opportunity to choose more than two or three courses in total. At the same time, my education was not as broad as it could have been.

Planning ahead is very useful. This can mean planning a semester ahead or even planning the next two to four years. While you will likely change several courses because they are no longer offered or because another, more interesting course appears on your radar, you save time and lower stress by minimizing the decisions needed each term. Even if planning your two or four years is not doable, you will save time and energy if you select each term's courses early and avoid adding too many courses after the semester has started.

Some majors offer a sample curriculum, partially filled with the required courses, or you can create your own based on the requirements for your enrollment year. If you find the curriculum difficult to understand, your academic advisor could be able to help you. You should not feel like you must do it on your own! As an academic advisor, I've seen both very streamlined, easy-to-follow curricula, as well as some I had serious difficulty understanding and had to reach out to the registrar for clarification.

Another benefit of planning all your undergraduate courses very early on is that you can make sure you are considering the course sequences—many courses need to be taken in a specific order or require you to have fulfilled certain requirements. Also, some courses may be offered only in one term per academic year (e.g., only in the fall) and missing that course could potentially mean an extra year of studying. You also need to make sure that your workload will be similar each semester. Student athletes or those who are or plan to engage in different activities that are term or season-bound need to account for the time and energy requirements and, for example, take fewer courses or less difficult courses when their sport is in season.

Your institution possibly offers hundreds or even thousands of courses. From those, you will only be able to take *maybe* a total of 40. When you are selecting courses don't think "I still need a three-credit course," which could lead to simply choosing an easy course regardless of the topic. It's much better to think that by choosing this three-credit course, you're *NOT* choosing another dozen or hundred courses you could take instead. By choosing courses you really care about, you will be able to graduate with the knowledge and skills you really want to achieve and that will help you in the future, and to take some that are truly interesting and fun. Your time and effort are valuable!

Planning and Organizing Each Academic Term

Adding and Dropping Courses

Planning your semester time and effort is a crucial part of time management. The optimal time to start planning your days and weeks is before the semester begins. However, there are practical reasons why this is not always possible. For example, you may not be completely sure you will remain on all the courses you're enrolled in, or you may be waiting to see if you will be able to enroll in courses that are currently full or require a permission code. Still, it is good practice to create a provisional plan—it may also show you if you're underestimating your commitments, or if you have more than enough time for an additional class.

It is also important to recognize that, even with careful planning, it's possible you won't be able to initially enroll in all your desired courses due to situations out of your control. In these circumstances, it is also important to carefully consider your options and what the consequences of each decision are. If you enroll late in a course, there will be a period of "catching on," mostly assignments to submit and chapters to read, and you will have missed lectures or discussions.

Students sometimes "overenroll," that is, they enroll in more courses than those they intend to keep. Many times, students do this with the idea of selecting between two elective courses. However, a few classes at the beginning of the term will not be representative enough of the coursework to make a truly informed decision. Overenrolling can lead to difficulties keeping up with all the material and assignments of all the courses and can cause unnecessary stress. A better way to compare two courses would be to talk to students who've taken the course, request the syllabus from the instructor if not available online, or speak with the instructor to clear out any questions about the curriculum or teaching style, for example.

Many of the students I advise make the mistake of dropping a course too late. A recent study by Borchers et al. (2025) suggests that enrolling or dropping late leads to a higher semester workload than when students don't change their enrollment. They also saw that students tend to drop courses with a high workload late in the semester, particularly if they also enrolled late in that course; the researchers consider that, in their study, students adding a course after the semester begins were unprepared for the additional workload of that course.

Consider this Scenario

A student is dedicating much of their time to a very difficult course, maybe going to tutoring or looking for additional textbooks or other sources of information. Despite the extra time and effort, they are unable to fully understand the concepts or solve problems as quickly as their classmates, and their grades are low. The student has given the course much attention and time, and has neglected other courses, which is reflected in lower grades in those courses. Disillusioned, the student finally drops the difficult course. By then, they cannot increase their grade in their other, neglected courses, and they finish the semester with lower grades and content mastery than if they had dropped the difficult course early. While the student *may have been able to* manage them all, the likelihood is lower with each passing week. That said, this is something that only the person facing that situation can properly gauge and the decision (and responsibility) is theirs too.

Distributing Your Workload Across the Term

Generally speaking, you will start a semester feeling like there's little to do. A few weeks after, you start having exams and quizzes. After this, it all seems like a blur. Here is where I see students being so stressed out and sleep deprived that they can no longer plan well. Vacation breaks help if students dedicate their time to sleep and relax, and if professors don't assign homework due immediately after, or schedule exams for the first or second day of classes after the break.

When students just "wing it" or go with the flow, worrying only about the assignment that is due next, they usually end up living in a state of unnecessary and constant emergencies, increasing stress and lowering performance. It also leads to sleep deprivation, not eating or exercising enough, neglecting friends and family, etc., and decreased well-being.

A full-term calendar, such as the *Semester Calendar* created by the Center for Academic Success at Louisiana State University (McGuire & McGuire, 2023), is a good tool to visualize what weeks will be very busy or relaxed. I adapted it for my class, having students add only very important points, as it is not meant to duplicate a regular calendar or planner. Based only on the key dates or tasks, students can estimate the workload for each week and designate them as having a low, moderate, or heavy workload, as seen on Figure 4.2. The main idea is to visually see how the semester "busyness" changes throughout the term and then to attempt to even it out. To even the

Semester Calendar (sample month)

	SUN	MON	TUE	WED	THU	FRI	SAT
Week 10	Oct **26**	Oct **27**	Oct **28**	Oct **29**	Oct **30**	Oct **31**	Nov **1**
HEAVY	*1 year anniversary!*	Chemistry problem set due		Biology quiz		**Game in Pittsburg**	**Game in Pittsburg**
Week 11	Nov **2**	Nov **3**	Nov **4**	Nov **5**	Nov **6**	Nov **7**	Nov **8**
MODERATE	**Game in Pittsburg**	Chemistry problem set due			History midterm exam		
Week 12	Nov **9**	Nov **10**	Nov **11**	Nov **12**	Nov **13**	Nov **14**	Nov **15**
HEAVY		Chemistry problem set due		Biology quiz		**Game in NYC**	**Game in NYC**
Week 13	Nov **16**	Nov **17**	Nov **18**	Nov **19**	Nov **20**	Nov **21**	Nov **22**
MODERATE	**Game in NYC**	Chemistry problem set due					*Mary's wedding!*
Week 14	Nov **23**	Nov **24**	Nov **25**	Nov **26**	Nov **27**	Nov **28**	Nov **29**
LOW				*Thanksgiving Break*	*Thanksgiving Break*	*Thanksgiving Break*	*Thanksgiving Break*

Figure 4.2 Term Calendar. Concept by Florencia Ardon, PhD, based on the Semester Calendar created by the Center for Academic Success at Louisiana State University (McGuire & McGuire, 2023). Design by Julia Felice, PhD.

workload as much as possible, students need to determine what work can be done ahead of time or could possibly wait until after a difficult week has gone by.

To make your own semester calendar, you can add *key academic dates*, e.g., first and last day of classes, deadlines to add or drop a course, exams, or due dates for big projects. Next, *student athletes* would add games or special training sessions. Dates related to *professional development* are also important, whether that is a poster session where you'll present your research, an internship application due date, or deadlines for law or medical school application. Finally, you also need to consider important personal dates. Maybe for your anniversary, October 26 in Figure 4.2, you won't be doing any academic work, just like on November 22, which is Mary's wedding on the same example. You should move work to other days; you don't want to be stressed out about a problem set during a celebration.

Planning Your Weekly Work Time

Once you are aware of the time you really have, the importance of maintaining a uniform workload through the semester and what tasks and activities you should focus on, you can plan your days. There are multiple ways to keep track of your schedule; many students use an online calendar, an online project manager, or to-do lists. Others prefer paper-based, be it a commercial planner, a plain notebook or even one containing unlined paper. The tool you use should be chosen *by you* and be useful *to you*. For example, I need to have my weeks start on Sunday. I have tried using calendars that start on Monday and kept making mistakes. The workable solution was not to force myself to adapt; it was to create and print calendars that started on Sundays. To avoid forgetting tasks or activities, it is fine to use as many reminders as you need, including redundant reminders (e.g., an email to yourself and an alarm on your phone), though you need to be careful to avoid all the reminders becoming overwhelming.

There are a few ways people organize their calendars, and what is overly complicated for one may be super useful to another. Some people only mark classes, practices, or meetings. In my case, being an ADHDer, I would struggle to decide what to do with the time in between or would overestimate what I can do. I've scheduled back to back meetings with no time in between, without considering the meeting places are 20 minutes away, or have not considered that for a virtual meeting I need to be in a quiet space, so I find myself in the middle of a busy corridor trying to understand what is said in the meeting. So, for me, it is also important to mark commute times and locations. To plan related activities, like studying, preparing for a meeting, calling someone, etc., you can either write all of them individually, which can seem overwhelming (certainly to me), or simply write "to-do," "prep time," etc.

Benjamin Franklin seems to be the first person to describe such a schedule, what he called "Scheme of Order": "The precept of Order requiring that every part of my business should have its allotted time, one page in my little book contain'd the following scheme of employment for the twenty-four hours of a natural day." He also added reflections, in the morning: "What good shall I do this day?" and in the evening: "What good have I done today?" Based on his Order, his day started at 5 a.m. From five to eight, he got up, washed, dressed, set goals for the day, and ate breakfast. Between 8 and 11 a.m., he worked. From 12 to 2 p.m., he "read, or overlook my accounts, and dine." He worked again from 2 to 6 p.m., and dedicated the time between 6 and 10 pm to "put things in their places. Supper. Music or diversion, or conversation. Examination of the day." From 10 p.m.–5 a.m., he planned to sleep (Franklin, 2006).

Franklin, by the way, adds that Order "was extremely difficult to acquire...having an exceeding good memory, I was not so sensible to the inconvenience attending want of method." He adds that some people who tried to put order in their days and failed kept telling him to give up. He continues: "[T]ho' I never arrived at the perfection I had been so ambitious of obtaining, ... I was, by the endeavor, a better and a happier man than I otherwise should have been if I had not attempted it." Your scheduling and planning may not be perfect, but they will be useful.

Scheduling Your Work in Order of Importance

a Classify as work hours only those that don't interfere with your sleep routine, e.g., 8 a.m.–9 p.m.
b Block the meeting times for your classes, field trips, office hours, athletic practice, etc.
c Mark the time you will be sitting down to eat. As discussed in the nutrition section, you don't have to eat a strict number of meals a day, or at specific times, but it is important to block time for this purpose.
d Select some blocks of time for academic work and to study. This is important; not doing so has led many of my students to forget they need to study for tomorrow's test or write an essay.
e Block time to spend with your friends and family. Getting together, speaking on the phone, writing emails, engaging in a group chat, all take time and are important.
f Finally, schedule breaks for nature walks. Detaching from work and screens is also crucial for your well-being.
g The spaces still open are those you can dedicate to activities in the "urgent, less important" and "less important and less urgent" categories of the Eisenhower Matrix, described earlier.

Scheduling time to work on specific tasks can be extremely helpful, as some of my students have found:

- Keeping a schedule and making to-do lists has helped me; even if it is not anything big, it's better that I can get something out of the way. (A student)
- Breaking bigger projects into smaller tasks gives me an itemized list to work through and achieve one by one, rather than forcing me to stare down the entirety of a monstrous task. (Pat O)
- Maintaining healthy habits is easier when my life has a schedule. I find myself slipping into unhealthy habits during times like finals week, breaks, or times when I'm unemployed. (Alexandra)

Starting Academic Work Early

Accurate estimates of time needed for each activity help you avoid overbooking yourself and avoid overestimating the time you have available to work on a paper or study for an exam. This is especially important for ADHDers, as one of ADHD's characteristics is an inaccurate perception of time.

There are a couple of options to do this: one is to have a calendar in which you create a plan and compare it to what you really do, side by side. Or you can simply make note of all deviations from your plan. When my students do this type of exercise in class, they recognize how often they get sick, need to spend time with a friend who is going through a rough situation, or have to fill in for a colleague at work, among other unexpected circumstances.

Many students postpone working on an assignment until shortly before the due date. That is, if they assume they need half a day, that would be the afternoon of the day an assignment is due by midnight. I propose the opposite: creating a "just in case" buffer between your internal deadline and the actual deadline set by your professor. If nothing extraordinary happens, you can enjoy the time, free of the pressure created by the pending work, which could subconsciously affect you. If something unexpected does happen, you would have started, thus having less work pending, consequently experiencing less stress. Starting early often leads to higher quality work, as one of my students mentions: "I have developed the habit of starting assignments at least one week before they are due, which gives me enough time to refine my work and make it the best it can be." (EA)

Thinking of Learning as a Cycle

Optimally, you should not *need* to "study for an exam," and should avoid cramming. You certainly need to ensure the knowledge is readily available in your memory and that you can quickly and efficiently perform activities such as writing essays or mathematical calculations.

But, sometimes students go to a class without knowing what they will learn or what they'll do. During class, they take notes and pay attention, or they are possibly halfway listening while writing a to-do list for later, or texting with a friend. After class, they don't read or do anything with the notes they wrote. Then, a few days before an exam, students start reading their notes and trying to make sense of them, reading the textbook, watching recorded lectures and so on.

This behavior is what some students mean when they say "studying for an exam." And it is the wrong approach for meaningful, deep, and long-term learning. It *may* ensure that you maintain the grades you want, but you would quickly forget what you learned. Optimally, you are taking mostly courses that you like, or that are needed for your future career. By engaging only as little as possible, you are wasting time twice: the time you are physically in class without paying enough attention, and the time needed to learn the material, essentially for the first time, just before the exam.

The learning cycle shown here is my adaptation of the Study Cycle created by the Center for Academic Success at Louisiana State University, described by McGuire and McGuire (2023). The Study Cycle was comprehensibly reviewed by Favero and Cesar (2022). I like the concept of a learning cycle because it shows that you don't learn topics in isolation; they feed upon each other, and your learning should be ever present. Additionally, it embeds reviewing concepts several times, which enhances your recall and understanding (Figure 4.3).

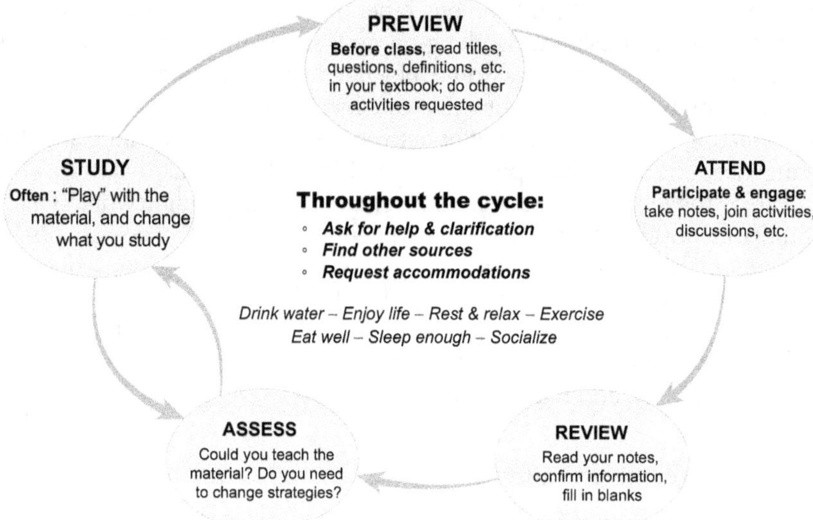

Figure 4.3 The Learning Cycle. Concept by Florencia Ardon, PhD, based on the Study Cycle developed by the Center for Academic Success at Louisiana State University, described by McGuire and McGuire (2023). Design by Julia Felice, PhD.

The Learning Cycle in Practice

Throughout, ensure your readiness by sleeping enough, eating well, exercising, and taking care of your well-being by resting, relaxing, and spending meaningful time with others. As the semester progresses, request accommodations if needed, keep asking for help and clarification of concepts, and find other sources of information to deepen your understanding. This is useful because sometimes the way a person explains a concept doesn't "click" with us, but we understand someone else's really well. Sources can include documentaries, your family and friends, podcasts, your textbook, blogs, free online courses, and generative artificial intelligence (GenAI). You need to verify information you obtain from sources not included in your course, especially when using GenAI. A useful way to use GenAI is described by Tyler, one of my students: "If you are going to use GenAI, in the long run it's much better to ask it to explain thought processes instead of giving you answers."

In a survey I conducted of my former students, they consistently mentioned asking for help was *useful and easy to do*, both to prepare for class, as mentioned by 64% of the students, and after class (for 62% of the students) (47 students answered this portion of the survey).

Preview up to a day before class. This includes doing any work requested, such as watching a video or practicing a language, as well as reading about the topic you'll see in class, and using the course material, such as slides or the textbook. For the reading portions, you don't need to do a deep dive, skimming the course material is enough. This preparation allows students to be familiarized with new vocabulary and concepts, and better understand the context (Favero & Cesar, 2022). The class can then be dedicated to discussions and application of the knowledge. This is deemed more engaging than listening to a lecture, and is preferred by students (Aagaard et al., 2014, corroborated by my students' feedback).

Two class preparation strategies selected by my former students as *useful and easy to do* were reading notes from previous lectures, for 53% of the respondents, and performing any activity required by the instructor as preparation for the class (also for 53% of them). At the same time, only 23% of them said the same about skimming the textbook before class. While it is good to read notes from a previous class, as it helps to create context for anything new you'll learn as well as for creating links between new and old knowledge, it can be seen as a look toward the past, while skimming the textbook, which the majority of my former students said they don't do, is a look at the future. It is a very useful and helpful strategy that doesn't take long, around 5–10 minutes could be enough.

Attend and participate during class. You will not learn what you don't hear or read. Actively participating will minimize "zoning out" or getting bored, and will improve your understanding of the material. Some engagement strategies are as follows:

a Taking notes of key concepts creates a base for future review and will keep you more engaged, as you actively listen or read, looking for key concepts. Your notes should not be elaborate or distracting, and you should use the method that works best for you. A recent study (Wiechmann et al., 2022) found no difference between handwriting on paper or using a tablet or laptop. Eighty-one percent of the students who answered my survey said taking notes and annotating slides was *useful and easy to do*.

b Receiving sensory input helps keep you alert. Depending on your professor's rules, this may look like drinking water, eating a snack, stretching, or even chewing gum. Seventy percent of my survey respondents agreed, finding these activities *useful and easy to do*. Another activity that helps you remain attentive is using fidget toys. Unfortunately, 43% of students who answered my survey stated they had not used fidget toys, even though fidgets are available for use during my class. Contrary to what many people believe, fidget toys don't distract you; they help you to stay "in the room" and attentive. Keeping your hands busy will make it less likely that you reach out for your phone and other distractors. Incidentally, 60% of the respondents to my survey said keeping their phone and other distractors away was *useful, but complicated to do*.

c For some students, it is helpful to use a transcription app, to simultaneously read and hear the lecture or in-class discussion, thus engaging more of their senses.

d Asking and answering questions, and participating in discussions, allows you to learn from your peers, establish friendships, and keep you "present" in class. Sixty-six percent of my former students answered in my survey that they found these actions *useful and easy to do*.

e On the other hand, while not as obviously detrimental as nodding off and multitasking in class, taking pictures of slides is a common strategy that hinders learning. It makes you *feel* like you paid attention and know what it was about, when in reality taking the picture distracted you from listening or reading, and it is likely you won't look at the picture after that.

Review the same day. After class, you can compare your class notes with slides, textbook, your peer's notes, etc. This allows you to make sure you don't miss anything and evaluate whether you understood the topic well. Based on my students' responses to the survey, reviewing after class is an area for improvement. Only 47% found reading notes after class was *useful and easy to do*, while 26% found it *useful but complicated to do*. Comparing their notes to slides, textbooks and other sources was deemed *useful and easy to do* for 30% of the students, while 36% considered it *useful, but complicated to do*. Finally, only 26% find starting assignments the day they're given is *useful and easy to do*, while the majority (53%) considered it *useful, but complicated to do*. At the same time, I'm not surprised by this, as students are generally involved in many courses, several of which are very difficult, as well as in a variety of extracurricular activities; they enjoy active social lives, and many of them have part-time jobs. I would still recommend taking a few minutes to take a look at their notes, to make sure they wrote everything important while the memories are fresh. Reading assignment instructions is valuable as well, as it helps estimate the time and material needed to complete the assignments, and taking this first step helps minimize procrastination.

Assess your knowledge before studying. This is a slight modification of the study cycle described by McGuire & McGuire (2023). Being aware of what you understand well and of what you didn't fully grasp early on gives you time to reach out to professors, TAs, or, if needed, to look for additional resources and materials. I've seen many students self-test only after spending a long time re-reading their textbooks or notes or trying to answer problem sets. By the time they realize they are missing some crucial information, it's very close to an exam or deadline, and as a result, they don't have enough time anymore, and their anxiety skyrockets.

Study often rather than *everything all at once*. You remember better if you recall the memory several times on different days; for example, to remember the name of a person, it's better to say it several times or recall their name when you look at their picture (Paller, 2024). This is also called *distributed practice* or *spacing*. It is not enough to study a topic once; remembering and understanding require several recollections, re-encoding and consolidation of the memory, and connecting new and old knowledge. This is another area of growth for my former students; only 34% of them found reviewing notes and other materials once a week was *useful and easy to do*, while 45% of the students found it *useful, but complicated to do*. Part of this may be lack of planning; blocking out time over the weekend to review one week's worth of information would not take much time and would keep memories salient.

Studying often will allow you to:

- a Schedule study sessions over several days. You need to sleep for the memory to be ingrained, organized with similar memories, and to be able to see the big picture and connections that are not readily visible. That's why cramming and all-nighters are detrimental.
- b Re-activate memories and understanding, enhancing your comprehension of the subject (Brod, 2021).
- c Pay attention to all your courses without falling behind in the "easy" courses.
- d Have time to reach out for help and clarify concepts, and to request any needed accommodations.

Making the Most Out of Your Study Sessions

Choose your study space in advance and make sure you have everything you need including timers or other tools you use. If you plan to study in a public space, keep in mind a second location you can go to if the first one is too crowded. Changing plans without warning is many times difficult for neurodivergent people and those that for other reasons (e.g., lack of sleep, or too much to do) face executive functioning issues. In the survey I conducted of my former students, I asked them to rank their optimal study environment. Forty-seven of them answered this portion of the survey. They considered being *alone in a quiet space* as the optimal study environment, followed in order by *alone with music, alone with background noise* (e.g., coffee shop–style sounds), *in a group working in silence*, and *in a group while talking*. They also commented:

- I've found that studying with a partner who experiences the same issue and handing each other our phones help us concentrate. (Anthony)
- I like studying in a classroom with a chalk board so that I can write and visualize what I am learning… I am forced to think deeper so that the information stays in my mind without the need for a reference in the future. (Hugo M)
- Studying with a friend just as determined as you to get work done makes for a great study partner! (Anthony)
- I feel that when I need to study or do well in an assignment, I am good at creating a quiet and secluded environment where I know I will perform my best. (Tyler)

Starting a study session may be the most difficult part. It may seem overwhelming, or you may feel like you're not in the correct mindset. Some strategies that may help is to dedicate the first session or at least a portion of it to "set the stage": writing down what it is you need to study, how long you believe you need, your motivation to study for that class, writing a checklist of materials to have at hand, and so on. And to make the transition from not-studying to studying easier, you can think of a *bridge activity*: something that gets you to, first, go to the study space and then open your notebook or your laptop. It is also helpful to remind yourself that you are not obligated to study for too long, that you can study for 5 minutes and stop. For many students, thinking they only need to study for 5 minutes is enough to get them going. Pep-talking yourself is a very useful strategy for many, as is counting down "three-two-one-go" or another short phrase of your choosing.

Self-testing, also called *retrieval practice*, has been demonstrated to enhance your memory. For instance, Walck-Shannon et al. (2021) reported that students with higher test scores were more likely to self-test as part of their study routine. Self-testing includes completing problem sets without looking at example problems or answer keys, or writing everything you remember on a blank piece of paper, using flash cards, reciting, or writing answers to questions (e.g., questions in a textbook). Teaching others is another powerful way to self-test. "Others" can mean your family and friends, your dog or cat, or even a plastic duck. The main idea is to externalize your knowledge by speaking or writing (many people, me included, need to write while explaining a concept). Sixty-eight percent of my former students answered in the survey that they find answering practice tests, study guides and similar without looking at answers as *useful and easy to do*. One of them, Hugo M, elaborated on this topic:

> When I am motivated and interested in a topic, I strive to understand it deeply. I learn it with the goal of being capable of teaching to someone else, which makes me focus on understanding and linking core ideas in ways that can't really be done if all I did was practice problems.

Practicing writing an essay. Walck-Shannon et al. (2021) determined that students with higher test scores were likely to practice writing essays as part of the self-testing. However, a whopping 57% of my former students stated in my survey that they don't practice writing essays (my survey didn't include any question about their grades, so I cannot infer a relationship with their academic performance). There are many reasons to practice writing. One is to acquire speed and accuracy when expressing your thoughts, making your ideas flow in order; this is particularly important for students who are ADHDers or who face difficulties when planning and organizing their thoughts. Another important aspect to consider is that when you write out your thoughts, you force your brain to connect ideas and concepts to draw conclusions, retrieve knowledge from long-term memory, and re-evaluate that knowledge based on newer information you learn, and much more. In many ways, writing shapes our thinking.

Spreading your study, as explained earlier. Combining spacing and self-testing is more effective than spacing alone (Rawson et al., 2013). This can also be seen in the short term. For example, Dobson and Linderholm (2015) found that self-testing in between two readings of the same material (reading, then self-testing, and then re-reading) led to better recollection than reading a passage several times or reading and taking notes, as evidenced by a test conducted after one week.

Alternating the subjects you study gives your brain a break from the material. It prevents you from narrowing your vision too much, which can happen when you focus on a detail for too long. This also prevents you from relegating or neglecting other courses.

Changing how you visualize and organize information, such as using mind maps or making drawings, charts or pictures were correlated to higher grades (Vemu et al., 2022; Walck-Shannon et al., 2021). This is what I call *playing with the material*: by using different representations or even media, depending on your skills and your brain's needs, you vary perspectives and engage different senses. This can be done writing on paper, using 3D representations by handling objects, or digitally, using a word processor or design software. Sixty percent of my former students responded they find this strategy *useful and easy to do*.

Evaluating why you made mistakes in exams. Analyzing why you answered some questions incorrectly, and attempting to find the correct answer, can help you clarify any misunderstandings you had, or be aware of the errors you committed due to paying insufficient attention during the exam. Reflecting and writing about this experience enhances your understanding and recall even more, with improved scores in a subsequent test (Mynlieff et al., 2014). This strategy was found by 53% of my former students as *useful and easy to do*.

Watching or listening to a recording of the lecture at a faster playback speed is helpful for some students, while not affecting concentration or retention (Merhavy et al., 2023). It is important, however, that you use strategies to ensure you don't get distracted while doing this, as listening or watching a video will not be as engaging as an in-person class.

Text to speech and speech to text apps are very useful for students facing difficulties reading or writing. It is possible that you could need permission from your instructors, or that it can be an academic accommodation (find more information about accommodations in Chapter 6).

Reading textbooks: note-taking and summarizing. When *reading* any dense or lengthy text, your notes should be clear and detailed enough to be sufficient so that you don't need to read the lengthy text again; at the same time, your notes should not be long or dense. If you use e-books, text to speech software may help you engage and understand better. If you learn better from hard copies, and only digital material is available, you could summarize the information to minimize your printing needs. Reciting what you just read and paraphrasing, as well as using words you are very familiar with, can be very helpful. For jargon, you could create a vocabulary list and then use it to create flash cards.

Enjoy your study sessions. Many students reward themselves for studying, for example, by eating their favorite food (say, chocolate). The problem with that is that you are focusing on extrinsic motivations, unconsciously reinforcing a mental image of studying as unpleasant. Additionally, your rewards may become distracting, as Anthony, one of my students, explains, "After a problem or two I would 'reward' myself by texting friends back or scrolling on social media." Instead, I propose you reward yourself *while* you are studying. Ensure you are comfortable in terms of temperature, noise level, seating comfort, and number of people around you. Also, have snacks and water at hand, and maybe eat that chocolate as you study. Fluorescent light can make you feel very uncomfortable, as you may notice the flicker of the lights and hear the sound. For some people, fluorescent lights can trigger headaches. If possible, use natural or soft lightning. Fluorescent light filters or covers, i.e., fabric panels that can attach to ceiling light fixtures using magnets, can help minimize the detrimental effects of fluorescent lights (Yuen et al., 2023).

Make it fun. Imitate entertaining instructors; walk around, move your hands, speak and change your tone of voice, sing, don't be afraid to be silly. Making hand gestures has been found to help both the listener and the speaker: a study where children had to repeat how to solve a problem remembered better when they had used hand gestures than when they only spoke (Clough & Hilverman, 2018). Even speaking while solving a problem and reading aloud what you write will make your learning more enjoyable and will show you mistakes in your process or your grammar that you probably wouldn't detect otherwise.

Apply the neuroscience of cognition to your learning strategies. The following tips can be used at any point when you're interacting with the material you're studying, whether that's in the classroom, laboratory, reading a textbook, etc.

a You can "tag" items to remember, that is, telling yourself that a piece of information is important (Mathias & Von Kriegstein, 2023).
b Since our memory is stronger when more than one sense receives the input (Alhamdan et al., 2025), you could use close captions or speech-to-text software during class (if your professor allows or if it's stated in your accommodation letter).
c Effective learning depends on repeatedly recalling and reprocessing what we learn, as well as connecting similar information, both new and old. These processes may be enhanced by using several ways of representing the information, depending on how your brain works. This may include *internal* visualization or dialogue, and *external* strategies like writing or drawing the information, sustaining an inner dialogue where you "hear" your thoughts, verbally explaining it to yourself, singing, using objects to show movement and interactions, making gestures to explain concepts like big, small, increasing, etc. (Mathias & Von Kriegstein, 2023).
d As the capacity of our working memory is very limited and short-lived, you need to avoid "cluttering" it with information you don't need. You should not use it as a to-do list. If you are studying *and* keeping in mind that you need to head to class at 4 p.m. *and* call your sister in the evening,

it's likely you'll need to spend more time and effort studying, making it feel more overwhelming, and you will learn less effectively. Having at hand a *to-do list* or a *worry list* can help you keep focused on the topic you're reviewing without feeling like you'll forget something important.

e When you are receiving or working with the material you're studying, you need to be *ready*: rested, fed, hydrated, and in a good mood. If you are in a good mood, you'll likely attach a positive *emotion* to the information. It is easier to recall positive memories or events that happened when we were in a good mood (Lopis et al., 2021).

f To learn in depth, focus on *recalling* the information, as when you test yourself by saying, writing, or drawing what you know without looking at the material. This will help you remember it better than *maintenance rehearsal*, i.e., further exposure to the material, e.g., reading, seeing, or hearing it again (Asuncion & Al, 2024; Paller, 2024).

g While reading or hearing information, *select* what is important; while your brain does this on its own, it will be more efficient if you are not "info-dumping" on it. Write your notes with only the most important information you are hearing, reading, seeing; this will save time and effort, as your brain doesn't have to comb through all the information (Li et al., 2025).

h *Sleep well*. Our brain manipulates our memories in several ways during sleep, in a way that makes them easier to remember. That is, our brain adds context that helps us understand and determine the meaning, relevance and importance of a piece of data. Our brain may link memories, so when the memory for one is triggered, the attached memories are also recalled. Another way that memories may be handled is to determine the differences and similarities between one memory and another. Thanks to these processes, we can distinguish a chimpanzee from a gorilla while keeping in mind that both are great apes, and we may recall what we know about a chimpanzee when asked about a gorilla (Paller, 2024).

Avoiding Mental Fatigue

The optimal duration of your study sessions depends on the difficulty or complexity of the assignment or topic you are working on. You need a lot of energy to concentrate, i.e., pay intense attention to one activity, while monitoring potential distractions or temptations and avoiding reacting to those distractions.

Fatigue decreases with rest: It is crucial to take breaks during study sessions. When the topic or activity is difficult for you, your breaks should be more frequent. It is also important to keep in mind that the purpose is to let your brain recover, without adding intense cognitive, physical, or emotional activities. That's not the time to "doomscroll," study something else, or run a mile.

To avoid reaching mental fatigue, it is best to play it safe: Start with short study sessions (e.g., 10 minutes) followed by a break. Based on how you are feeling after those study sessions, you could increase the duration of the next study session. After a few cycles, you may need to take a longer rest or stop for the day. Sixty-two percent of my former students said taking breaks while studying is *useful and easy to do*.

An additional perk of taking breaks is that they foster your "creative cognition"—that is, your capacity to merge seemingly unrelated knowledge sets. For "creative cognition" to take place, you need to be able to think in abstract, rather than in concrete terms, and this cannot happen when you are intensely focused on a task or piece of information. Breaks will also help you visualize more and possibly better solutions to a problem (Pietsch et al., 2024).

Metacognitive skills will be affected and you may not be able to properly reflect if you are overwhelmed by the amount of knowledge and skills you need to learn in a short period of time, you task-switch (multitask), are sleep deprived, hungry, sad, lonely, or dealing with stress, depression or anxiety (Fraiwan et al., 2025). You could support your metacognitive skills by reaching out for help, joining a supportive community, and keeping at a manageable level your academic load, extracurricular activities, and other commitments.

In Brief

In college, you spend much of your time learning and applying what you learn. Studying using strategies that work well for you will make your learning more enjoyable and engaging, as well as long-lasting. Keep in mind that there is no method that works for all; it's a matter of fit. Don't think that if you got a lower grade than expected it is a "you" problem. It's most likely a "strategy" problem. Choose a few (or more) of the strategies mentioned in this chapter, visualize how to implement them, try them out, and if they don't work after a couple of weeks in which you consistently used them, tweak them or change them to different ones.

References

Aagaard, L., Conner Li, T. W., & Skidmore, R. L. (2014). College textbook reading assignments and class time activity. *Journal of the Scholarship of Teaching and Learning*, 132–145. https://doi.org/10.14434/josotl.v14i3.5031

Alhamdan, A., Pickering, H., Murphy, M., & Crewther, S. (2025). From senses to memory during childhood: A systematic review and Bayesian meta-analysis exploring multisensory processing and working memory development. *European Journal of Investigation in Health, Psychology and Education*, *15*(8), 157. https://doi.org/10.3390/ejihpe15080157

American Psychological Association (n.d.). Study. In *APA dictionary of psychology*. Retrieved February 14, 2026, from https://dictionary.apa.org/study

Asuncion, R. M. D., & Khalili, Y. Al. (2024). Short-term memory impairment. In *StatPearls* [Internet]. Treasure Island, FL: StatPearls Publishing. Retrieved February 22, 2026, from https://www.ncbi.nlm.nih.gov/books/NBK545136/

Bahrami, Z., Heidari, A., & Cranney, J. (2022). Applying smart goal intervention leads to greater goal attainment, need satisfaction and positive affect. *International Journal of Mental Health Promotion*, *24*(6), 869–882. https://doi.org/10.32604/ijmhp.2022.018954

Borchers, C., Xu, Y., & Pardos, Z. A. (2025). Workload overload? Late enrollment leads to course dropout. *Journal of Educational Data Mining*, *17*(1), 126–156. https://doi.org/10.5281/zenodo.14907388

Brod, G. (2021). Predicting as a learning strategy. *Psychonomic Bulletin & Review*, *28*(6), 1839–1847. https://doi.org/10.3758/s13423-021-01904-1

Cambridge Dictionary (n.d.). Important. In *Cambridge Dictionary*. Retrieved November 1st, 2025, from https://dictionary.cambridge.org/us/dictionary/english/important

Clough, S., & Hilverman, C. (2018). Hand gestures and how they help children learn. *Frontiers for Young Minds*, *6*, 29. https://doi.org/10.3389/frym.2018.00029

Covey, S. (2014). *The 7 habits of highly effective college students: Succeeding in college … And in life* (1st ed.). FranklinCovey.

Covey, Stephen R. (2009). *7 habits of highly effective people: Restoring the character ethic* (Online-Ausg). RosettaBooks.

Dobson, J. L., & Linderholm, T. (2015). Self-testing promotes superior retention of anatomy and physiology information. *Advances in Health Sciences Education*, *20*(1), 149–161. https://doi.org/10.1007/s10459-014-9514-8

Eisenhower DD, 1954. *Address at the second assembly of the world Council of Churches, Evanston, Illinois* [Speech transcript]. The American Presidency Project. Retrieved November 1st, 2025, from https://www.presidency.ucsb.edu/node/232572

Favero, T. G., & Cesar, C. E. (2022). Using the study cycle model to support better student learning: A faculty guide. *Advances in Physiology Education*, *46*(4), 735–741. https://doi.org/10.1152/advan.00168.2022

Fraiwan, M., Almomani, F., & Hammouri, H. (2025). Prevalence and contributing factors of executive cognitive dysfunction symptoms in university students. *PLoS One*, *20*(6), e0323783. https://doi.org/10.1371/journal.pone.0323783

Franklin, B. (2006). *Autobiography of Benjamin Franklin*. Ed. F. W. Pine. Project Gutenberg. https://www.gutenberg.org/cache/epub/20203/pg20203-images.html

Li, Q., Tang, W., & Liu, X. (2025). Value-directed remembering: A dual-process perspective. *Behavioral Sciences*, *15*(8), 1113. https://doi.org/10.3390/bs15081113

Lopis, D., Le Pape, T., Manetta, C., & Conty, L. (2021). Sensory cueing of autobiographical memories in normal aging and Alzheimer's disease: A comparison between visual, auditory, and olfactory information. *Journal of Alzheimer's Disease*, *80*(3), 1169–1183. https://doi.org/10.3233/JAD-200841

Mathias, B., & Von Kriegstein, K. (2023). Enriched learning: Behavior, brain, and computation. *Trends in Cognitive Sciences*, *27*(1), 81–97. https://doi.org/10.1016/j.tics.2022.10.007

McGuire, S. Y., & McGuire, S. (2023). *Teach yourself how to learn: Strategies you can use to ace any course at any level* (1st ed.). Routledge.

Merhavy, Z. I., Bassett, L., Melchiorre, M., & Hall, M. P. M. (2023). The impact of lecture playback speeds on concentration and memory. *BMC Medical Education*, *23*(1), 515. https://doi.org/10.1186/s12909-023-04491-y

Merriam-Webster (n.d.-a). *Study*. In *Merriam-Webster.com Dictionary*. Retrieved February 2nd, 2026, from https://www.merriam-webster.com/dictionary/study

Merriam-Webster (n.d.-b). *Urgent*. In *Merriam-Webster.com Dictionary*. Retrieved November 1st, 2025, from https://www.merriam-webster.com/dictionary/urgent

Mynlieff, M., Manogaran, A. L., St, M., & Eddinger, T. J. (2014). Writing assignments with a metacognitive component enhance learning in a large introductory biology course. *CBE—Life Sciences Education, 13*(2), 311–321. https://doi.org/10.1187/cbe.13-05-0097

NCAA (2025). *Understanding today's student-athlete experience: Key findings from the 2025 NCAA goals study*. Retrieved February 22, 2026, from https://ncaaorg.s3.amazonaws.com/research/goals/2026RES_GOALS-AWEdSession.pdf

Office of Postsecondary Education, Department of Education (2010) *Credit hour*. 34 CFR 600.2. Retrieved November 10, 2025, from https://www.ecfr.gov/current/title-34/part-600/section-600.2

Paller, K. A. (2024). Recurring memory reactivation: The offline component of learning. *Neuropsychologia, 196*, 108840. https://doi.org/10.1016/j.neuropsychologia.2024.108840

Pardos, Z. A., Borchers, C., & Yu, R. (2023). Credit hours is not enough: Explaining undergraduate perceptions of course workload using LMS records. *The Internet and Higher Education, 56*, 100882. https://doi.org/10.1016/j.iheduc.2022.100882

Pietsch, S., Riddell, H., Semmler, C., Ntoumanis, N., & Gucciardi, D. F. (2024). SMART goals are no more effective for creative performance than do-your-best goals or non-specific, exploratory 'open goals'. *Educational Psychology, 44*(9–10), 946–962. https://doi.org/10.1080/01443410.2024.2420818

Rawson, K. A., Dunlosky, J., & Sciartelli, S. M. (2013). The power of successive relearning: Improving performance on course exams and long-term retention. *Educational Psychology Review, 25*(4), 523–548. https://doi.org/10.1007/s10648-013-9240-4

Seifert, K., & Sutton, R. (2009). *Educational Psychology* (2nd ed.). Orange Grove.

Swann, C., Keegan, R., Crust, L., & Piggott, D. (2016). Psychological states underlying excellent performance in professional golfers: "Letting it happen" vs. "making it happen". *Psychology of Sport and Exercise, 23*, 101–113. https://doi.org/10.1016/j.psychsport.2015.10.008

Vemu, S., Denaro, K., Sato, B. K., & Williams, A. E. (2022). Moving the needle: Evidence of an effective study strategy intervention in a community college biology course. *CBE—Life Sciences Education, 21*(2), ar24. https://doi.org/10.1187/cbe.21-08-0216

Walck-Shannon, E. M., Rowell, S. F., & Frey, R. F. (2021). To what extent do study habits relate to performance? *CBE—Life Sciences Education, 20*(1), ar6. https://doi.org/10.1187/cbe.20-05-0091

Wiechmann, W., Edwards, R., Low, C., Wray, A., Boysen-Osborn, M., & Toohey, S. (2022). No difference in factual or conceptual recall comprehension for tablet, laptop, and handwritten note-taking by medical students in the United States: A survey-based observational study. *Journal of Educational Evaluation for Health Professions, 19*, 8. https://doi.org/10.3352/jeehp.2022.19.8

Yuen, H. K., Wood, A. L., & Chen, J. (2023). Emotional responses of college students to filtered fluorescent lighting in a classroom (v3). *Health Psychology Research, 11*, 70169. https://doi.org/10.52965/001c.70169

5 Changing Habits That May Be Detrimental to Your Learning

From Perfectionism to Excellencism

Perfectionism has a somewhat positive connotation; when we start talking about this topic in my class, my students typically consider "perfectionist" as a compliment. It has long been considered a double-edged sword, with positive and negative consequences. Some researchers differentiate between "adaptive" and "nonadaptive" perfectionism (e.g., Jiang & Jiang, 2025). Recently, though, researchers started to use "excellencism" instead of "adaptive perfectionism" (Gaudreau, 2019). I'll use *excellencism* to clearly differentiate it from perfectionism.

Gaudreau (2019) defines excellencism as the "tendency to aim and strive toward very hard yet attainable standards in an effortful, engaged and determined yet flexible manner." *Perfectionism* is defined by the American Psychological Association (n.d.-b) as "the tendency to demand of others or of oneself an extremely high or even flawless level of performance, in excess of what is required by the situation."

People who strive for excellence and those who want to achieve perfection both want to do a good or even a great job. One difference is that while "excellencists" are more likely to consider failure as a normal part of learning, perfectionists find their work has to be flawless when submitted; they keep finding faults with their work and consequently remain frustrated and disappointed with themselves. Another characteristic of perfectionism is to ruminate on their perceived challenges or shortcomings, while hiding them from others (An et al., 2025). Because of the unrealistic nature of "perfection," students who aim for it create a gap between their goals and what they can really achieve, leading to more dissatisfaction with their results (Fernández-García et al., 2022; Flett et al., 2024). One of my students mentioned that perfectionism "is a detrimental habit I continue to face in all aspects of my life—I continue to strive for something that doesn't exist." (DK)

DOI: 10.4324/9781003750246-6

Striving for perfection is associated with negative emotions such as depression, anxiety, stress, self-doubt, and self-criticism; frustration, fear of failure, performance anxiety, low sense of belonging and social support; procrastination; and considering dropping out (Fernández-García et al., 2022; Gaudreau & Benoît, 2025; Goulet-Pelletier et al., 2025; Leath et al., 2025). Chen et al. (2024) found similar negative self-perceptions in undergraduate, medical, and law students. Students in all three groups felt pressured to be perfect and to project an image of perfection, which led to unwillingness to ask for help or to accept when they had committed a mistake. Furthermore, perfectionists who show a need to be "number one" will experience distress whenever a peer receives a higher grade or appears to understand the topic more easily than them (Flett et al., 2024).

Perfectionism can lead to procrastination, as one of my students expressed: "perfectionism prevents me from starting my assignments, thinking I can't do the assignment justice, leading to procrastination." (Shy Cabbage)

In comparison, striving for excellence is associated with several positive emotions and outcomes, including improved academic performance, well-being, self-esteem, believing in one's self, setting a high bar for oneself, enjoying positive experiences, being willing to engage in new experiences, and feeling satisfied with life, as well as with research productivity, in the case of graduate students (Chen et al., 2024; Gaudreau & Benoît, 2025; Koutra et al., 2023).

Environments that foster perfectionism include those that emphasize high performance and hypercompetition, praise hard work, self-sacrifice, and full dedication, adopting a culture of "good is never good enough" (Gaudreau & Benoît, 2025). Demanding degrees, hypercompetitive careers, and extremely high parental expectations also play an important role (Fernández-García et al., 2022; Fung et al., 2023; Lasalle & Hess, 2022). While these conditions can lead to great achievements, they come at a high personal cost, as academic work and career are prioritized above well-being (Gaudreau & Benoît, 2025).

Members of marginalized identities are at a higher risk of the adverse effects of perfectionism. Many of them already consider they need to *work twice as hard to be considered good enough*. For instance, both Fernández-García et al. (2022) and You and Yoo (2021) found that perfectionism in women led to worse psychological outcomes than perfectionism in men; Leath et al. (2025) found that perfectionism in Black women is related to both racism and sexism in education, and Fung et al. (2023) reported a significant effect of family perfectionism among Asian and Latinx youth.

The pressure may be even higher when expectations are unclear, as it is difficult to gauge when one has reached excellence, particularly when there is no opportunity to improve after submission. Faculty can support students by writing clear rubrics, offering them opportunities to submit assignments for a preliminary review, allowing them to improve their work based on feedback, and sharing examples of completed work that the instructor deemed excellent.

I can imagine you are thinking, "How do you know when your work is excellent and you can submit it without getting a bad grade?" First, consider this statement by Gabriel Garcia Marquez (1992) in an interview:

> [T]he pleasure of writing [is] the most intimate and lonely you can imagine, and if you don't stay correcting the book your whole life it's because the same iron rigor needed to start the book is needed to finish it.

Garcia Marquez had good reasons for meticulously correcting his books; after all, they are still being sold worldwide to thousands of people. Even so, an imperfect manuscript submitted is better than an unsubmitted perfect manuscript. He realized the need to strive for excellence rather than for perfectionism, and knew he needed to force himself to stop editing.

You could consider a task is excellent or at least good enough when (a) you are fulfilling requirements, according to the rubric and instructions and (b) when you review your work, you cannot find glaring errors: if you keep editing and re-editing the phrasing on an essay, you are likely at an excellent level. If you still have doubts, you can (c) Ask a trusted classmate or peer for their opinion.

Also, you can limit the amount of time dedicated to finding information online. After a preset period of time, you could either consider you've found the best available information, or you can reach out to a librarian or other faculty or staff member who can help you. Sometimes you search for information that literally doesn't exist yet or is not available in the precise way you want it, and you will simply not find it regardless of how long you keep looking for it.

Practicing self-compassion and mindfulness has been found to be helpful (Koutra et al., 2023; Nepon et al., 2024); if you are not sure how to initiate or sustain these practices, reach out to a therapist or another trusted professional.

A useful tool when assessing the time and effort invested in an assignment or when studying a particular topic is the *law of diminishing returns*. This is an economic theory proposed by Anne Robert Jacques Turgot in the 18th century (Brue, 1993) and adapted to learning by Gaudreau (2019). According to the law of diminishing returns, any effort and time given to a particular course will highly increase your grade and understanding of the topic (zone of increasing returns). After a certain point, additional work will only marginally improve the quality of your work (zone of diminishing returns). And after another point, it is possible that more time and effort will be counterproductive, as you may start to doubt yourself and, for example, change correct answers to incorrect ones (zone of decreasing returns). This is illustrated in Figure 5.1.

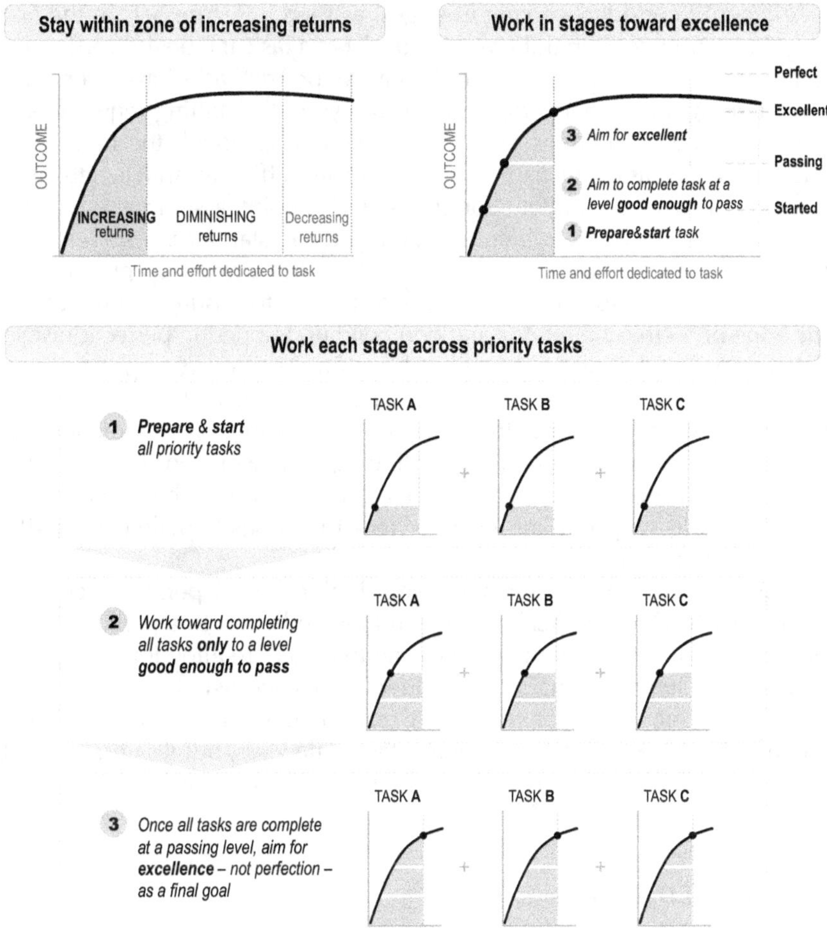

Figure 5.1 Working in stages toward excellence, staying within the zone of increasing returns. Concept by Florencia Ardon, PhD and Julia Felice, PhD, loosely based on the "rate of returns" analogy created by Gaudreau (2019). Design by Julia Felice, PhD.

Since you only have 168 hours a week and you need to make progress in all your classes, as well as maintain a healthy balance between academics and personal life, the time you can allocate to each topic is limited. If you set a limit on the time and effort you will dedicate to each task, making sure that you pay attention to all your courses and personal life, you will probably remain in the zone of increasing returns in all areas, keeping any perfectionistic tendencies in check.

You could consider working in stages, as seen in Figure 5.1. In the *first stage*, you prepare everything you need to start a task and begin working on it, and then move on to another task, until all priority tasks have been initiated. During the *second stage*, you ensure you are fulfilling requirements and following instructions for each assignment. Although the time dedicated to each task will vary according to its difficulty and length, it is important to set time and/or effort limits. At this point, assignments will not be excellent but can be submitted. Then, you can start a *third stage* where you aim for excellence, starting with the task that is your top priority. You would again need to set time and/or effort limits to ensure you remain in the zone of increasing returns and don't end up trapped in perfectionism.

You may feel that doing this will risk not finishing a very important task. However, preparing and starting that task, then moving on to others, doesn't mean you will forget about them (if you feel you might, set a reminder!). The space between starting and continuing your work on that task may enrich your work, as your brain will be evaluating approaches, other material that could support your ideas, or recall previous knowledge or skills that can come in handy.

Working in this way ensures that you don't risk your performance on a course because you dedicate too much time and effort to a particular task of another course. Emotionally, knowing that you are allowing yourself to go back and improve what you consider unsatisfactory may make it easier to stop working on a "not-yet-perfect" assignment. As expected with perfectionism, you will likely never feel a task is flawless, but it's possible that once you are not focused on that task, the urge to continue perfecting it decreases or disappears.

Getting Stuff Done, Today

Another name for procrastination is behavioral delay. Svartdal et al. (2018) define procrastination as the "unnecessary and unwanted delay of an action, despite knowing it will have detrimental consequences." This implies that (a) the activity or task can be done immediately, (b) the person has the opportunity to, at the very least, start the activity, (c) there will be negative consequences if the task is not done, and (d) the person anyway decides not to engage with that task or activity.

Gabriel Garcia Marquez (2018) warned about procrastination:

> I woke up and discovered I didn't have anything else to do but write.... I told myself: I don't need to "work" anymore; I can write or not write, if I want to. Soon, I understood the danger that such liberty meant to me, because if I didn't write today, I wouldn't do it tomorrow and probably never. I kept on writing.

Procrastination is common among college students, e.g., 52.5% of participants in a recent study (Kuai et al., 2025), and is associated with a variety of habits, situations, and conditions. While procrastination is commonly thought to be linked to long-term projects, it can be present in short-term conditions, as seen by Di Nocera et al. (2023). In their study, students were assigned projects lasting three or five days; in both cases, procrastinators delayed most of the work until the deadline was imminent.

Procrastination is correlated with a variety of negative emotions and outcomes, including decreased academic performance and likelihood of reaching own's goals, lower self-esteem and life satisfaction, increased stress, and discomfort, and is related to depression and anxiety.

Some procrastination sources and possible solutions are as follows:

a *Coping style*—that is, how people react to stressful situations—is also linked to procrastination. Di Nocera et al. (2023) found that people who distributed their effort throughout the duration of three- and five-day projects showed a "task-oriented" or "problem-focused" coping style, meaning that when facing stressful situations, they focus on the task at hand and place their efforts into solving the situation. Task-oriented behaviors are considered positive coping styles. In contrast, *Avoidance* is considered an "emotion-focused" or negative coping strategy. Xue et al. (2025) found that high academic stress increased the likelihood of students utilizing negative coping strategies, leading to procrastination. There are two possible solutions here: one, lowering academic stress, which can be addressed at the individual level by maintaining a reasonable workload and extracurricular commitments (addressed in Chapter 4), and, two, through therapy and/or medication (Ihara et al., 2024).

b *Reward after finishing is too far into the future*. Long-term projects can lead to procrastination when the reward expected (e.g., a good grade) is not enough to prompt you to start working. It is also possible that your time perception is inaccurate, and you perceive the deadline and the reward you would receive for your hard work to be much farther into the future than they really are. Inaccurate time perception is also called "temporal discounting" or "time agnosia" among other terms. Kuai et al. (2025) found that moderate-to-vigorous physical activity increases alertness, which makes estimation of time more accurate. Zhang and Ma (2024) propose two solutions: mindfulness-based training, resulting in a higher capacity to sustain your focus on the project, and "episodic future thinking," meaning visualizing the project as completed, and imagining the feeling of satisfaction you would feel, which would increase the motivation to complete a task. Another strategy is to break down a long-term project into several sections with shorter deadlines, each with their own reward, if needed. My students' experiences are varied, with some benefiting from having several short-term deadlines. For others, multiple short-term deadlines become overwhelming and lead to even more procrastination. You may need to evaluate if this strategy is good for you. When testing out any strategy, I encourage you to write down the results and how it made you feel, to ensure you remember the outcome. This will make it easier to choose a strategy in the future, as you can easily discard the strategies that didn't work for you before spending time evaluating them again.

c *Lack of motivation when tasks are too easy*. As discussed in Chapter 2, we require a certain amount of stress to feel motivated. As Alexandra, one of my students, explained, "If I do not feel any urgency, such as an upcoming deadline, my studying becomes sporadic and broken up with phones, friends, and food." There are tasks that are too easy, simple, or would take just a few minutes of your time. These are very likely to be forgotten or neglected. An option is to set a time every day or every week, depending on how frequent the deadlines are, to work on all those small tasks. For example, answering emails or submitting small assignments every morning.

d *Feeling overwhelmed when tasks seem too hard*. We get overwhelmed when we perceive tasks as being too hard, difficult, or unclear. The stress it causes prevents us from clearly analyzing the task or sometimes you may hesitate to even read the instructions. In reality, the task may be much easier than you expect, and you may be able to get it done very quickly. Also, the longer you wait to start, the more overwhelming the task will appear. Moderate-to-vigorous physical activity enhances working memory and improves the capacity to regulate emotions, including *anxiety*, which plays a role in task avoidance (Kuai et al., 2025). This is one situation where working alongside your peers or requesting help from your academic advisor or a peer tutor may help you get ready to start the task, and break it down into smaller pieces, if necessary and helpful for you.

e *Sedentary behaviors*, like sitting or lying down, decrease our cognitive capacity, which in turn affects our motivation and efficiency, especially when facing complex tasks.

f *Lack of sleep or low-quality sleep* can lead to tiredness and procrastination. Maier et al. (2022) evaluated procrastination in the workforce and determined that procrastinating behaviors were more likely to occur after the shift to daylight saving time, which leads to the population "losing" an hour of sleep, as the shift occurs at 2 a.m., which suddenly becomes 3 a.m. Maier et al. (2022) assert that sleep helps people restore physical and mental resources that are critical for self-regulation. When this restoration process is disrupted, people's self-regulation decreases the next day and leads to procrastination. Sleep is discussed in more depth in Chapter 1.

g *Neurotype*. Procrastination is related to your executive function, which is influenced by your neurotype. ADHD, depression, anxiety, and other neurotypes may make it difficult to start, continue working, finishing, and even submitting a completed assignment. This can be due to suboptimal short-term memory, inaccurate perception of time, increased impulsivity, and other executive function-related characteristics (Netzer Turgeman & Pollak, 2025; Niermann & Scheres, 2014; Oguchi et al., 2023). ADHD and other neurotypes are discussed in more detail in Chapter 6, and executive function in Chapter 3.

h *The inertia of not doing anything*. Sometimes you are not motivated to engage with academics because you're relaxing, and it's hard to change from a pleasurable activity to a not-so-pleasant one. Fortunately, the opposite can be true as well, with productivity begetting productivity. Amy, one of my students, describes this situation:

> I like the saying "if you need a job well done ask a busy man"—I reckon anyone who is busy will be good at time management because you are constantly in a productive state. It's getting started with being productive that's the hardest, but once you are productive it's easier to stay productive and slowly cross all the assignments off your to do list.

Productive Procrastination

Feeling overwhelmed by a task may lead students to avoid a difficult task by busying themselves with easier activities, like organizing materials, which make them feel accomplished and no longer feeling guilty for "not doing anything." This is a type of productive procrastination: you are doing something, just not what you should be doing (Kuai et al., 2025).

However, productive procrastination can be positive. People's energy and cognitive capacity vary throughout the day in a pattern that is unique to each person. Many projects require difficult *and* easy tasks. For you as student, this can mean working on easy tasks when you feel your cognition is not optimal, or you don't have enough time to immerse yourself in tasks that require intense focus.

Easy tasks can also be used as "bridge activities," meaning an easy or even fun task that helps you get going. A former student of mine used statistical analyses, which she likes doing, as a bridge activity that helped her open her computer and continue writing her dissertation. These bridge activities work well when they cannot be done other than on your desk or your computer, or wherever the task you may otherwise avoid is located. The bridge activity should not be one that could make you hyperfocus on it, and should be easily done in a few minutes. I encourage students to have a to-do list of "10-minute" or "3-minute" tasks they can work on as bridge activities or simply to continue working on a project or academic work when they're short on time.

Realistic Estimation of Task Difficulty and Your Capabilities

Overconfidence is defined by the *American Psychological Association* (n.d.-a) as "a cognitive bias characterized by an overestimation of one's actual ability to perform a task successfully, by a belief that one's performance is better than that of others, or by excessive certainty in the accuracy of one's beliefs."

Overconfidence in academic settings fits into what is commonly called the "Dunning-Kruger effect." Kruger and Dunning (1999) evaluated if people are able to recognize when their performance is poor in a variety of situations, finding that people who performed poorly overestimated their capabilities and believed themselves to be better than the mean. Their findings revealed that less skilled participants had lower metacognitive skills.

In several studies, college students overestimate their knowledge and skills, and evaluate themselves as being more competent and successful than their peers in a variety of scenarios. Güner Gültekin and Akıncı (2025) found that students overestimated their ability to guess their instructor's favorite songs and believed themselves to have guessed better than their peers. This is a very innocuous situation; however, the bias is present when students evaluate their academic performance, which can lead to procrastination if students believe they can easily and quickly learn a great amount of information for an exam or write a superb essay in a couple of hours.

Additionally, students may not learn from experience or feedback. Foster et al. (2017) found this to be particularly true of students with low academic performance. Over the course of an academic term that included 13 exams, students who obtained lower grades continued to overestimate their future exam scores. Karaca et al. (2023) obtained similar results in their study, where "low-performing" students continued to overestimate how well they would do on a test, and their confidence in their prediction remained stable even after seeing their actual scores, which were lower than what they predicted (e.g., a group of 16 students predicted having an average grade of 86.52 while their real average grade was 65.41).

Furthermore, students may attribute the discrepancy between the competence they believe they have and their actual grades not to their lack of preparation or knowledge but to other factors, such as a course being extraordinarily difficult or a professor being extremely harsh in their grading. This can have long-term consequences if students react by dropping courses, changing their majors, or even dropping out of college (Serra & DeMarree, 2016).

Since Kruger and Dunning's influential 1999 article, metacognition has proven to be crucial to accurately evaluate one's competence. They found two ways in which overestimation can be minimized: improving participants' metacognitive skills, and increasing their competence. The best way to improve your own metacognitive skills is to practice it until it becomes a habit. This means intentionally questioning yourself, comparing your estimations with actual outcomes, and readjusting your learning strategies as needed.

As explained in more depth in Chapter 4, self-testing helps you evaluate more accurately how much you know about a topic. Self-testing is best done without having access to the information you need to learn. When you have the information at hand, e.g., when you are re-reading your notes, it is more likely that you will be *recognizing* and not actually *recalling* the information, which could lead to having overconfidence in your knowledge. Instead, self-test by writing down everything you know about a topic on a blank piece of paper or explaining it to someone (or to your pet).

Avoid Multitasking and Remove Distractions

True multitasking, as in "the performance of multiple tasks at one time" (*Merriam-Webster*, n.d.) is not a realistic expectation. You can certainly perform two tasks at once if you mean walking and talking, eating and writing. The vast majority of people cannot really think about two different things at once or solve a math equation while writing an essay at exactly the same time. Even with movement, there are limits. A tennis player would not want to be talking to the audience or even listening to them while preparing to serve, and when you are driving during rush hour, you probably need your full focus on the road and not on the conversation you're having with your friend.

What we do is "task-switching," meaning we stop one activity, do another activity for a few minutes, stop that second activity, go back to the first one, and so on. Every time you stop and start represents a distraction. It sounds simple, but every one of those actions requires a specific executive function skill and taxes your brain, in addition to taking time. Maybe it's milliseconds, but milliseconds add up!

It's possible that what many people mean by "multitasking" is the capacity to manage several tasks and projects and not forgetting about any of them. That's related to organizing and planning skills, not really to going back and forth between two or more activities every few minutes.

When you task-switch, or when you get distracted by your phone, someone walking by, a sound, etc., the brief loss of focus is enough to reduce your accuracy and make you lose your train of thought. As a result, your work could have errors you would otherwise not commit, and you will need more time to finish. Multitasking leads to lower job performance (Pluut et al., 2024). In a study with student pharmacists, multitasking led to careless verification of prescription information, which could have serious consequences for their clients' health (Enz et al., 2021).

Students often multitask while studying. As can be expected, students are less likely to multitask when engaged in an activity they like or find important, and more prone to multitask when they feel they "should" or "must" do the activity (Bachmann et al., 2024).

It is so common to speak about multitasking that students may believe everyone should be able to multitask, and if they can't, there's something wrong with them. Rest assured: nobody can truly multitask; human brains don't work that way (Madore & Wagner, 2019).

At a certain level, you *know* that you cannot multitask. I am sure many times you have had to rewatch a portion of a movie or series episode because you looked at a message you received and then you didn't understand what was happening. To show this, I challenge students in my class to listen to a podcast and read an article at the same time; both contain information that is easy to understand, although the topics are different. Invariably, students pay more attention to one or the other. Some are more interested in one of the topics or tend to pay more attention to what they hear or to what they read. Immediately after, students answer a questionnaire covering the information given in the podcast and on the article, and as you can imagine, the majority fail to accurately answer most of the questions, or can answer questions about only the podcast or only the article. I invite you to try this out, if you are not convinced that multitasking is a myth. It would be optimal to use a podcast and article (or similar combination of media) chosen by someone else, who would then ask you questions about both topics.

Once you accept that you cannot multitask and that multitasking is really another distraction, you will be able to start planning and organizing how you'll tackle tasks, one at a time. Then you can add breaks, rest, clear your brain, and avoid mental fatigue. You will be able to do all tasks that can realistically be done in a certain period of time, do them well, and not overwhelm yourself.

In Brief

There are some habits you may fall into that are detrimental to your learning. When evaluating their effect, it is important to consider that you are evaluating habits, not yourself. There may be a personality component that leads you to engage in procrastination, perfectionism or to overestimate your ability; however, the force of habit has a large influence, and you have the capability of modifying your habits. In this chapter, I discuss perfectionism, procrastination, and overconfidence, all of which can have severe consequences to your academic performance and to your well-being. I invite you to focus on excellence rather than perfection, and to spread your work across several tasks. This will prevent you from focusing on perfecting a task while neglecting others, which can lead to lower grades in the neglected courses. Procrastination has many sources, and it's necessary for you to reflect and pinpoint the reasons you procrastinate to find solutions tailored to those causes. Finally, you can minimize overconfidence by using metacognitive reflection and learning strategies that work well for you. This will allow you to continuously improve and refine your learning methods, become more skilled and knowledgeable, and increase your academic performance along with your self-confidence.

References

American Psychological Association (n.d.-a). *Overconfidence*. APA Dictionary of Psychology. Retrieved February 17, 2026, from https://dictionary.apa.org/overconfidence

American Psychological Association (n.d.-b). *Perfectionism*. APA Dictionary of Psychology. Retrieved January 2, 2026, from https://dictionary.apa.org/perfectionism

An, D., Wang, J., Xia, Y., & Xing, W. (2025). The effect of cognitive avoidance on rumination in college students: The chain mediating role of perfectionism and stress. *Frontiers in Psychology, 16*, 1562927. https://doi.org/10.3389/fpsyg.2025.1562927

Bachmann, O., Grunschel, C., & Fries, S. (2024). Multitasking while studying – Grit moderates the relationship of situational motivation and multitasking. *Frontiers in Psychology, 15*, 1404767. https://doi.org/10.3389/fpsyg.2024.1404767

Brue, S. L. (1993). Retrospectives: The law of diminishing returns. *Journal of Economic Perspectives, 7*(3), 185–192. https://doi.org/10.1257/jep.7.3.185

Chen, S., Saklofske, D. H., Flett, G. L., & Hewitt, P. L. (2024). Assessing and evaluating the perfectionism social disconnection model: Social support, loneliness, and distress among undergraduate, law, and medical students. *Journal of Psychoeducational Assessment, 42*(6), 743–767. https://doi.org/10.1177/07342829241244951

Di Nocera, F., De Piano, R., Rullo, M., & Tempestini, G. (2023). A lack of focus, not task avoidance, makes the difference: Work routines in procrastinators and non-procrastinators. *Behavioral Sciences, 13*(4), 333. https://doi.org/10.3390/bs13040333

Enz, S., Hall, A. C. G., & Williams, K. K. (2021). The myth of multitasking and what it means for future pharmacists. *American Journal of Pharmaceutical Education, 85*(10), 8267. https://doi.org/10.5688/ajpe8267

Fernández-García, O., Gil-Llario, M. D., Castro-Calvo, J., Morell-Mengual, V., Ballester-Arnal, R., & Estruch-García, V. (2022). Academic perfectionism, psychological well-being, and suicidal ideation in college students. *International Journal of Environmental Research and Public Health, 20*(1), 85. https://doi.org/10.3390/ijerph20010085

Flett, G. L., Nepon, T., Hewitt, P. L., Su, C., Yacyshyn, C., Moore, K., & Lahijanian, A. (2024). The social comparison rumination scale: Development, psychometric properties, and associations with perfectionism, narcissism, burnout, and distress. *Journal of Psychoeducational Assessment, 42*(6), 685–704. https://doi.org/10.1177/07342829241238300

Foster, N. L., Was, C. A., Dunlosky, J., & Isaacson, R. M. (2017). Even after thirteen class exams, students are still overconfident: The role of memory for past exam performance in student predictions. *Metacognition and Learning, 12*(1), 1–19. https://doi.org/10.1007/s11409-016-9158-6

Fung, J., Cai, G., & Wang, K. (2023). Personal and family perfectionism among Asian and Latinx youth. *Cultural Diversity & Ethnic Minority Psychology, 29*(2), 235–246. https://doi.org/10.1037/cdp0000555

Garcia Marquez, G. (1992). Prologue: Why twelve, why short stories, and why pilgrims. In *Strange pilgrims: Twelve stories*. Sudamericana Buenos Aires, Edit.

G Garcia Marquez (2018). The writer's trade (interview). In *El Correo de la UNESCO*. Retrieved November 23, 2026, from https://courier.unesco.org/es/articles/gabriel-garcia-marquez-el-oficio-de-escritor-entrevista

Gaudreau, P. (2019). On the distinction between personal standards perfectionism and excellencism: A theory elaboration and research agenda. *Perspectives on Psychological Science, 14*(2), 197–215. https://doi.org/10.1177/1745691618797940

Gaudreau, P., & Benoît, A. (2025). Distinguishing perfectionism and excellencism in graduate students: Contrasting links with performance satisfaction, research self-efficacy, burnout, and dropout intentions. *British Journal of Psychology, 116*(4), 907–929. https://doi.org/10.1111/bjop.12798

Goulet-Pelletier, J.-C., Beaudin, M.-F., & Cousineau, D. (2025). Investigating the negative link between perfectionism and emotional divergent thinking. *Discover Psychology, 5*(1), 9. https://doi.org/10.1007/s44202-025-00330-x

Güner Gültekin, D., & Akıncı, F. N. (2025). Overestimating the self, outranking the group: An experimental study of overconfidence biases in young decision-makers. *Behavioral Sciences, 15*(12), 1671. https://doi.org/10.3390/bs15121671

Ihara, S., Katayama, N., Nogami, W., Amano, M., Noda, S., Kurata, C., Kobayashi, Y., Sasaki, Y., Mitsuda, D., Ozawa, M., Matsuoka, J., Takemura, R., Uchida, H., & Nakagawa, A. (2024). Comparison of changes in stress coping strategies between cognitive behavioral therapy and pharmacotherapy. *Frontiers in Psychiatry, 15*, 1343637. https://doi.org/10.3389/fpsyt.2024.1343637

Jiang, Y., & Jiang, C. (2025). The impact of maladaptive perfectionism on college students' bedtime procrastination: The chain mediating effects of nomophobia and physical exercise. *Acta Psychologica, 260*, 105504. https://doi.org/10.1016/j.actpsy.2025.105504

Karaca, M., Geraci, L., Kurpad, N., Lithander, M. P. G., & Balsis, S. (2023). Low-performing students confidently overpredict their grade performance throughout the semester. *Journal of Intelligence, 11*(10), 188. https://doi.org/10.3390/jintelligence11100188

Koutra, K., Mouatsou, C., & Psoma, S. (2023). The influence of positive and negative aspects of perfectionism on psychological distress in emerging adulthood: Exploring the mediating role of self-compassion. *Behavioral Sciences, 13*(11), 932. https://doi.org/10.3390/bs13110932

Kruger, J., & Dunning, D. (1999). Unskilled and unaware of it: How difficulties in recognizing one's own incompetence lead to inflated self-assessments. *Journal of Personality and Social Psychology, 77*(6), 1121–1134. https://doi.org/10.1037/0022-3514.77.6.1121

Kuai, F., Wu, X., Zhou, X., & Liu, W. (2025). Association and benefits of 24-h activity behavior and academic procrastination among Chinese college students based on the isotemporal substitution model. *Frontiers in Public Health, 13,* 1700750. https://doi.org/10.3389/fpubh.2025.1700750

Lasalle, M., & Hess, U. (2022). A motivational approach to perfectionism and striving for excellence: Development of a new continuum-based scale for post-secondary students. *Frontiers in Psychology, 13,* 1022462. https://doi.org/10.3389/fpsyg.2022.1022462

Leath, S., Latimer, A., Inniss-Thompson, N. M., Seward, M. D., & Ball, P. (2025). The pressure to be perfect: Stereotype management, (mal?) adaptive perfectionism and well-being among black college women attending predominantly white institutions. *Psychology of Women Quarterly, 49*(2), 182–204. https://doi.org/10.1177/03616843251329013

Madore, K. P., & Wagner, A. D. (2019). Multicosts of multitasking. *Cerebrum,* April 1, 2019:cer-04-19. https://pmc.ncbi.nlm.nih.gov/articles/PMC7075496/

Maier, T., Kühnel, J., & Zimmermann, B. (2022). How did you sleep tonight? The relevance of sleep quality and sleep–wake rhythm for procrastination at work. *Frontiers in Psychology, 12,* 785154. https://doi.org/10.3389/fpsyg.2021.785154

Merriam-Webster Dictionary (n.d.) *Multitasking.* Retrieved February 18, 2026, from https://www.merriam-webster.com/dictionary/multitasking

Nepon, T., Flett, G. L., & Hewitt, P. L. (2024). Perfectionism, self-image goals and compassionate goals in health and mental health: A longitudinal analysis. *Journal of Psychoeducational Assessment, 42*(6), 650–667. https://doi.org/10.1177/07342829241239997

Netzer Turgeman, R., & Pollak, Y. (2025). Adult ADHD-related poor quality of life: Investigating the role of procrastination. *Scandinavian Journal of Psychology, 66*(5), 729–737. https://doi.org/10.1111/sjop.13117

Niermann, H. C. M., & Scheres, A. (2014). The relation between procrastination and symptoms of attention-deficit hyperactivity disorder (ADHD) in undergraduate students: Role of procrastination in ADHD-related symptoms. *International Journal of Methods in Psychiatric Research, 23*(4), 411–421. https://doi.org/10.1002/mpr.1440

Oguchi, M., Takahashi, T., Nitta, Y., & Kumano, H. (2023). Moderating effect of attention deficit hyperactivity disorder tendency on the relationship between delay discounting and procrastination in young adulthood. *Heliyon, 9*(4), e14834. https://doi.org/10.1016/j.heliyon.2023.e14834

Pluut, H., Darouei, M., & Zeijen, M. E. L. (2024). Why and when does multitasking impair flow and subjective performance? A daily diary study on the role of task appraisals and work engagement. *Frontiers in Psychology, 15,* 1384453. https://doi.org/10.3389/fpsyg.2024.1384453

Serra, M. J., & DeMarree, K. G. (2016). Unskilled and unaware in the classroom: College students' desired grades predict their biased grade predictions. *Memory & Cognition, 44*(7), 1127–1137. https://doi.org/10.3758/s13421-016-0624-9

Svartdal, F., Granmo, S., & Færevaag, F. S. (2018). On the behavioral side of procrastination: Exploring behavioral delay in real-life settings. *Frontiers in Psychology, 9,* Article 746. https://doi.org/10.3389/fpsyg.2018.00746

Xue, C., Helian, Z., & Li, Y. (2025). Academic pressure and academic procrastination: The mediating role of negative coping strategies. *PLoS One, 20*(12), e0338956. https://doi.org/10.1371/journal.pone.0338956

You, S., & Yoo, J. (2021). Relations among socially prescribed perfectionism, career stress, mental health, and mindfulness in Korean college students. *International Journal of Environmental Research and Public Health, 18*(22), 12248. https://doi.org/10.3390/ijerph182212248

Zhang, P. Y., & Ma, W. J. (2024). Temporal discounting predicts procrastination in the real world. *Scientific Reports, 14*(1), 14642. https://doi.org/10.1038/s41598-024-65110-4

6 Self-Advocacy

The Key to Receiving the Support You Need to Learn Well

What Is Self-Advocacy?

Learning to understand and to clearly explain your needs to others is a key component of adult life. These skills enable decision-making and facilitate independence. In many disability circles, this is known as self-advocacy.

The Autistic Self Advocacy Network (n.d.), a US disability rights organization led by autistic people, defines self-advocacy as

> taking control of our own lives. That can mean making choices about how we live our lives, like choosing what we do at home, at school, at work or in our relationships. It can also mean working as a community to take control of how society views disabled people, how the media talks about us, and policies that affect our lives.

Understood (n.d.), a national nonprofit serving people who have learning and thinking differences in the US, describes three elements of self-advocacy: *understanding* your needs, *knowing* what support is helpful to you, and *communicating* your needs to others.

Before College: Your Caregivers May Have Served as Your Main Advocates

Your caregivers may have been your biggest advocates until now, requesting evaluations, supports and services, participating in the decision-making process, monitoring your progress toward agreed-upon goals, and managing meetings with the special education staff in your school. It is possible that over time they switched over to you the responsibility of managing meetings and deciding what accommodations and supports you needed. Nonetheless, they possibly were the main advocates for you. Additionally, your caregivers "owned" the rights to your educational records, under the Family Educational Rights and Privacy Act of 1974 (FERPA, n.d.). They were able to disclose information if needed, e.g., to your pediatrician.

DOI: 10.4324/9781003750246-7

In College: You Are in Charge and Can Request Help!

FERPA (n.d.) states that all the rights to your education records must be transferred to you when you turn 18 or start college. This means that your caregivers are no longer able to see your grades, know if you attended class, etc., unless you inform them or expressly allow the college to let them know. In practice, this means your instructors and advisors will not talk to your caregivers unless you have consented to it, most likely at a meeting where you and your caregiver or caregivers are present.

Similarly, healthcare professionals are bound by the Health Insurance Portability and Accountability Act of 1996 (HIPAA, n.d.) to keep your health information private. This means that if you are recommended to meet with a mental health counselor, the counselor will keep all information related to your visit confidential, including whether you made an appointment, if you went to the appointment, or what you said during the appointment.

It can be incredibly challenging for caregivers not to be able to advocate for you, especially in the case of disabled and neurodivergent students. In turn, neurodivergent students may still want to have their caregivers' support. If you want them to be in the loop, you may need to sign a consent-to-disclosure for each individual office or provider. You can also give your caregivers the information yourself, and/or ask your professor, advisor, or other staff member for permission to have your caregivers present at a meeting.

Everyone Needs to Ask for Help: Attending Office Hours, Reaching Out to Advisors

Consulting with your professors, teaching assistants (TAs), and tutors is a fantastic way to make sure you fully understand the topic. Research shows that students who engage with professors and TAs tend to have better grades than those who do not (Guerrero & Rod, 2013). In addition to improving your academic performance, engaging with your instructors outside of class creates a connection with them. If professors know you better, it is much easier for them to, for example, write a letter of recommendation for an internship, program, or graduate school. They may think of you when they hear about certain opportunities, such as a program abroad, or even invite you to be their TA or work in their laboratory.

Typically, consultations with instructors take place during tutoring or review sessions and during "office hours" i.e., time set aside by professors and TAs to provide additional instruction, which commonly recur weekly at a specific location. Most office hours are optional and open to all students on a course. They can be used to clarify anything not understood during class, ask for academic or career advice, request permission to submit an assignment after the deadline, ask about research positions, etc.

In a study by Ritter et al. (2021), over 90% of students who attended office hours reported that they found office hours helpful for understanding course material and working through grade-related information. Students often need time to understand how and why they should use office hours efficiently and effectively. This research demonstrates that becoming more familiar with how office hours work helps students engage more and with more confidence.

Among the reasons my students mention as preventing them from attending office hours or tutoring are some beliefs that don't match reality, as detailed in Table 6.1.

Table 6.1 Beliefs and reality about office hours and tutoring

Common Belief	*Reality*
"I have had professors seem annoyed by questions and instruct me to attend office hours with a TA only for these office hours to be overly crowded and I feel I am wasting time waiting for over 3 hours and only being allowed to ask one question." (Maddy)	It is unfortunately possible that instructors are in a rush or otherwise show lack of patience or empathy. In those cases, talk to a person you trust on campus, be it your academic advisor, the ombudsman, or a therapist. You should also be able to submit a complaint to your institution.
"I find it easier to reach out to help from friends rather than faculty. The proximity of a friend versus the formal office and potentially crowded office hours makes me more comfortable going to someone I know personally." (Racquel)	Faculty can signal their commitment to support students, as Dahlia mentioned: "I feel more at ease reaching to faculty who put less barriers in place to signing up or simply encourage us to arrive to their office." With regard to crowded office hours, while there are weeks with peak attendance, in other weeks there are very few students present.
"I think the major issue I have when asking for help is the inner critic inside me that says I am asking for too much when I reach out for help from others, which is a direct side effect of growing up in an emotionally neglectful household where I was taught to not ask for anything but the bare minimum unless my family was in a good mood." (Lidia)	Teaching faculty and staff have a job BECAUSE you don't understand everything. If you did, we'd be jobless. When considering asking for help, think that you're doing us a favor!

(*Continued*)

Table 6.1 (Continued)

Common Belief	*Reality*
"I have trouble trying to articulate what I am having trouble with when asking for help, and sometimes I do not know what question I should begin with." (John Doe)	"I am trying to combat this by learning that it is ok to go into a conversation without preparing." (Hugo M)
"The biggest challenge I face is the initial fear of appearing underprepared or not having a 'perfect' question ready." (Racquel)	
"I'd rather stare down a problem myself, even if I know a TA could probably help me with it - I don't like the idea of committing time to going to office hours or waiting on an email response." (Pat O)	You could do both! Work on the problem yourself AND verify your answer with the TA or professor.
I understand everything, there's no point in going.	While it is *possible* you understand everything, it's also *possible* you don't. Just like mentioned earlier, hearing others talk about the material will enrich your knowledge of the topic.
Office hours are scheduled at the same time as another of my classes.	You could email the professor or TA, or ask them if you could set up an appointment if that's not already stated in the syllabus.
"Reaching out for help is extremely difficult, since it feels like I'm admitting I haven't studied enough." (Curjot)	The "spotlight effect" in psychology is when you believe other people notice you more than they really do. Briefly, most of your peers won't remember you attended office hours or what you asked, just as you won't remember most of the other students who attended, or what they asked.

Elaborated by Florencia Ardon, PhD, based on her own student comments and descriptions by Dauber and Hsu (2025), Ritter et al. (2021); and Guerrero and Rod (2013).

Several of my students have mentioned that attending office hours, reaching out to the instructor or TA, and talking to classmates helps them:

- Talking with peers is super helpful, and chances are they've got questions that I could help with in return. (Pat O)
- When I encounter academic hurdles, I typically reach out to my peers for collaborative problem-solving or visit faculty during office hours for clarification on more technical subjects. (A student)

Staff, Faculty, and Peer Advisors

Advisors are another valuable source of information. There are several types of advisors, and that may become confusing. Two common types are faculty advisors and staff advisors. *Faculty* advisors are commonly in charge of a group of students in the department where they teach. That faculty member usually offers advice in relation to their focus of research and/or teaching, career paths, and courses related to their major and department. Your faculty advisor should be named in your student portal.

Staff advisors and their offices may have a variety of names, such as student support centers, academic advising, or academic support centers. Advisors can help you understand general graduation requirements for your college; you can talk about the possibility of adding a major or minor, or of changing your major, and much more. Also, in many cases, you may need their signature for some academic petitions, such as adding or dropping a course.

Peer tutoring, coaching, and mentoring are valuable because your peers are or may have been in the same situation. They are also about your age and could have more in common with you than staff or faculty advisors. Peer advisors offer advice and assistance about navigating college, specific coursework, learning strategies in general, and more.

Other Resources and Support

There is a wide range of additional support services, some of which are specific to a subject or skill, such as math, statistics, writing centers, use of technology, literature research, among others. For your desired career path, there may be specific advisors, e.g., pre-law, pre-health, pre-business. Other offices may support study abroad programs, or other specific opportunities. Additionally, your college may have identity- or interest-based support, and much more. It is worth spending a day or two navigating your college web pages and bookmarking the pages of the different offices and centers you believe may be helpful to you. If you are not sure with whom you need to speak, reach out to any advisor you know and ask for their help identifying the person you can reach out to with a particular concern.

Prevalence of Neurodivergent People in College

It is extremely difficult to determine how many neurodivergent students are in college, for several reasons. One is that many students may be neurodivergent, but unaware; I've met many students who realized they are neurodivergent in graduate school, as well as many people who self-identified or were diagnosed late in life (e.g., I was diagnosed as ADHDer at 48). Others may have a diagnosis or self-identify, but don't disclose. Others may have two or more neurotypes or co-occurring conditions but only disclose one. Additionally, the forms used to report disability may group some neurotypes into broad categories, e.g., dyslexia and dyscalculia are under "learning disabilities" (New York State Department of Education, n.d.). Thus, different situations can lead to undercounting the prevalence of specific neurotypes. The prevalence of some common neurotypes is described in Table 6.2.

Table 6.2 Common neurotypes. Neurotypes are ranked according to their prevalence

Neurotype	*Responses*	*Students Who Have Been Diagnosed*		*Students Who Have Seen a Healthcare or Mental Health Professional about Their Diagnosis*	
	(n)	*(n)*	%	*(n)*	%
Anxiety	46,779	16,371	35%	11,888	73%
Depression	46,732	12,168	26%	8,785	72.5%
ADHD	46,715	7,282	15.6%	5,054	69.8%
Post-traumatic stress and related conditions	46,665	3,558	7.6%	2,432	68.6%
Obsessive-compulsive and related conditions	46,674	3,260	7.0%	2,177	67.1%
Autism	46,488	1,666	3.6%	843	51.2%
Bipolar and related conditions	46,697	1,231	2.6%	858	70.1%
Borderline, avoidant, dependent, or another personality-related condition	46,726	805	1.7%	521	65.1%
Traumatic brain injury	46,540	588	1.3%	258	44.6%
Schizophrenia and related conditions	46,626	217	0.5%	109	51.7%
Tourette's and other neurodevelopmental not mentioned above	46,555	347	0.7%	149	43.4%

Elaborated by Florencia Ardon, PhD, based on the American College Health Association's, 2025 report (ACHA-NCHA III, 2025).

Useful Information If You Need Accommodations

Relevant Laws

Colleges are required to follow several laws that prohibit discrimination. For this chapter, important laws to know are the American with Disabilities Act ("ADA," 1990). ADA is a federal law that prohibits discrimination against people with disabilities. Another important law is the Section 504 of the Rehabilitation Act ("Section 504," Section 504 of the Rehabilitation Act of 1973, 29 U.S.C. § 794, n.d.) a federal law that protects the rights of disabled people in programs that receive federal financial assistance. Finally, the Title II of the ADA prohibits discrimination against disabled people in state and local government services, programs, and activities, regardless of whether they receive federal financial assistance ("Title II," 2011).

What Does It Mean to be Disabled?

Under the ADA,

> the term "disability" means, with respect to an individual, (A) a physical or mental impairment that substantially limits one or more major life activities, (B) a record of such an impairment; or (C) being regarded as having such an impairment.
>
> (ADA, 1990)

Section 504 defines a physical impairment as a physiological disorder or condition, cosmetic disfigurement or anatomical loss affecting one or more body systems, including some crucial for learning such as neurological, special sense organs and speech organs. Mental impairments include intellectual disabilities, emotional or mental health conditions, and specific learning disabilities (US Department of Education, n.d.). Many of these conditions can be considered hidden disabilities, which include a wide variety of illnesses, conditions, and neurotypes, such as learning disabilities, diabetes, low vision, or being hard of hearing (US Department of Education, n.d.).

Major life activities are an extremely broad category. In the case of neurodivergent students, impairments that affect learning include those limiting their ability to sleep, eat, speak, process information, concentrate, read, and communicate. For any disability, the impediment can be episodic, e.g., "flare up" or be in remission (ADA, 1990).

Supports and Accommodations in College

The support given to disabled students at the college level is different in several ways from that provided to students up to high school, and the regulations differ. An accommodation that may be considered reasonable in high school may not be deemed reasonable in college. Additionally, while schools are required to identify all students with a disability to "meet the individual educational needs of [disabled] persons as adequately as the needs of [non-disabled] persons are met," and provide them with "an equal opportunity to participate in nonacademic and extracurricular services and activities," *colleges are not obliged to identify disabled students*. Additionally, the regulation speaks of "qualified" individuals, meaning "a [disabled] person who meets the academic and technical standards requisite for admission to, and participation in, the college's education program or activity." Colleges are, however, required to inform applicants and students of the availability of auxiliary aids, services, and academic adjustments, as well as the name of the coordinator of these services (US Department of Education, n.d.).

You may be familiar with or have heard different names for supports and accommodations; some of them are as follows.

Offered from Kindergarten to High School (K–12) But Not in College

Interventions: Specialized teaching to support students who need assistance to fully understand a particular skill or topic.

Modification or *adjustments*: It means that the content of the curriculum and learning objectives change. This means, for example, reducing the content, grading using different criteria, assigning easier math problems, etc. These are included in an Individualized Education Plan (IEP) and go beyond the academic adjustments that are provided at the college level.

Response to intervention: This refers to short-term support, based on a specific need. For example, a school occupational therapist may notice that a child is not holding the pencil properly, which may cause pain and strain in the hand, wrist, and arm. The therapist would teach how to grasp a pencil and ensure the child learns that skill; all of this with permission from the caregivers.

Offered at All Levels

Accommodations, modifications, or academic adjustments: The content of the curriculum and difficulty level remain the same; the student is provided with some support that may help them listen better, be present in the classroom, engage with the material, and demonstrate what they know. While the learning objective of a course doesn't change, a decreased academic courseload could be allowed.

Auxiliary Aids and Services: This includes *Accessible Educational Materials* and *Assistive Technology Devices or Services*. For example, textbooks may be converted to Braille, a student may be allowed to use text-to-speech or speech-to-text software, use of closed captioning, notetakers, written material (instead of only verbal), sign language interpreters, etc. (ADA National Network, n.d.-a).

Students' familiarity with accommodations when they arrive at college can fall into three groups: (a) They are familiar with accommodations, as they received special education services based on an IEP. (b) They are familiar with accommodations, as they received special education services based on a "504 Plan." (c) They didn't receive any special education services and are not familiar with accommodations. The following are brief descriptions of those plans; more information can be found on the Department of Education website and through advocacy organizations.

If You Had an IEP in High School

IEPs are based on the 1990 Individuals with Disabilities Education Act (IDEA, n.d.). Under IDEA, K–12 schools have an obligation to:

a Evaluate any child who may have a disability that could hinder their learning, conducting evaluations of the children at no charge to families. These evaluations are different from a diagnosis and may not be valid in other institutions (e.g., college).

b In addition to accommodations and services to ensure access, such as offering books written in Braille for blind children, IDEA also includes *modifications* to the curriculum itself, as explained earlier, and other services such as speech, physical and/or occupational therapy.

c IEPs are legal contracts and are typically reviewed every year. The IEP committee can include caregivers, students, special education staff, a case manager, special education teacher, etc.

d During IEP meetings, educators submit "present level of performance" (PLOP) reports stating the students' academic, physical, and social skills and strengths. The IEP also mentions specific issues the student is facing, for example it may be hard for autistic people to understand non-autistic people's pragmatic language, that is, how non-autistic people use figurative language, implied meanings and more. *Non-autistic people's pragmatic language differs from that of autistic people.*

e Students' progress is monitored through annual goals based on PLOPs. For instance, students may be enrolled in classes that are co-taught by a general education teacher and a special education teacher, who will be paying attention to the student's progress, providing direct instruction as needed.

A student may be disabled but not eligible for an IEP. Only 13 disabilities are covered by IDEA. The disability must have a negative effect on the student's performance at school that can only be minimized through an IEP; that is, it is determined that accommodations provided under a 504 plan (described next) would not be enough to support the students' success.

IDEA does not apply to colleges. As mentioned earlier, colleges are not required to find students who may be disabled or to conduct evaluations to identify those students. The student is responsible for requesting accommodations; if a student does not request accommodations, the college does not have an obligation to offer them. There are also no PLOP evaluations or annual goals, and, generally speaking, the curriculum cannot be modified. It can be a shock to transition to college and lose much of the support that was received in high school.

If You Had a 504 Plan in High School

As mentioned earlier, Section 504 prohibits exclusion, denial of benefits or discrimination under any program or activity that receives federal financial assistance. This includes K–12 schools, and all colleges and universities in the US. Accommodations and supports you received in high school are like those you can receive in college.

Colleges are forbidden from asking applicants about their ability status and cannot require students to undergo testing to determine whether they are disabled. At the same time, colleges are not obligated to offer or pay for any disability-related testing. Colleges are required by the US Department of Education (n.d.) to inform applicants and current students about the supports offered and to designate a person responsible for coordinating Section 504-related accommodations and services.

Like an IEP, a 504 Plan is a legal contract between the school and the student's caregivers. However, 504 Plans focus on having the same opportunity to engage with the course material and their faculty and peers, to meet the same requirements and expectations as non-disabled students. This means they ensure *access*, not *success*. That is, the 504 Plan does not create an obligation to make sure a student excels in class.

If You Didn't Receive any Services in High School

More and more students are arriving at college with a diagnosis and having had accommodations and supports in high school. That is an optimal situation since you already know what you need *and* what supports can help you.

Many other students realize they need accommodations once they start facing challenges in college. It may be a surprise or shock to students who used to study very little and do very well. If you are in this situation, know that this only means that the compensatory strategies you unknowingly developed in K–12 are no longer enough for college courses. It can also show that there is a vast difference between the rigor of your high school and that of your college.

It is good to always keep in mind that you are still you. You are smart and capable, and in the past were supported by the structure and routine that exist at the high school level. Some college students, such as student-athletes, have a routine imposed by a team. For most of the students, however, the routine and schedule they had in high school disappears suddenly. This creates novel needs to plan and organize your time, which are skills that need to be developed over time. These skills are part of your executive function, covered in Chapter 3.

Once you realize you need support, the next step is to reach out to the disability support office. All higher education institutions must have one; your academic advisor should be able to connect you with them if needed.

Requesting Accommodations from the Disability Support Office

Remember that you are NOT required to disclose a disability to anyone, be it college staff or an employer. You DO need to disclose your needs, and you may have to provide evidence (e.g., a diagnosis) to receive accommodations and support.

It is very important to familiarize yourself with the disability support offices processes, including whether there is a deadline to request accommodations; some institutions allow you to request accommodations throughout the term, while others require that you submit your request within the first few days. Read through the documentation requirements; it is possible that they request current evaluations (College Board (n.d.), for example, requires evaluations made within the last five years). They may also request a copy of your IEP or 504 Plan, if you received such services in high school. You can trust that, by law, the disability support office cannot share any information about you with anyone, except for the accommodation letter mentioned in the following section, which does not state your disability or disabilities.

You will be a more successful self-advocate if you know what accommodations you received as part of your IEP or 504 Plan, and how they helped you, so reading that documentation before reaching out to the disability support office would be helpful. Similarly, familiarizing yourself with your evaluations can give you ideas of what accommodations and services can support your learning; some diagnostic reports include such recommendations. It may be good to read them in the company of a supportive person such as your therapist or an advisor who is familiar with disability support, as the language may focus more on what could be perceived as "deficits" instead of on your strengths.

It is not necessary for you to be failing a course or courses; accommodations can help you sustain academic excellence. Students may hesitate to request support, comparing their need to that of others and thinking, "Maybe someone needs it more than I do." But the law does not limit the number of students who should be accommodated! For example, if you are allowed more time to complete an exam, that doesn't mean someone is having less time.

In some cases, you may be demanding too much of yourself. For example, some students believe that because they can finish an exam on time, they don't need extended time, when what is likely happening is that they're hurrying to keep up with everyone else's pace and end up making mistakes, or not being able to do a final check of their responses or writing. While they *technically* turned in the exam on time, their answers don't reflect what students truly know. If you are in this situation, remember that according to the ADA, testing accommodations ensure that the score you obtain *reflects your aptitude or knowledge about the topic* and *should not be a measure of your disability*.

Your neurotype makes you *"you,"* and some of your traits, related to your neurotype, are very positive, such as perseverance or creativity. Other traits, also related to your neurotype, may create some difficulties. In Table 6.3, you can read about the effect of some neurotypes on students' academic performance, as reported by the ACHA-NCHA III 2025. Many of the difficulties you may face could be minimized by using accommodations.

Still, you may hesitate to request accommodations, thinking that you may end up not needing to use them every time or may not want to request accommodations if the prior semester you didn't use your accommodations or supports. However, each semester you are taking different courses, probably with more specialized information or more rigor, with different instructors, etc., so you cannot know for certain that you won't need accommodations. If you have extended time for an exam and finish early, you can leave. If you don't need an extension for an assignment, turn it in by the regular deadline. Having accommodations doesn't force you to use them. It's much better to have them and not use them every time, than needing them and not have them yet, as accommodations are not retroactive.

The goal of accommodations given in college is to provide an equal opportunity to participate in and benefit from educational programs or activities. When you start the process of requesting accommodations, it's possible that you will not have an idea of what you need and not even know what's available. However, disability support offices don't have a comprehensive "menu" to show you. A good reason for this is that disability support staff should not assume what might help you. People may have the same diagnosis yet need different support and services. Additionally, sometimes the most effective solution is new or a composition of several tools and strategies that is created specifically for you. Section 504 protects students in this regard, as institutions are required to provide students with services and aids that are effective specifically for *them*.

Table 6.3 Effect of common neurotypes on academic performance. Neurotypes are listed in alphabetical order

Neurotype	*Responses*	*Does not Experience This Issue*		*Did Not Affect Academic Performance*		*Negatively Impacted Performance in a Class*		*Delayed Progress toward Degree*	
	(n)	*(n)*	%	*(n)*	%	*(n)*	%	*(n)*	%
ADHD	46,637	36,911	79.1%	3,374	7.2%	5,290	11.3%	1,062	2.3%
Anxiety	46,328	15,958	34.4%	15,483	33.4%	13,298	28.7%	1,589	3.4%
Concussion or Traumatic Brain Injury	46,647	44,949	96.4%	838	1.8%	714	1.5%	146	0.3%
Depression	46,424	29,250	63.0%	7,211	15.5%	8,286	17.8%	1,677	3.6%
Post-Traumatic Stress and Related Conditions	46,446	42,740	92.0%	2,077	4.5%	1,247	2.7%	382	0.8%

Elaborated by Florencia Ardon, PhD, based on the American College Health Association's, 2025 report (ACHA-NCHA III, 2025).

If you are not sure of which accommodations could help you, reach out to the disability support office anyway; once you explain the challenges or barriers you are facing, they can likely identify an accommodation that may help you, as they may have worked with another student who faced the same challenges. Similarly, if you receive an accommodation and find out it is not helpful, or you believe you need additional accommodations, or for any other reason you want to speak to a disability support specialist, you can reach out to the disability support office at any point of your academic career, not just at the beginning of each academic term.

The ADA (1990) states that *every single* student that demonstrates a need should be provided "appropriate accommodations." Accommodations mentioned in the ADA (1990) are extremely broad and include not only those related to architecture (e.g., ramps), but several related to invisible disabilities.

Accommodations given by Section 504 due to a disability include, among many others (see the website of the Pennsylvania State Education Association (n.d.) for a very comprehensive list):

a *Class attendance*: be allowed to miss class, arrive late, take breaks, sit in front of the class, sit in a low-distraction area, or near a door, have access to fidget items.

b *Exams*: be given study guides in advance, be able to present an exam orally instead of in writing, in a quiet space, dictating answers, be given "extended time," e.g., if the exam has a time limit of 60 minutes, the student may be given 1.5x, i.e., 90 minutes.

c *Assignments*: be allowed to submit them after the due date, have long projects broken down into smaller pieces, be given examples of what the finished assignment should look like, submit assignments as audio or video recordings, and be given clear feedback.

d *Notetaking*: be allowed to record the class or type notes instead of writing by hand or use speech-to-text software. In some cases, accommodations may mean having a notetaker (e.g., another student in the class) who takes notes that will be provided to the student.

e *Materials and reading*: access to text-to-speech software and audiobooks, receive slides in advance if not regularly provided, have materials available in Braille or written in dyslexia-friendly fonts.

f *Communication*: clear and concise rubrics, expectations, and instructions, presented in different formats (e.g., visual and written); easily available, making sure the student understands them.

Accommodations must be *"reasonable."* This means they should not create an *undue burden*; i.e., it should not be exceedingly difficult or extremely expensive to offer a given accommodation. If it is, the college and professor should try to find another solution that does not cause the *undue burden*.

Additionally, an accommodation must not *fundamentally change* the service provided; as an extreme example, an accommodation for swimming cannot state the student cannot get wet.

And, as explained earlier, Section 504 focuses on *access*, not *success*. This means that offering an academic coach you can meet with on a daily or weekly basis is not considered *reasonable*: You would presumably meet with an academic coach to succeed in your courses, which goes beyond being able to access the course materials.

Some institutions have specialized programs that offer these types of services, and in many cases, the services are fee-based. It is important to consider that those fees, since they are additional and only charged to participants in a specific program, are not part of the regular "cost of attendance" of colleges and may not be included in your financial aid package. There may be programs that help you pay that fee, depending on your college and your home state, but it's not guaranteed, and it may be your responsibility to secure that support.

You can create your own "premium service" by taking advantage of all the resources that are in place in your university. Most colleges have a student success program, as well as academic advisors, peer mentors, student organizations, etc. Depending on the size and structure of your institution, you may need to spend a few hours navigating their web pages or may need to reach out to a few staff members, but it is worth it!

Lastly, I want to mention service and emotional support animals, as there can be some confusion about the two categories:

a *Service animals* are defined by ADA as "a dog that is individually trained to do work or perform tasks for an individual with a disability" (ADA National Network, n.d.-b). The task must be directly related to the disability, e.g., they may remind you to take your medication or warn you if you are about to have a seizure. They must be allowed to go with you anywhere that's open to the public, including classrooms, residencies, restaurants, etc. *Service animals* are intrinsically different from *emotional support animals*.

b *Emotional support animals* are considered assistance animals "that provide emotional support that alleviates one or more identified effects of a person's disability." Emotional support animals are not covered by ADA; they are covered by the Fair Housing Act (US Department of Housing and Urban Development, n.d.). Emotional support animals must be allowed in the place where you live but no other space is required to admit them, and you may be required to provide your property-owner with a letter written by a licensed mental health professional stating your need for the emotional support animal. In college, that means you could have your emotional support animal in your dorm room, but likely not in the classroom, dining halls, etc.

Discussing Accommodations and Support with Your Professors and Other Staff

HIPAA and FERPA regulations prevent the disability support office from disclosing your disability to faculty and staff. Typically, after the disability support office has determined what accommodations are appropriate for you, they send a "accommodation letter" to faculty teaching the classes you're taking, stating what accommodations you have been granted for that class. You need to speak with each faculty member to discuss what those accommodations mean for you in that particular class. In rare cases, the faculty member may disagree with an accommodation if they feel that granting it would fundamentally alter their course. In that instance, they can request a review, stating the essential components or requirements of their course and how the accommodation would alter or nullify one or more components.

Significant stigma around accommodations still exists, and faculty may not fully understand that a student *really* needs the accommodation they are requesting, or faculty may feel that the accommodation will create issues for the student in the long term. For example, if a student is granted extended time to complete assignments, and for any number of reasons ends up not working on them until late in the semester, the student could end up having ten assignments to do in two days and ultimately not submit most of them, leading to a lower grade.

However, students, faculty, and staff need to keep in mind that the issue is not the accommodation itself; the accommodation is valid and needed. What may be happening in these cases is that the students are still learning how to best use accommodations, and they may benefit from explicit instruction and mentoring. It's possible you can request this instruction from the disability support office on your campus. Other people who can help you are academic advisors, tutors and peer mentors.

There are also misunderstandings about accommodations. Something I've heard often is that extended time during an exam is akin to cheating or an unfair advantage. When I hear that "everyone would have a higher grade if they got more time," my thinking is "then everyone should get more time." When you are facing a difficult exam question, and you have the knowledge, more time can help you express that knowledge in a more cohesive, clear manner. In contrast, if you don't know enough about the topic, all the time in the world won't provide you with the answer.

Other accommodations may be misunderstood in a similar manner. It would be helpful for you to be aware of potential false assumptions about the accommodations you are requesting, as well as of concerns faculty may have, to be prepared to address them when you explain your needs.

I recognize that speaking to faculty may be hard and cause an emotional and cognitive load. Explaining the same issue to multiple people can be tiresome and stressful, as your experience may have been that people ask you several follow-up questions that may feel invasive, or their demeanor may imply they are not believing you. Preparing ahead of your conversation with faculty may help decrease your worries and give you tools and the language you need for a successful dialogue.

Keep in Mind

a You are in control of what you *disclose*. As mentioned earlier, the accommodation letter does not state your disability, and you don't need to explain more than you are comfortable sharing. It's also important to note that faculty are prohibited from disclosing to others anything they learn about your disability or accommodation needs.
b You may want to request an *appointment*. This is not the kind of conversation you want to have in the hallway right after class, in a rush and surrounded by other people.
c Alternatively, if it is more helpful to you, you could ask if it's possible for you to communicate via *email* or have an advisor or other staff member accompany you to the meeting.

To Prepare for the Meeting

a You want to feel satisfied about your explanations and advocacy after the conversation. When you are speaking to your instructor, you may find you are not able to rapidly answer their questions or concerns. It could be helpful for you to *write down* your concerns about specific portions of the syllabus, assignments, or projects ahead of time. You may also ask for follow-up meetings if for some reason you feel your needs were not discussed well enough or an adequate solution was not found.
b If not stated in the syllabus, you could ask your instructor what *learning objectives* are met with the assignments or projects you want to address during the meeting, to prepare your arguments showing how the accommodations will help you fulfill the learning objectives for the class.
c Look for *examples* of helpful accommodations online, ask peers or the disability support office staff, or base your request on your own experiences in other courses.
d *Anticipate* the concerns the professor could express and questions they may have and write down your answers and explanations. Practicing the conversation with a friend can help you prepare your responses, both the content and how to express it.

During the Meeting

- Frame your conversation around a *common goal*: Your instructor is invested in supporting everyone's learning and loves the course's topic. You are interested in the course and want to learn, and this desire to understand the topic is what drives your request for accommodations.
- *Assume good intent*. Many faculty are eager to support you but are unsure how to do so; they will appreciate your ideas. As mentioned earlier, your instructor may not understand your lived experience; there are many nuances that are almost impossible to comprehend unless they are explicitly expressed.

It is important to note that many accommodations covered by Section 504 could benefit all students. Universal Design for Learning (UDL, CAST, 2024), which can be understood as the learning equivalent of ramps for buildings, was conceived in the late 1990s and focuses on making learning accessible to all. It includes (a) providing the information or skills students should learn in multiple ways, to cover the needs of diverse learners; (b) allowing students to engage with the material using different approaches; and (c) enabling students to demonstrate their understanding and skills in a variety of manners.

While UDL is an extremely useful framework, it can be difficult to transfer the theory to practice, especially for busy faculty. To facilitate UDL implementation, some colleges offer training about UDL's framework and what that looks like in the classroom. Another way colleges help faculty is by offering logistical support. For instance, a common issue is how to offer extended time for an exam, if the classroom is needed by someone else after the regular exam time, or if the faculty member or their TAs have other commitments. Some disability support offices are offering an alternative space, staffed by the office, helping ensure the student receives the accommodation while minimizing the burden on faculty. It would be good from an advocacy point of view for you to speak to the disability support office or some other offices on campus to understand what training and other supports are available for faculty.

Your Options If an Accommodation Is Denied or Not Appropriately Given

As explained earlier, accommodations are a right you have, based on your disability. It should be seen as a win-win situation, fulfilling your goal to learn and the instructor's to teach you. Sometimes, an accommodation may be denied by the disability support office, and in other situations, the accommodation is granted, but not provided in a way that is useful.

Before Applying: Research the Institutions You Want to Attend

When you are deciding what college to apply to, be it during high school, or if you are planning to go abroad or transfer to a different college, it is crucial to evaluate their attitude toward disabled and neurodivergent students. You can look for signs that help you determine if they will respect you as a scholar who requires support to thrive academically and as a member of their community.

The college's websites may give you an idea of their general attitude toward differences and willingness to support students. Positive signs include offering a wide range of support to the general student population, including tutoring, one-on-one coaching or consultations on study skills and other subjects. Language is important! A college that intentionally mentions disability and neurodiversity acceptance and inclusion will be more likely to create a welcoming environment for everyone.

The disability support office website will be another great source of information. You can evaluate how easy it is to register as a disabled student, how much, how recent, and what type of documentation they require, and whether they offer students meetings with their staff to better understand their needs. Their choice of words will be another clue. Do their web pages read as friendly and amicable, willing to help you? Or does it seem like they will only offer the support they are legally obliged to provide? Are there clear processes to request accommodations and to appeal a decision?

A third area to explore is student organizations. Is there a club for neurodiversity and/or disability? Do they offer events where you can meet other students with your same neurotype or access and support needs? Do they advocate for more inclusion and acceptance, as well as better services?

While the websites can give you an initial idea, visiting the college in person, or meeting virtually with staff from the disability support office, and academic support centers would provide you with very valuable information to help you choose an institution.

Your Accommodation Request Was Denied. What Now?

Even though you will hopefully not be denied reasonable accommodations, it can happen, and it is helpful to be familiar with the processes to appeal and if necessary present a complaint, just in case you need them.

Many times, accommodations are denied because there is some documentation missing, or the reasons behind your request are not clear. You can request a written decision that states the reasons for denial. You can then provide any documentation needed or meet with them to explain why the accommodation helps you.

The request could be denied even though there is nothing missing and you have clearly described your needs. You should be able to appeal the decision and/or pursue a formal grievance, i.e., file a complaint. A common path would be to look first for an informal process where you write to the staff at the disability support office or fill out a form if available.

If that doesn't solve the problem, the next step would be to submit a complaint at the campus level. Your college should have an office dedicated to support students filing complaints related to violation of civil rights, and an ombudsman's office. If you are not sure who to reach out to, your academic advisor should be able to help you file the complaint.

If these steps don't lead to a satisfactory solution, you can certainly reach out to the Civil Rights Office (or Human Rights Office) of the state where your university is located, and to the US Department of Education Office for Civil Rights.

Steps You Can Take If the Accommodations You are Receiving Are Not Helpful

It is possible that you are being provided accommodations, but in a way that is not helpful. This can be a very distressing and frustrating situation for you; you may feel like you are not keeping up with class material, are not able to sleep properly, and you cannot find food you can eat, among other possibilities.

The process described earlier would be appropriate for this situation as well, only you would start by speaking to the professor, residence or dining hall staff, etc.; if the faculty or staff member is still not understanding how to provide the accommodation in a way that is helpful to you, you can speak to the disability support office staff. They could facilitate a conversation with the professor or staff member.

It is possible that for several reasons the instruction you are receiving on a required course is not accessible or clear, even with accommodations in place. This is a possibility for all students, regardless of whether they receive accommodations, as the way a professor explains a concept may be unclear or even increase your confusion.

For all students, the campus academic support center is a valuable resource. Supplemental classes, tutoring, and consultations could help you fill gaps in your knowledge or understanding. Peer mentoring and tutoring, as well as study groups, can be very helpful too. External resources can be very valuable; this includes a variety of sources from textbooks, online videos, courses available through free online learning platforms, to generative artificial intelligence (GenAI). Some of my students use GenAI to understand certain topics, prompting the bot to provide them with detailed explanations at different levels of expertise. If you use GenAI, remember to fact-check the information it gives you to make sure it's accurate.

It is also important to listen to your intuition. Is the disconnect with your professor or staff member related to the person or the course not being a good fit for you? Or can it be related to a civil rights violation? Is the course or service accessible? If you feel uneasy, don't hesitate to reach out to your advisors and peers, who can also serve as a soundboard to help you determine what the issue is and talk about possible solutions. And believe that the ombudsman, regulatory agencies on and off campus, and advocacy organizations, exist for a reason: to help you and others in similar situations.

Deciding Whether to Pursue a Diagnosis and Consider Medication

It is possible that you are facing challenges, and although you are receiving some support, it's not enough. Or you start to feel too different from your peers or go through a difficult situation that makes you realize that maybe there's something else that goes deeper than *not trying hard* or *not studying enough* or some other self-blaming statements you tell yourself (or others tell you). While it is important to give yourself time to consider if you want to dig further into this issue, it is also important not to wait too long.

There are two main reasons for getting a diagnosis sooner rather than later: one, very crucial, is that many disability support offices require a diagnosis to provide accommodations, and the benefit of accommodations is not retroactive; i.e., it's not applicable to what has already happened. They will be honored *after* your instructor receives an accommodation letter but anything that happened before is unmodifiable; you cannot change the past. This can mean an incredibly low exam grade, not being able to submit missing assignments, and so on. Diagnoses are also needed to receive medication.

There are shockingly few people who offer high-quality diagnoses, and most have a several-month waitlist. The sooner you get on those waitlists, the sooner you will be able to obtain a diagnosis and use it to request and receive accommodations and/or medication. Additionally, many people find having a diagnosis helps them feel better, like the difficulty they're having is not "in their head" and that they are not "imagining things." Diagnosis can provide a path forward in many ways.

The disability support office, the health center, or your family physician can refer you to healthcare professionals who will offer high-quality, comprehensive, and useful diagnostic evaluations and reports. It is particularly important that the healthcare professional is someone you feel comfortable with. Optimally, the person would be someone who is trained to diagnose the particular disability you suspect or identify with and its possible co-occurring conditions, and who has experience working with people like you, meaning your age range, capabilities, gender, and more. Some of the students I advise have been told by a healthcare professional that they cannot be autistic because they're in college, or have a partner, or similar biased statements. If a healthcare professional says something similar, that means they are starting your diagnostic evaluation with biases that may affect their assessment. People who have developed coping mechanisms that include "masking," that is, imitating non-disabled people behavior and actions, such as making eye contact even when it is painful or uncomfortable, may find it hard to obtain an accurate assessment.

Relatedly, keep in mind that diagnoses are mostly based on what others can *see and hear*. The internal experience may differ quite dramatically, and answering questionnaires may be difficult. For example, the Autism-Spectrum Quotient (Baron-Cohen et al., 2001) includes questions like "I would rather go to a library than a party." Many autistic people (very reasonably) need more nuanced information: What type of library? What type of party is it, and who is there? What day? You could say that the way people react to the question can give you a good idea of whether the person is autistic, but that doesn't make the question easy to answer.

In addition to the healthcare professional's expertise in the use of current and validated questionnaires, a holistic evaluation will provide more accurate information and a better view of the different challenges the person faces. Adamou et al. (2024) propose a standard for ADHD evaluations that includes an account of challenges faced by the person, as well as a "life narrative," school, college, or work reports; information given by family and friends; a diagnostic interview; evaluation of other possible co-occurring conditions; and a discussion about treatment options and accommodations or services that may be useful for the person. The healthcare professional should be able to explain the diagnosis in plain language, describe the different options of treatment and supports, and offer referrals for further evaluations, if needed. Adamou et al. (2024) also state that the ADHD evaluation should be part of a full psychiatric and neurodevelopmental evaluation.

Young et al. (2020), offering a consensus approach for diagnosing people who are autistic and ADHDers (colloquially called AuDHD), concur with Adamou et al. (2024) and further recommend taking in consideration that family members who offer information about the person may be autistic or an ADHDer, even if undiagnosed, and this may impact their judgment of what "typical" behavior looks like. They also caution that norms for many screening tools are often based on the expected presentation of autism and/or ADHD in males and could affect the evaluation of those who don't identify as males.

The recommendations mentioned earlier also apply to mental health-related diagnoses; Walter et al. (2023) additionally recommend considering the effects of medications or other substances, as well as the presence of medical conditions that may influence the person's behaviors, thoughts, or feelings.

When receiving a diagnosis, it is useful to remember that, by definition, diagnoses are given based on the presence of issues or deficits. The many strengths and positive traits of these neurotypes are not considered during a diagnosis. It may be helpful to have someone you trust to offer you support and affirmation present when you read your diagnosis or when you discuss it with the person who provided the evaluation.

If you are not planning to request accommodations, or for any other reason decide not to pursue a diagnosis, self-identification is a valid path. It can help you understand yourself; come to terms with your need to use alarms and reminders, for example; and explore other tools and strategies. It also helps you understand why your academic performance doesn't reflect your hard work or intelligence. You can certainly benefit from joining support or social groups where you can find others who have strengths and challenges like yours. They can help you feel you're not alone.

The ACHA-NCHA III 2025 results show that, with few exceptions, a majority of students diagnosed as neurodivergent reach out for healthcare or mental health support, which is very positive from a well-being perspective (see Table 6.2). Therapy and medication can help you deal with some traits that are upsetting to you or creating issues you would prefer not to experience. However, engaging in therapy or taking medication is an extremely personal decision. Many neurodivergent people don't receive either, and some others have no formal accommodations in place. If you decide to use medication, it's good to keep in mind that finding the correct type and dosage can take several trials and some time, so it may be better to work that out over an academic break like the summer or during a nonstressful part of an academic term.

Mapping Out Your Resources and Support

Get to Know Students Like You

Since individual privacy is protected, and many students don't disclose at all or only do it on a need-to-know basis, you may feel as if you are the only person dealing with a particular issue. This may make you feel extremely lonely, especially as you transition to college or during your first year. It is important to identify your resources and the people who can help you. While your family and close friends will be invaluable sources of support, getting to know other disabled and/or neurodivergent students can help you feel accompanied. Many colleges have student organizations of disabled and/or neurodivergent students or those who identify with another social identity you hold. They are a valuable source of help and information; members may share your disability, use similar accommodations, or know of other supports that could help you. These organizations can also offer or advocate for programming and support that can benefit everyone.

Support Network: What You Need and Who Can Help

Areas in which you are likely to need support in college include academic, financial, career development, identity-related, campus living (housing and dining), mental health, religious and/or spiritual, and social life.

Several offices and people can support you in each of those areas. Depending on your college and situation, some offices or people may support you in two or more areas, or you may need to reach out to two or more different offices and people for one specific need. For instance, staff in the office dedicated to education abroad will be able to help you find a good program, while the disability support office staff can provide you with documentation once you've been accepted.

People who can help you in an unofficial manner include your classmates, members of organizations, clubs, and project teams you belong to, friendly faculty and staff, trusted religious leaders, etc. They don't have to know the ins and outs of your disability or even know you have one. Their support may be emotional, economic, academic, and so on.

Among college staff whose job is to support you are staff from the disability support office, faculty you are taking courses with, academic advisors in your college or major, faculty advisors, staff in offices who support any or several of your social and academic identities, etc.

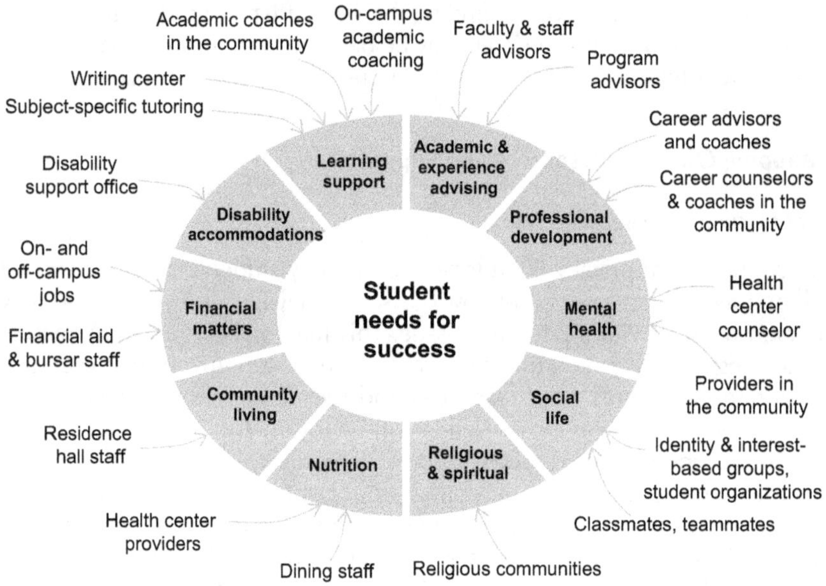

Figure 6.1 Needs and sources of support for a student in a residential college. Concept by Florencia Ardon, PhD. Design by Julia Felice, PhD.

Outside of your college, there are several organizations that can assist you. This may include doctors, therapists, academic coaches, employers, nonprofit organizations, and much more. Figure 6.1 shows a simplified example of a support network.

In Brief

Self-advocacy involves understanding and clearly explaining your needs, as well as requesting supports that ensure you are given equal opportunity to participate in educational and other programs offered at your institution. While college students are not required to disclose to anyone any disability they may have, they may need to disclose their disability or disabilities to receive accommodations. While some students may have received accommodations and services all along, some may realize their needs once they are in college, at which point they may start the process of self-identification and pursuing a diagnostic evaluation, if they desire one. If you are in this situation, it is immensely helpful to know other students who face challenges like yours; this would help you to feel accompanied and part of a community, and your peers can guide you through the process of requesting accommodations and discussing them with faculty and staff. If you want to pursue a diagnostic evaluation, the disability support office or the health center could refer you to a reputable healthcare professional who is known to conduct comprehensive, high-quality diagnostic evaluations. Regardless of whether you have or could have a diagnosis, there is a network of support that can assist you with a variety of needs you may have in college.

References

ADA National Network (n.d.-a). *Effective communication*. Retrieved January 23, 2026, from https://adata.org/factsheet/communication

ADA National Network (n.d.-b). *Service animals and emotional support animals*. Retrieved January 17, 2026, from https://adata.org/factsheet/postsecondary.

Adamou, M., Arif, M., Asherson, P., Cubbin, S., Leaver, L., Sedgwick-Müller, J., Müller-Sedgwick, U., Van Rensburg, K., & Kustow, J. (2024). The adult ADHD assessment quality assurance standard. *Frontiers in Psychiatry, 15*, 1380410. https://doi.org/10.3389/fpsyt.2024.1380410

American College Health Association (2025). *American College Health Association-National College Health Assessment (ACHA-NCHA III). Reference group data report – Spring 2025*. Retrieved December 20, 2025, from https://www.acha.org/wp-content/uploads/NCHA-IIIb_SPRING_2025_UNDERGRADUATE_REFERENCE_GROUP_INSTITUTIONAL_DATA_REPORT.pdf

Americans with Disabilities Act of 1990, 42 U.S.C. § 12101 (1990). Retrieved January 17, 2026, from https://www.ada.gov/law-and-regs/ada/

Americans with Disabilities Act Title II Regulations (2011). Retrieved February 22nd, 2026, from https://www.ada.gov/law-and-regs/regulations/title-ii-2010-regulations/

Autistic Self Advocacy Network (n.d.). *Self-advocacy*. Retrieved December 18, 2025, from https://autisticadvocacy.org/self-advocacy/

Baron-Cohen, S., Wheelwright, S., Skinner, R., Martin, J., & Clubley, E. (2001). The autism-spectrum quotient (Aq): Evidence from Asperger syndrome/high-functioning autism, males and females, scientists and mathematicians. *Journal of Autism and Developmental Disorders, 31*(1), 5–17. https://doi.org/10.1023/A:1005653411471

CAST (2024). CAST Universal Design for Learning Guidelines version 3.0. Retrieved June 3, 2026, from https://udlguidelines.cast.org

College Board (n.d.) *Documentation guidelines: Learning disorders*. Retrieved December 18, 2025, from https://accommodations.collegeboard.org/request-accommodations/provide-documentation/by-disability/learning-disorders

Dauber, G. R., & Hsu, J. L. (2025). Factors influencing student motivations and experiences in stem course office hours. *CBE—Life Sciences Education, 24*(2), ar28. https://doi.org/10.1187/cbe.24-08-0214

Family Educational Rights and Privacy Act of 1974, 20 U.S.C. § 1232g. (n.d.) Retrieved December 18, 2025, from https://studentprivacy.ed.gov/ferpa#0.1_se34.1.99_15

Guerrero, M., & Rod, A. B. (2013). Engaging in office hours: A study of student-faculty interaction and academic performance. *Journal of Political Science Education, 9*(4), 403–416. https://doi.org/10.1080/15512169.2013.835554

Health Insurance Portability and Accountability Act of 1996, (n.d.) Pub. L. No. 104–191, 100 Stat. 1936. Retrieved December 18, 2025, from https://aspe.hhs.gov/reports/health-insurance-portability-accountability-act-1996

Individuals with Disabilities Education Act (n.d.) Retrieved December 18, 2025, from https://sites.ed.gov/idea/

New York State Department of Education (n.d.) *Enrollment of college students with disabilities*. Retrieved December 20, 2025, from https://www.nysed.gov/information-reporting-services/higher-education-reports

Pennsylvania State Education Association (n.d.). *504 Accommodations guide*. Retrieved December 19, 2025, from https://www.psea.org/contentassets/ac6695903bd94d27aa14e85c3a12d90e/504-accommodations-guide.pdf

Ritter, L., Scherrer, C., Vandenbussche, J., & Whipple, J. (2021). A study of student perceptions of office hours. *Journal on Excellence in College Teaching, 32*(4), 81–115. https://celt.miamioh.edu/index.php/JECT/article/view/183

Section 504 of the Rehabilitation Act of 1973, 29 U.S.C. § 794. (n.d.) Retrieved December 18, 2025, from https://www.ed.gov/laws-and-policy/civil-rights-laws/disability-discrimination/frequently-asked-questions-section-504-free-appropriate-public-education-fape

Understood (n.d.) The importance of self-advocacy. Retrieved December 18, 2025, from https://www.understood.org/en/articles/the-importance-of-self-advocacy

US Department of Education (n.d.). *The civil rights of students with hidden disabilities and section 504*. Retrieved December 19, 2025, from https://www.ed.gov/laws-and-policy/individuals-disabilities/section-504/civil-rights-of-students-hidden-disabilities-and-section-504

US Department of Housing and Urban Development (n.d.) *Assistance animals*. Retrieved December 19, 2025, from https://www.hud.gov/helping-americans/assistance-animals

Walter, H. J., Abright, A. R., Bukstein, O. G., Diamond, J., Keable, H., Ripperger-Suhler, J., & Rockhill, C. (2023). Clinical practice guideline for the assessment and treatment of children and adolescents with major and persistent depressive disorders. *Journal of the American Academy of Child & Adolescent Psychiatry, 62*(5), 479–502. https://doi.org/10.1016/j.jaac.2022.10.001

Young, S., Hollingdale, J., Absoud, M., Bolton, P., Branney, P., Colley, W., Craze, E., Dave, M., Deeley, Q., Farrag, E., Gudjonsson, G., Hill, P., Liang, H., Murphy, C., Mackintosh, P., Murin, M., O'Regan, F., Ougrin, D., Rios, P., … Woodhouse, E. (2020). Guidance for identification and treatment of individuals with attention deficit/hyperactivity disorder and autism spectrum disorder based upon expert consensus. *BMC Medicine, 18*(1), 146. https://doi.org/10.1186/s12916-020-01585-y

For Product Safety Concerns and Information please contact our EU
representative GPSR@taylorandfrancis.com
Taylor & Francis Verlag GmbH, Kaufingerstraße 24, 80331 München, Germany

www.ingramcontent.com/pod-product-compliance
Lightning Source LLC
LaVergne TN
LVHW011929250726
844069LV00031B/339